Rethinking Sustainability

Evolving Values for a Capitalist World

In most of the world today, the issue is not whether or how to embrace capital-ism, but how to make the best of it. The currently dominant capitalist values include competitive individualism, instrumental rationality, and material suc-cess. The series will explore questions such as: Will these values suffice as a basis for social organizations that can meet human and environmental needs in the twenty-first century? What would it mean for capitalist systems to evolve toward an emphasis on other values, such as cooperation, altruism, responsi-bility, and concern for the future?

Titles in the series:

Neva R. Goodwin, Editor. *As if the Future Mattered: Translating Social and Economic Theory into Human Behavior*

Severyn T. Bruyn. *A Civil Economy: Transforming the Market in the Twenty-First Century*

Jonathan Harris. *Rethinking Sustainability: Power, Knowledge, and Institutions*

Rethinking Sustainability

Power, Knowledge, and Institutions

Edited by
Jonathan M. Harris

Ann Arbor

THE UNIVERSITY OF MICHIGAN PRESS

*This book is dedicated to my students at
the Tufts University Fletcher School of Law and Diplomacy,
who give me hope for a democratic and sustainable future.*

Copyright © by the University of Michigan 2000
All rights reserved
Published in the United States of America by
The University of Michigan Press
Manufactured in the United States of America
∞ Printed on acid-free paper

2003   2002   2001   2000   4   3   2   1

A CIP catalog record for this book is available from the British Library.

Library of Congress Cataloging-in-Publication Data

Rethinking sustainability : power, knowledge, and institutions /
    edited by Jonathan M. Harris.
        p. cm. — (Evolving values for a capitalist world)
    Includes bibliographical references and index.
    ISBN 0-472-11142-6 (acid-free)
    1. Sustainable development.   2. Environmental economics.   3.
Economic development—Sociological aspects.   4. Economic
development—Social aspects.   I. Harris, Jonathan M.   II. Series.
HC79.E5 R48 2000
333.7—dc21   00-008651

Contents

Preface and Acknowledgments   vii

Introduction: An Assessment of Sustainable Development   1
Jonathan M. Harris

Part 1. Institutional Perspectives on Sustainable Development

1. Sustainability and Systemic Issues in a New Era   13
   Gar Alperovitz

2. The Case for the Global Commons   33
   Baylor Johnson and Faye Duchin

3. Development Connections: The Hedgerow Model   50
   Neva R. Goodwin

4. Wealth, Poverty, and Sustainable Development   77
   David Barkin

5. Free Trade or Sustainable Trade? An Ecological
   Economics Perspective   117
   Jonathan M. Harris

Part 2. Sustainability and Institutions in Practice

Introduction to Part 2: Power, Knowledge, and
Institutions in Development Practice   141
Jonathan M. Harris

6. Stories People Tell: The Cultural Construction of
   Environmental Policy in Africa   151
   Allan Hoben

7. Political Power and Environmental Sustainability
   in Agriculture   173
   Robert L. Paarlberg

8. Toward a Learning Paradigm: New Professionalism and
   Institutions for Agriculture   189
   Jules N. Pretty and Robert Chambers

9. Does Food Security Require Local Food Systems?   228
   Molly D. Anderson and John T. Cook

10. Community, Ecology, and Landscape Change in
    Zambrana-Chacuey   249
    *Dianne Rocheleau, Laurie Ross, Julio Morrobel, and
    Ricardo Hernandez*

   Contributors   287

   Index   289

Preface and Acknowledgments

This volume bring together the thoughts of economists, political scientists, anthropologists, philosophers, and agricultural policy professionals. The question it addresses — that of sustainability in development — is of necessity interdisciplinary. A theory of sustainable development must take into account economic, social, and environmental dimensions. Until recently, the question "what constitutes development?" was often answered in a one-sided manner, with the economists' perspective dominating, and a high priority — sometimes the only priority — being assigned to expansion of economic output. The social, political, institutional, and ethical aspects of development have often been neglected. But now that "sustainable development" has become a broadly accepted concept, entering the lexicon of even such previously resistant institutions as the World Bank, it is impossible to maintain a narrowly economistic view of development. For this reason, the varied perspectives offered by the contributors to this volume are crucial to understanding the process of development as it relates to environmental sustainability and human well-being.

The selection of articles in this volume is meant to be stimulating and provocative rather than comprehensive. They are roughly divided between those which deal with broad theoretical issues concerning the economic, political, and social aspects of development (part 1), and those which present more applied analysis (part 2). The common thread is a concern for examining which factors contribute to making development socially just and environmentally sound. The issues that are addressed range from international trade to political power, gender roles, legal institutions, and agricultural research. Each author has something unique to offer. Their perspectives may not always be compatible, but I hope will all be complementary in the sense that they will provide the reader with varied insights into complex issues.

For support in the preparation and editing of this volume, I am indebted to the Tufts University Global Development and Environment Institute (G-DAE), and in particular to its codirector, Neva Goodwin. Financial support was provided by the Ford Foundation.

John Nordgren assisted in editing the articles, and G-DAE research associate Kevin Gallagher provided important information for the section on the North American Free Trade Agreement in my article on trade issues. I am also indebted to two anonymous readers for numerous specific suggestions. Many of the ideas discussed in this volume have been percolated through my courses on environment and development at the Tufts University Fletcher School of Law and Diplomacy. My students have been a never-failing source of enthusiasm and intellectual vitality, and it is to them that this volume is dedicated.

Introduction: An Assessment of Sustainable Development

Jonathan M. Harris

In 1987 the World Commission on Environment and Development (WCED) introduced the term *sustainable development,* defined as "development which meets the needs of the present without compromising the ability of future generations to meet their own needs." Since the publication of their report, *Our Common Future,* the term has been appropriated by so many analysts and practitioners holding widely differing perspectives that it is now difficult to determine whether it has any clear meaning. Does it represent a workable new concept, or simply a gloss on established forms of development?

Interpretations of sustainable development consistent with the original intent of the 1987 WCED report have been presented by such authors as Holmberg (1992), Pearce, Barbier, and Markandya (1990), Reid (1995), and others. Economic and accounting techniques for measuring sustainable development have been advanced under the auspices of the World Bank (1993a, 1993b, 1995a, 1995b) and the United Nations (1993), as well as by independent researchers (Pearce 1993). A thoroughgoing application of the principles of sustainability seems to imply a basic change in patterns of agricultural and industrial growth, an emphasis on renewable energy and energy efficiency, an integration of population policy into macroeconomic policy, a sustainable management policy for natural resources, and new instruments of macroeconomic measurement, as well as new social and institutional structures.

In general, however, what we observe in the real world embodies little change from earlier development patterns. Economic development is still characterized by fossil-fuel dependence, "modernized" agriculture, automobile-centered transport, and traditional industry: steel, petrochemical, paper, and so on, with heavy demands on natural resources and increasing flows of waste. Inequality of distribution, urban slums, forced migration, and social problems of crime and racial/ethnic conflict are commonly accentuated rather than relieved in the process of development. Globalization of markets means that it is increasingly difficult for individual nations or regions to choose a different development path, and it increases the power of multinational corporations to shape development. And the traditional measurement of GNP or GDP[1] still dominates economic theory and policy-making.

Some theorists have challenged the whole concept of sustainable development. According to Beckerman (1992), "the aggregative concept of global 'sustainability' that is so widely encountered these days . . . seems to be either morally indefensible or devoid of operational value." In Beckerman's view, it is morally indefensible to limit economic growth when such growth offers the world's poor both their best chance to climb out of poverty and the resources to improve those environmental problems that most severely impact human health and well-being, such as polluted water and inadequate sanitation. Moreover, he argues that no clear criterion exists for distinguishing "sustainable" from "unsustainable" economic activity, or balancing the interests of present and future generations. A similar criticism is made by Dasgupta and Maler (1995), who argue that the concept of sustainability is unworkably vague, and not based on any clearly defined concept of social welfare.

Can sustainable development be said to have made any headway at all? Certainly the discussion of the concept has evolved from generalities to a wealth of technological and economic specifics, as presented by many authors including those cited above. Even Beckerman, somewhat grudgingly, acknowledges the importance of renewable energy and energy-efficient development paths. Recognition of the importance of sustainable agricultural systems is also widespread (Breth 1996). There has been significant work on the theory and application of industrial ecology (Ayres and Simonis 1994). Financing for environmentally sound development has expanded dramatically in the decade since 1987 (World Bank 1995c). The theoretical criticisms raised by Beckerman and by Dasgupta and Maler have been answered by Howarth and others, who argue that the incompatibility of sustainability with standard economics indicates excessive narrowness in neoclassical economic theory, rather than any inconsistency in the inherently normative concept of sustainability as intergenerational justice (Howarth 1995, 1997; Pezzey 1997; Norton and Toman 1997).

Despite this theoretical and practical progress, it is clear that there are significant barriers to the implementation of sustainable development on a broad scale. The theme of this volume is that those barriers arise especially as a result of issues of power, knowledge, and institutional structures. The contributors to this volume offer both theoretical analysis and empirical evidence to support a crucial proposition: *when the existing social institutions are such as to deny many people access to the power and knowledge they need to affect the development process, sustainable development is impossible.* However, there are many examples — mostly small-scale — of more equitable and democratic conditions that allow people-centered sustainable development. It is important to move beyond the rhetoric of sustainability to examine what works, what does not, and how it might be possible to multiply examples of success to achieve more substantial progress toward a more inclusive concept of what Neva Goodwin has identified as "SAEJAS" — "socially and environmentally just and sustainable" development.[2]

The Economic and Political Context

It is worthwhile to start by placing the discussion on sustainability into a broad context of economic and political theory. It was only relatively recently, following World War II, that economic development emerged as a distinct field of study. Two models of economic development contended in the postwar world: the socialist/communist system and the capitalist one. Much of the effort in development theory in the West was oriented toward presenting an alternative to communism, as set forth, for example, in W. W. Rostow's *The Stages of Economic Growth: A Non-Communist Manifesto* (1960). With the collapse of most communist systems in the late 1980s, this would appear to leave only one model for economic development — although many cumbersome state and parastatal bureaucracies throughout the developing world still attest to the legacy of the centrally planned model. Although a few cases — such as the state of Kerala in India — provide examples of apparently workable capitalist/socialist mixed systems, in most instances the global market mechanism is increasingly dominant. The standard market-oriented approach to development, however, pays scant attention to resource and environmental issues and makes no provision for long-term sustainability. Can sustainability be grafted onto the standard market-oriented model, or does it require some rethinking of fundamentals?

Gar Alperovitz suggests that the issue of sustainability can only be properly understood in terms of such a rethinking. The disastrous record of communist regimes in the environmental area can be traced to their fixation on industrial growth through centralized management, together with a political system that suppressed dissent. But capitalist systems are also strongly oriented toward economic growth, resulting in a steady increase in what Herman Daly has called "throughput" — input of natural resources and output of wastes and pollutants (1991). The profit motive that is basic to capitalism creates pressures to externalize environmental costs, both through economic production techniques and through the political lobbying power of corporations. The growth ideology that accompanies capitalism also encourages people in market economies to believe that growth at the expense of the environment is necessary to avoid unemployment and escape poverty, and it teaches them to identify well-being with increased consumption of goods. All these tendencies in market capitalist systems militate against sustainability.[3]

Alperovitz suggests that community-based institutions are more likely than capitalist firms to respect sustainability principles. He also identifies an important link between ecological and social equity issues: individual income and job security are essential to civic freedom. Without fully participating citizens, sustainability itself would have to be imposed from above — although what would more likely be imposed are unsustainable policies favored by powerful corporations or bureaucrats. Thus a free citizenry in an equitable society is a crucial component of a broad vision of sustainability.

Private and Common Property Institutions

Baylor Johnson and Faye Duchin pursue the issue of appropriate institutions for sustainability through a reconsideration of common property institutions. They provide evidence that common property institutions are robust, workable, and often more conducive both to participatory democracy and to environmental preservation than a private property regime. The concept of common property has been viewed too negatively by economists, they argue, due to a confusion with an open-access resource regime. There is a sound theoretical basis, as well as ample empirical evidence, to support the assertion that open-access regimes are destructive to natural resources and ecosystems. But true common property resource systems differ from open-access regimes, being characterized by a well-defined set of rules for management of the commons. In addition, common property institutions often include a strong presumption in favor of conserving the resource for future generations — a principle of intergenerational equity that is lacking in private property institutions.

Johnson and Duchin propose the extension of common property institutions, frequently present in traditional societies, to the modern problems of the global commons such as atmosphere and oceans. Their argument can also be applied to other issues that have a partly national and partly transnational character, such as the conservation of species diversity, the management of transboundary water resources, and the conservation of soils. In all these areas a good case can be made that the solutions to environmental problems require not just modified national policies or specific international agreements, but also the development of new institutions reflecting the principles of common property. Certainly the limitations of privatization and market institutions for dealing with these problems are evident.

In some cases, such as allocation of transferable water rights, private ownership can play a role, but the maintenance of watersheds and water ecosystems clearly has a common property character. The same is true of species conservation, which in some instances might benefit a private owner or single nation, but more usually is a "common heritage" issue.[4] Soil conservation may be in the interest of the individual farmer, but often national soil conservation initiatives are required to overcome the limited time horizon imposed on farmers by current economic pressures. There is also a less clearly perceived but nonetheless real supranational interest in preservation of the global soil base.

Neva Goodwin suggests a "hedgerow model" of development to link local and traditional institutions with those at the national and transnational level. Too often, powerful transnational institutions together with national-level elites have overridden local and community interests in the pursuit of development. Not coincidentally, they have also often pursued policies that are environmentally destructive. While it is not certain that greater respect for local institutions will always be consistent with environmental protection, Goodwin's hedgerow strategy implies that unless the interests of all the actors and interests in the development process are fully taken into account, including the general interest in maintaining ecosystem functions, the goals of sustainable development will remain elusive. This perspective is clearly consistent with the suggestion by Johnson and Duchin that common property institutions have much greater importance, both at the local and global levels, than they have traditionally been accorded in economic theory.

Goodwin moves away from the neoclassical economic definition of development as essentially equivalent to growth in gross domestic product. Her approach is more consistent with the "Human Development" concept that has been introduced in the annual reports of the UN Development Program (1990–98). She emphasizes the importance of human, social, and natural capital as well as manufactured capital in development. Thus, rather than the standard economists' recommendation of "letting markets work," Goodwin suggests a focus on the institutional and cultural bases of development. Her specific examples concern agricultural development, public health, small business development, and solar energy. In each case, the institutional relationships — between national and multinational organizations on the one hand, and local and community groupings on the other — are crucial to shaping development. The goal she defines is "socially and environmentally just and sustainable" (SAEJAS) development. In pursuing this goal, the growth of market-oriented supply and demand (as measured by GDP) is only a part of the picture. Institutional factors will determine whether the benefits of development flow to the few or to the many, and whether current activities support or undermine future well-being.

Globalization, Trade, and Local Sustainability

A more sharply drawn distinction between global market development and local sustainability is evident in David Barkin's article. Barkin argues that the process of globalization and the spread of the market mechanism throughout the developing world is fundamentally hostile to sustainability. According to Barkin, the international market works to homogenize processes of production, in contradiction to the need to preserve social and ecological diversity for sustainable development. This process disrupts local communities, destroys traditional methods of cultivation, and creates a floating population of migrants, increasing ecosystem stresses and worsening urban social and environmental problems. While globalization creates wealth, it also results in an increase in economic inequality and a large population cut off both from their former communities and from any access to political power in the broader society, in which the political process is dominated by the interests of wealthy elites and transnational corporations.

Achieving sustainability thus requires a consciously dualistic development strategy. In those areas where marketization is already complete, the standard economic techniques for "internalizing externalities" and promoting energy and resource efficiency have potential to limit environmental damage. However, in many rural areas where traditional economies survive, further marketization will only worsen the situation. Barkin proposes strategies to promote self-sufficiency in rural communities, including the areas of food production, crafts and light industry, resource husbandry and ecosystem maintenance, and the use of renewable energy sources. He sees the role of nongovernmental institutions (NGOs) as being crucial in promoting this alternative model of development.

Barkin's critique of globalization echoes the arguments of other analysts who have suggested that the free-trade paradigm is in conflict with sustainability. My article on trade attempts to develop this theme further. In standard economic theory, free trade works to increase the wealth of nations. However, free trade may also increase inequality both within and between nations, as well as undermine the power of national and local political institutions. There is no theoretical reason to expect that free trade will itself promote long-term sustainability, and at the same time it may weaken the political institutions that could do so. In other respects — such as the promotion of greater resource exploitation and energy use — free trade may increase environmental stresses. Specific institutional reforms are therefore required to promote the goal of sustainable trade.

Trade is not merely a question of exchanging goods. It also involves culture, information, and the environment. Thus the narrow economic perspective, focused only on deriving utility from goods, fails to capture the social, political, and ecological dimensions of trade. Free trade may succeed on its own terms by increasing the volume of goods production and consumption, but at the expense of damaging communities and the environment. The cultural and political responses to social and environmental issues take place at various levels, from local to regional to national to global. The integrity of institutions at these different levels is threatened by unrestricted free trade, which subsumes all other considerations under the single logic of the global marketplace.

To promote sustainable trade, a number of reforms are necessary. The role of nongovernmental organizations in the North American Free Trade Agreement, while very limited, establishes an important principle: the interests of communities and of groups advocating environmental protection should be represented in international trade agreements. Greater transparency is essential for this more democratic involvement (replacing the notorious secrecy of many GATT and WTO bodies).[5] The integrity of multinational environmental treaties and of national health and environmental protection laws must be respected, as well as national rights to restrict exploitation of natural resources. Barkin's point about the need to protect local communities from the disruptive effects of unrestricted trade is relevant here, and my argument on trade is compatible with his advocacy of local autonomous development.

Reinterpreting Sustainable Development

The discussion thus far suggests a fresh interpretation of the first decade of "sustainable development." Many significant efforts have been made to advance both the theory and practice of development in response to the challenge set forth in the 1987 World Commission on Environment and Development report. But these efforts have been limited by the resistance of established institutions to yielding power. Wherever there has been progress, it has been linked to some degree of institutional reform. At the global level, the effective implementation of global environmental agreements requires some surrender of national prerogatives to a transnational authority. Where this has occurred, as in the Montreal Protocol on Ozone Depletion, there has been measurable progress. Where it has not occurred, little change is observed from established patterns of development. For example, since the Framework Convention on Climate Change was adopted at Rio de Janeiro in 1992, fossil fuel use and carbon emissions have continued to rise, and it is not yet clear whether the "binding" commitments of the 1997 Kyoto conference will be implemented in practice.

At the regional level, the establishment of authoritative bodies with a social and environmental mandate, along with input from NGOs, has been essential. This has occurred in the European Union, but only to a very limited extent in the NAFTA agreement.[6] At the local level, the participation of local residents, their acquisition of skills as well as the application of traditional knowledge and their sense of "ownership" of sustainable development efforts, has proved to be crucial.

In the first part of this volume, we hope to offer an overview of these issues of power, knowledge and institutions as they relate to sustainability. In the second part, we seek to illustrate some of these general themes with practical applications. We hope that this collection of diverse theoretical and empirical perspectives will contribute to efforts to carry forward the principles and practice of sustainable development, in which the original insights set forth in *Our Common Future* will be combined with a more sophisticated appreciation of the political and institutional basis of socially and environmentally just and sustainable development.

NOTES

1. The difference between GNP and GDP is whether or not the foreign earning of individuals and corporations are included in the total. GDP, which includes all income earned within the country, regardless of the nationality or residence of the recipient, is commonly used as a measure of development.

2. See Goodwin, this volume.

3. For a more extensive discussion of this issue, see Martin O'Connor (ed.), *Is Capitalism Sustainable?* (1994).

4. For example, the government of Costa Rica will gain financial benefit from an agreement with Merck Corporation for the pharmaceutical exploitation of rain-forest species, while conserving the rain forest.

5. GATT is the General Agreement on Tariffs and Trade, set up in 1947 both as an organization setting rules for international trade and as a forum for continuing negotiations. WTO, the World Trade Organization, replaced GATT in 1995.

6. See Harris, this volume.

REFERENCES

Ayres, Robert U., and Udo E. Simonis. 1994. *Industrial Metabolism: Restructuring for Sustainable Development.* Tokyo: United Nations Press.

Beckerman, Wilfred. 1992. Economic Growth and the Environment: Whose Growth? Whose Environment? *World Development* 20 (4): 481–96.

Breth, Steven A., ed. 1996. *Integration of Sustainable Agriculture and Rural Development Issues in Agricultural Policy.* Morrilton, AR: Winrock International.

Daly, Herman. 1991. *Steady-State Economics* (2d ed.) Washington, DC: Island Press.

Dasgupta, P., and K. G. Maler. 1995. Poverty, Institutions, and the Environmental-Resource Base. In J. Behrman and T. N. Srinivasan, eds., *Handbook of Development Economics.* Amsterdam: North Holland.

Holmberg, Johan, ed. 1992. *Making Development Sustainable.* Washington, DC: Island Press.

Howarth, Richard B. 1995. Sustainability under Uncertainty: A Deontological Approach. *Land Economics* 71, no. 4 (November): 417–27.

———. 1997. Sustainability as Opportunity. *Land Economics* 73, no. 4 (November): 569–79.

Norton, Bryan G., and Michael A. Toman. 1997. Sustainability: Ecological and Economic Perspectives. *Land Economics* 73, no. 4 (November): 553–68.

O'Connor, Martin, ed. 1994. *Is Capitalism Sustainable? Political Economy and the Politics of Ecology.* New York: Guilford Press.

Pearce, David, et al. 1993. *Blueprint 3: Measuring Sustainable Development.* London: Earthscan.

Pearce, David, Edward Barbier, and Anil Markandya. 1990. *Sustainable Development: Economics and Environment in the Third World.* London: Earthscan.

Pezzey, John C. V. 1997. Sustainability Constraints versus 'Optimality' versus Intertemporal Concern, and Axioms versus Data. *Land Economics* 73, no. 4 (November): 448–66.

Reid, David. 1995. *Sustainable Development: An Introductory Guide.* London: Earthscan.

Rostow, W. W. 1960. *The Stages of Economic Growth: A Non-Communist Manifesto.* (2d ed. 1971) New York: Cambridge University Press.

United Nations Development Programme (UNDP). 1990–98. *Human Development Report.* New York and Oxford: Oxford University Press.

United Nations, Division for Economic and Social Information and Policy Analysis. 1993. *Integrated Environmental and Economic Accounting.* New York: United Nations.

World Bank. 1993a. *Valuing the Environment: Proceedings of the First Annual International Conference on Environmentally Sustainable Development,* Ismail Serageldin and Andrew Steer, eds. Washington, DC: World Bank.

———. 1993b. *Towards Improved Accounting for the Environment: An UNSTAT-World Bank Symposium,* Ernst Lutz, ed. Washington, DC: World Bank.

———. 1995a. *Monitoring Environmental Progress: A Report on Work in Progress.* Washington, DC: World Bank.

———. 1995b. *Defining and Measuring Sustainability: The Biogeophysical Foundations,* Mohan Munasinghe and Walter Shearer, eds. Washington, DC: United Nations University and World Bank.

———. 1995c. *Mainstreaming the Environment: The World Bank Group and the Environment since the Rio Earth Summit.* Washington, DC: World Bank.

World Commission on Environment and Development. 1987. *Our Common Future.* Oxford: Oxford University Press.

Part 1
Institutional Perspectives on Sustainable Development

CHAPTER 1

Sustainability and Systemic Issues in a New Era

Gar Alperovitz

For most of the twentieth century the progressive vision of the future in many parts of the world revolved around the socialist theory — namely, that equality and democracy could best be achieved by a system in which ownership of society's wealth (the means of production) is vested in a structure beholden to, and controlled by, society. This system theory has now collapsed.

However, the crisis of mainstream liberalism (or social democracy) leads to a closely related problem: What happens if socialism's distant cousin — the welfare state — also loses its capacity to achieve the fundamental value goals its core theory affirms? A less commonly recognized question concerns the implications when the fundamental basis of the conservative theory of liberty falters. All three issues, I shall suggest, point to a shared regime problem: the disintegration of traditional articulations of the relationship between values and systems.

The Conservative Critique

It is instructive to begin with the last issue first: Against the socialist idea, thoughtful conservatives (as opposed to demagogues and self-serving right-wing politicians) have for more than a century argued that vesting both economic and political power in one institutional structure must inevitably lead to the destruction of individual rights, of democracy, and of the human spirit. They have applied a similar structural critique to the expansive welfare state.

Friedrich Hayek, whose book *The Road to Serfdom* became a conservative bible, pushed this argument well beyond narrow economic ideas: "The most important change which extensive government control produces is a psychological change, an alteration in the character of the people." Hayek quoted de Tocqueville approvingly:

The will of man is not shattered but softened, bent and guided; men are seldom forced by it to act, but they are constantly restrained from acting. Such a power does not destroy, but it prevents existence; it does not tyrannize, but it compresses, enervates, extinguishes, and stupefies a people, till each nation is reduced to be nothing better than a flock of timid and industrial animals, of which government is the shepherd. (Hayek 1972)

Most progressives have generally been unsympathetic to this conservative position because it seemed oblivious to the moral and political importance of equality, and because it often served to mask a cruder form of conservatism willing to use any argument to justify private enterprise exploitation. They urged that to vest the ownership of the means of production in private hands inevitably produced great inequalities of income and wealth, powerful private interests that tend to subvert democracy, the desecration of the environment, and an equally disastrous spiritual result — the worship of money, of materialism, and of greed.

These strong criticisms of unrestrained capitalism led most progressives to underestimate the importance of the basic conservative argument regarding political and economic power. Only a very few argued the importance of listening to the main point of the critique, and of engaging serious conservatives in a serious dialogue over theory. Through most of the past half-century, cold war polarization focused progressives' attention on critiques of conservative policies, permitting many to avoid reflecting deeply upon the conservative structural argument and upon similar themes in anarchist and libertarian antistatist thought.

It is undeniable that the socialist ideal in the Soviet Union and Eastern Europe was severely handicapped by the devastation of World Wars I and II and also because it was introduced into essentially underdeveloped societies that had only a minimal historic experience with democracy. Further, the cold war generated an environment that gave priority to "national security," military expenditures, rigorous "internal security" measures, and a Soviet imperial occupation. However, the fatal underlying structural problem cannot be denied, and it has now demonstrated its tremendous importance as millions in the East have undertaken a sweeping rush away from a disaster they know directly to a seeming solution they know only vaguely: democratic capitalism.

In practice, the experience of capitalism in the former communist areas these last years, however, has also been radically different from its promise, as unemployment, social dislocation, ecological horror, and massive disillusionment have set in (sometimes even leading to the election of old communists as the least bad alternative!). If — as many in the West know so well — democratic capitalism also contradicts important values, what possible alternative can be conceived and affirmed for the future?

Serious conservatives are aware of another profound difficulty at the very heart of their preferred option: the conservative argument against statist socialism held not only that the concentration of economic and political power in the institution of the state was dangerous, but also that there had to be alternative sources of independent support for the individual, else liberty could never be sustained over time.

The essential notion involves a balance of forces: at the same time they contended against a strong state, such conservatives argued the importance of small-scale, entrepreneurial enterprise. In this system the underlying structural support for the principle of liberty cannot be compromised: a free political culture requires that society rest upon the foundation of a citizenry sustained by economic independence.

"It is widely believed that politics and economics are separate and largely unconnected," conservative economist Milton Friedman observes,

> that individual freedom is a political problem and material welfare an economic problem; and that any kind of political arrangements can be combined with any kind of economic arrangements. . . . such a view is a delusion . . . there is an intimate connection between economics and politics . . . only certain combinations of political and economic arrangements are possible. (Friedman 1962)

Thomas Jefferson urged a broadly similar theory of the requirements of a meaningful political-economic system. In his *Notes on Virginia,* Jefferson wrote: "Dependence begets subservience and venality, suffocates the germ of virtue, and prepares fit tools for the designs of ambition" (1781). His hope for the new system in early-nineteenth-century America also had a very specific structural foundation:

> everyone may have land to labor for himself, if he chooses; or, preferring the exercise of any other industry, may exact for it such compensation as not only to afford a comfortable subsistence, but wherewith to provide for a cessation from labor in old age. . . . such men may safely and advantageously reserve to themselves a wholesome control over their public affairs, and a degree of freedom. (Jefferson 1813)

For all its other difficulties, pre-twentieth-century American society did in fact rest upon a footing of millions and millions of *individual* entrepreneurs: they were mostly farmers (or, more accurately, farmer-businessmen — an entrepreneurial breed very different, for instance, from the farmer-peasants of many societies). A majority of the society (including spouses and children) actually had the experience of individually risking capital and being directly responsible for their own economic enterprises.

By the late twentieth century, however, only a very small fraction of Americans, no more than 15 to 16 percent, can in any sense reasonably be called *individual entrepreneurs.* The United States has become a society of employees, most of whom work for large or medium-sized bureaucracies, private or public. "As the consolidation of economic power progresses," traditionalist conservative Russell Kirk admonished in 1957, "the realm of personal freedom will diminish, whether the masters of the economy are state servants or servants of private corporations."

From this essential perspective, the difference between a system dominated by General Motors and Exxon and one based upon the individual landholding farmer and small businessman of an earlier day in American history may very well be as important in the actual life experience of the average person as the difference between a system based upon large private bureaucracies in the United States and public bureaucracies in "socialist" nations.

Moreover, irrespective of the hopes of conservatives and largely irrespective of who has been in power — including Herbert Hoover and Ronald Reagan — the state has generally grown in size and power. The government accounted for less than 8 percent of the GNP at the turn of the twentieth century and has grown to roughly 34 to 35 percent in recent years (U.S. Census 1975; Council of Economic Advisers 1995).

The dangers of statism in socialism are now clear to all. However, the truth is that serious conservatives, like serious progressives, also confront a direct contradiction of both aspects of their most dearly held theory in the experience of the West.

Democracy and Equality

Is there any meaningful way forward that promises to honor equality, liberty, and democracy, to say nothing of ecological rationality and even, perhaps, community? Might it be possible to begin to define a viable third structural option other than traditional socialism and traditional capitalism?[1]

What is needed is not a set of rhetorical goals, but a serious discussion of the outlines of an alternative system of institutions and relationships that might one day nurture, rather than erode, cherished values in an ongoing fashion over time. Space permits only an introductory set of notes and elements that might help contribute to a dialogue aimed at ultimately fashioning such a vision. Let us begin with *equality*.

Democracy obviously requires a reasonable degree of equality to be a meaningful expression of the idea not only of one person–one vote, but of "each and all" having equal capacity to impact the governing decisions that determine the fate and shape of the society in which they live. By this test the underlying condition of "democracy" in the United States is clearly weak, given an income distribution characterized by marked — and increasing — inequality.

Money and television, many studies show, increasingly tend to dominate elections. Even more fundamental is that when there are vast differences in income, wealth, education, free time, and personal security, those with low incomes are systematically disadvantaged: they do not have the wherewithal to influence politics, their educations do not give them as many skills, they don't have the time, and, often fearful of losing their jobs, they must be silent rather than speak their minds (Dahl 1996).

Any American reporter in any American city easily finds innumerable individuals chosen at random who express extraordinary disillusionment with the actual operation of democracy. They do not need to be instructed in the limits of what some have called "electionism" — a process in which mudslinging, distorted advertising, and a lack of significant issues make a mockery of the idea of democratic decision making in connection with important public matters.

The traditional American progressive or liberal answer to inequality has been that "reform" or "activism" or "political demands" or "organizing" can correct such imbalances and move society toward greater equality. In a sense, "politics" is seen as somewhat independent from and able to correct the essential functioning and structural basis of the system. This idea, in fact, is at the very core of the social democratic or liberal system theory.

The statistical record, however, confirms that there are obviously deep linkages between the structure of the economic system and the kind of politics it generates or permits (Thurow 1980; Rodriguez 1998; Roemer 1998). There is little evidence, for instance, that what we commonly understand as "reform," "activism," "political demands," or "organizing" has had the capacity to move the American system toward greater economic equality in the twentieth century; and if so, this theory also falters.

In fact, the only times there have been brief positive improvements in the relative distribution of income have been as a result of major crises: during World War I, during the Great Depression, and during World War II. But these shifts, indisputably, were associated with fundamental, system-shaking explosions — they are clearly not evidence that politics on its own in "normal" times has the capacity to alter the underlying trend.

With the U.S. economy buoyed by the postwar boom, the Korean War, the cold war, and the Vietnam War, the U.S. distribution of income held reasonably constant for two decades. However, the painful deterioration that has now been in process for a number of years resumes and points to a much older trend of growing inequality.

To be sure, the situation would undoubtedly be worse without progressive political activities. However, it is one thing to say that politics may have prevented or slowed down a trend toward even more regressive patterns of inequality and it is quite another to say that it has had the capacity to move society toward greater equality as the traditional theory argued.

Today, roughly 54 million people among the top one-fifth of American society receive approximately 49 percent of household income (including interest, rent, and dividends). Just about the same number of human beings among the bottom one-fifth of society make do on 3.6 percent of such income (U.S. Census 1999a). Still lower, at the very bottom of the system there is extreme poverty concentrated overwhelmingly among women, children, and minorities. In 1998, for instance, 12.7 percent of American society lived in poverty by official definitions — 34.5 million *people*. 36.7 percent of all black children (including 60 percent of all black children under six in female-headed households) and 34.4 percent of all Hispanic children (including 67 percent of Hispanic children under six in female-headed households) were living in poverty (U.S. Census 1999b).

But this clearly understates true inequality: If you receive $1,000 in one year and I receive $50,000, and a few years later you have $2,000 and I have $100,000, the ratio between our incomes has not changed. Economists will tell you, correctly, that the "relative" distribution of income has not been altered. But, self-evidently, in the real world the gap between us has jumped from $49,000 to $98,000, and the "real-world inequality" between persons has increased dramatically.

This, in fact, is precisely what has been happening in the United States. One recent study, for instance, concludes that the real-world gap between those at the top and those at the bottom of the American income pyramid more than doubled in the postwar period: The income gap between families in the bottom 20 percent and families in the top 5 percent, for instance, exploded from $31,000 in 1947 to more than $68,000 in 1987 (measured in 1985 dollars) (Winnick 1989). Another congressional study calculates that the gap (in 1993 dollars) between a family of four at the 80th percentile of income and a family of four at the 1st percentile of income grew by more than $98,000 in the brief period 1977 to 1989 alone (House Ways and Means Committee 1992). More recent U.S. Census data indicate that the real-life gap between a family at the 5th percentile and 80th percentile of income distribution increased from $74,623 to $89,549 between 1980 and 1992 (in 1992 dollars) (U.S. Census 1994).

It may be that in some special cases "social democratic politics" can achieve sufficient momentum so that the underlying structural tendencies of capitalism can be countered by a politics sufficiently powerful to significantly alter the trends and patterns of "real" inequality between people. The evidence from countries like Sweden is mixed, but even if it were not, this possibility would clearly be an exception to the general rule especially as that rule is exhibited in twentieth-century American experience.

The essential system theory as it relates to the affirmed value of equality has lost all serious operational meaning.

Community-Based Institutions

To those who reject the traditional conservative, socialist, and liberal (social democratic) alternatives, another commonly discussed structural possibility as the basis of still another system theory is worker ownership of the means of production. This is an arrangement in which it is hoped that the dangers of statism, on the one hand, and private capitalist ownership and exploitation, on the other, can be avoided.

There are many important advantages to worker ownership schemes, especially those that offer some real degree of participation. However, they are clearly no panacea.

First, there is very little evidence that worker-owned firms significantly alter society's *overall* distribution of income. Within the local or national community, for instance, privileged workers in rich industries do not easily share their advantage with the community as a whole or with workers in other industries, with the elderly, with the poor, or with women and children outside their own families. Second, worker-owned firms tend to develop their own "interests." Worker-owned steel mills, for instance, generally seek similar kinds of subsidies (and trade protection) as privately owned mills. Nor, for that matter, do worker-owners have any great interest in expensive pollution controls that may advantage the larger community but cost them money.

Some worker-owned firms or worker co-ops have more equitable internal pay scales, all teach that structural alternatives different from either major "system" are at least possible, and many yield experience with participation in general and with economic matters in particular that may be important to the future development of still other forms. Any open vision of the future would be wise to include a rich variety of small scale co-ops, worker-owned firms, neighborhood corporations, and so forth.

But the structural principle of worker-ownership does not provide a fundamental answer to the problems entailed in a serious and comprehensive vision or for a "system" of institutions that might undergird that vision in ways that can hope to nurture such fundamental values as liberty, equality, or democracy.

Another structural formulation worth reviewing involves the principle of "community" and institutions that give it power through specific forms related to everyday life. The idea of community is inclusive: in principle it extends beyond "the workers" in a firm (or even as a class) to include everyone. The philosopher Martin Buber urged that this required the creation of local institutions embodying the idea that the community as a whole should own and benefit from "wealth." Traditional conservatives have stressed the parallel idea that strong structures of local community are required to support individual liberty, that community and liberty are mutually reinforcing values.

"Society is naturally composed not of disparate individuals," Buber held, "but of associative units and associations between them." What is required is a particular form and structure that nurtures cooperative democratic activity through direct experience: "an organic commonwealth and only such commonwealths can join together to form a shapely and articulated race of men will never build itself up out of individuals but only out of small and ever smaller communities: a nation is a community to the degree that it is a community of communities" (Buber 1950).

"Community" must be sufficiently small and local so that those affected can participate in decisions. And, in general, the social principle of involvement, of participation, of subsuming strictly economic goals to larger social goals, must be given priority: the fundamental question How do we wish to live together? is more important than more limited questions such as How do we compete? How do we become number one? How do we increase the national product?

A number of modern ecological thinkers have also urged the importance of building new structural relationships upon the principle of community. Thus, Herman E. Daly and John B. Cobb Jr., in their book *For the Common Good* (on the economics of a sustainable future), urge rebuilding local economic community institutions. And ecologist Murray Bookchin has put forward a concept he terms "libertarian municipalism":

> A gap, ideological as well as practical, is opening up between the nation-state, which is becoming more anonymous, bureaucratic, and remote, and the municipality, which is the one domain outside of personal life that the individual must deal with on a very direct basis. . . . Like it or not, the city is still the most immediate environment which we encounter and with which we are obliged to deal, beyond the sphere of family and friends, in order to satisfy our needs as social beings. (1990)

A related question is how to provide structural means to alter the dynamic that commonly develops when private interests move into the political arena to secure special benefits. The notion of the community as a whole locally owning substantial wealth-producing firms at least in principle attempts to negate this feature of capitalism. It also counterposes local community structures to statist socialist forms (for a more detailed discussion, see Alperovitz, Williamson, and Campbell 2000).

Community-based institutional experiments from public land trusts to community- and worker-owned firms have multiplied as national social and economic difficulties have increased over the last several years. Many are important as suggestive and preliminary prototypes. Simply by way of illustration, a recent U.S. survey by Dawn Nakano found close to 10,000 worker-owned firms; more than 40,000 co-ops; numerous municipalities that have "communitized" capital ownership including community-owned cable systems, hotels, fertilizer-manufacturing companies, towing services, real estate development efforts, and thousands of city-owned electric utilities; many forms of neighborhood ownership dating back to the original community development corporations of the mid-1960s; and "eco-city" projects that combine innovative environmental technologies, democratic planning, and alternative living arrangements (Nakano 1994; also Howard 2000).

The Institutional Basis of Liberty

"Liberty" defined as a requirement of a comprehensive vision is rarely assessed in systemic or structural terms in modern discussions. However, if the individual must have an independent "place to stand" and if the small entrepreneurial basis of "liberty" can never be retrieved, what then?

The vast majority of both liberals and conservatives have simply avoided this issue: conservatives especially have mostly looked away even as the institutional basis at the heart of their system theory has largely disappeared. Only a very few have had the courage to acknowledge with Henry C. Simons, founder of the Chicago School of Economics, that the corporate-dominated economy is not the same as a true competitive free-enterprise system. In 1948 Simons noted that "the corporation is simply running away with our economic (and political) system" and warned that "the cause of economic liberalism and political democracy faces distinctly unfavorable odds."

Nor, avoiding the gaping hole in their theory, have many confronted the possibility that without some secure new footings for liberty the present system can all too easily be shaken by the scapegoating of minorities, unpopular political groups, or nonconformists in general. That a new institutional *theory* is needed if liberty is to have meaning has rarely been acknowledged.

One of the few even to have stated the problem is Peter Drucker who points out that in Western society "the overwhelming majority of the people in the labor force are employees of 'organizations' . . . and the 'means of production' is therefore the job." He affirms that, accordingly, jobs should (and in many ways have already) become a form of property; the *right* to a job should therefore be accepted as fundamental. Such an approach, in the modern era, Drucker argues, "is compatible with limited government, personal freedom" (Drucker 1980).

If "the job" is to provide the foundation for "liberty," it must obviously be made secure. Some liberals and socialists have proposed mainly on equity grounds (since few have confronted this aspect of the institutional problem of liberty) that there be a legal right to a job. But to be meaningful, to be truly a *right,* not merely a "hope," this requires certain guarantees: in the mid-1970s the initial drafts of the Humphrey-Hawkins full employment legislation contained provisions allowing an individual to go to court to secure a government guaranteed job if no other possibility were available.

Another solution involves the direct provision of a substantial share of income to individuals as a matter of right. The aim of such income is not simply "to help the poor," nor to assist the "aged," nor for any reason other than the most fundamental one that if liberty and democracy are to have meaning, then ultimately individuals must have substantial economic security: simply put, there must be a structural basis for liberty.

In his book *The State* the British political theorist Bill Jordan argues that in "order to reconcile political authority with individual autonomy the state needs to take certain steps to ensure a basis of equality and freedom amongst its citizens. . . . The new principle is that the state should pay to each citizen, simply by virtue of his or her citizenship, an income sufficient for subsistence. This should be unconditional, and paid equally to all, employed and unemployed, men and women, married and single. . . . This state-guaranteed subsistence income (sometimes referred to as the social dividend or social wage) would give every citizen the *basis* for equal autonomy" (1985).

Again, to be quite clear, the issue here is not one of "social justice." Rather, it is how to ensure that the conditions necessary for democratic participation and liberty are met in societies that are long past the era of the individual yeoman farmer and small entrepreneur.

Only a few decades ago the idea that individuals should receive direct funding from the government as, for instance, in the Social Security program, was regarded as illusory. One of the most interesting modern political innovations is the Earned Income Tax Credit, a system supported by both Democrats and Republicans that puts cash directly into the hands of ordinary citizens who work but receive inadequate pay. The concept is very different from welfare payments, which increase the dependency of a class of poor people on the state (as well as the state's coercive power over the person's life). It points ultimately to a much more powerful possibility: allocating part of the wealth created by the community to each individual in order to provide sufficient independence and security to make liberty meaningful.

The notion that there must be an alternative guarantee for some degree of economic security is also a core element in the very long-term system vision proposed by such diverse theorists as Paul and Percival Goodman, on the one hand, and Jacques Maritain, on the other. In their book *Communitas,* the Goodmans suggested a dual vision based on the distinction between necessities and luxury production: part of each day would be devoted to "necessary work" important to the entire community, and income would be assured. The other part would be free for the individual to work in whatever way and at whatever intensity each desired (Goodman and Goodman 1947).

Planning and Accountability

If at least part of the solution to the system problem requires not only the buildup of local structures embodying the principle of community but also the provision of a degree of direct individual economic security so that there can be individual independence, and, hence, substantive liberty, then there must obviously be a way to ensure that this happens. This means some form of planning.

Neither progressives nor conservatives like the idea of planning. In practice, planning has often been bureaucratic and inefficient, perpetuating top-down elite management. However, if stable structures of community are a goal, it is all but impossible to ensure this unless there is some overall capacity to deal with the economic problems involved. There is also no way to ensure some degree of individual economic security without a similar capacity.

The crucial issues are whether "planning" can be made accountable, whether it can be made reasonably efficient (not as compared with an absolute ideal, but with the inefficiencies of real world capitalism and real world socialism), and whether other elements of a long-term solution can confine planning to a supportive, rather than a domineering role.

Obviously, a full-blown account of how planning might become an effective feature in an alternative system formulation is beyond the scope of this essay. However, even to begin, we need a more balanced appraisal of the pluses and minuses of planned and market systems than that which is conveyed in most accounts.

For instance, it is difficult to reconcile conventional criticisms of "planning" and "nationalized industries" with the successes of the early Soviet space program both on its own terms and in comparison with the American record. Again, to choose an example on the other side of the ledger, the disastrous productivity experience of private American steel companies during the 1970s and early 1980s must be included in any serious assessment.

Above all, it is important to recognize that the United States is not a poor Eastern European country struggling to establish its industrial base and to inaugurate its first true consumer era: for all their difficulties, the United States and other major Western nations stand on the threshold of a postindustrial new century, a period when social, individual, and ecological goals could at least in theory plausibly take greater precedence over all-out efforts to achieve ever greater production and consumption.

It is also important to understand that a vision that accords importance to ideals both of community and of liberty does not require a totalist form of planning and should not urge such planning. What is required is sufficient predictability to give stability to local community structures, and to allow the long-term buildup of a serious culture of both liberty and community.

In any community of, say, 100,000 people, there are now full-time jobs for roughly 45,000. Children, the elderly, young people in school, people at home taking care of children and the elderly, those in hospitals, and so forth make up the rest. If, say, 15–17,000 jobs can be assured, then the people employed through "multiplier" effects can give substantial stability to up to twice as many others especially if combined with community-building "import substitution" programs. Planning to stabilize a certain percentage of jobs can allow paychecks to "re-circulate" as people pay for groceries, houses, teachers, doctors, and so on, and these people in turn pay for (and give work to) still others.

A form of planning is also needed if the notion of a guaranteed *right* of employment for each individual is to be meaningful: there is no other way to assure that real jobs exist when they are needed. (One aspect of planning long urged here and abroad involves establishing an inventory of future plans for the construction of needed school, road, bridge, rail, water, and other projects to be taken down off the shelf in time of need.)

Similarly, if ecological goals are important, there must be a systematic way to assure new jobs, for instance, for coal miners thrown out of work when provisions aimed at curbing acid rain are implemented. The same is true in connection with conversion from military production. In these and other cases, several goals — individual equity, a secure basis for individual liberty, ecological balance, movement toward a peace-oriented economy, and the ability to maintain community stability — all require a meaningful planning capacity.

Community Investment

A further feature of planning for community and liberty involves still another possible element of a longer range solution. Businessmen and conservatives commonly argue that a society's wealth should belong to those who take risks and invest capital. Labor organizers and progressives commonly argue that those who work should receive the fruits of their labor. A more fundamental understanding, both economic and moral, involves an emphasis somewhat different from either traditional view.

Compare the living standards of most African countries with the United States. Entrepreneurs invest in both Africa and the United States, and workers work, often very long and hard hours, in both societies. However, income levels are obviously radically different in the two settings. Enormous differences between "the wealth of nations" are related to the long, long history of the much older and larger *community investment,* the many generations of schooling, the historic construction of highways and waterways, the steady evolution of overall skill levels, and the slow buildup of a highly productive culture.

Still more fundamental, of course, is the even longer and larger community investment that produced centuries of science from before Newton to after Einstein and the development of technologies and inventions (and education in the skills to use the technologies) among hundreds of thousands of scientists and engineers, on the one hand, and millions of skilled working people, on the other.

When a young computer inventor produces an innovation that makes him a billionaire, he commonly thinks he "deserves" all that he has received. His "invention," however, is literally unthinkable without the generations of the community's prior accumulation of knowledge, skills, and wealth. He picks the ripe fruit from a tree that grows from a huge mountain of human contribution; the very broad history of community investment is obviously the central factor. Often, too, this involves specific public investments, such as American wartime investments in computer technology.

It is rare that we explicitly recognize this *community inheritance* (Alperovitz 1994). An alternative theory might make it a central feature of a new "system," both morally and politically. Building on inheritance laws as well as public land precedents, conceivably we might evolve our thinking so that major wealth (but not necessarily small businesses and homes, etc.) would regularly be returned to the community that ultimately made the creation of this wealth possible.

A tiny, tiny group of Americans today own huge shares of the nation's wealth. Edward Wolff of New York University, a leading researcher of these trends, has shown that the top one percent's share of household wealth has more than doubled since the mid 1970s: from 19.9 percent in 1976 to 40 percent in 1997 (Collins et al. 1999). The top one percent now owns more than the entire bottom 95 percent of Americans combined and Bill Gates alone owns more than the bottom 45 percent combined (more than 120 million people) (Wolff 1999). The moral case for this wealth being passed on through inheritance to those who do not even claim to have earned it is exceedingly weak. Tightening inheritance laws is clearly one element of a new approach. At the same time, a new approach might wisely allow true individual entrepreneurs to pass on to their chosen heirs a significant share of what each *personally* earns in one lifetime.

Within local communities, over time major buildings and major land ownership (again, not necessarily individual family homes) might pass slowly to the local community as a whole. This shift could also yield revenues and help in the development of new community-building land use and location strategies. A more creative use of eminent domain powers might also ultimately play a role in a comprehensive strategy.

A public trust to establish community ownership of major wealth at the national, state, regional, and local levels could also produce a positive income stream for public use. Part of this might be allocated by the community as a whole to offset taxes and to provide needed services; part might be used to provide security to individuals in the interest of a new structural basis for liberty and democratic participation. Control of substantial economic wealth as a public trust could also obviously help in the implementation of planning for more stable communities.

I have already cited the precedent of the Earned Income Tax Credit. Also particularly noteworthy in this connection is the current Alaskan practice in which an acknowledged communitywide interest in oil royalties has built up a large "permanent fund" that presently yields a direct cash payment of over $1,000 to each resident. In addition to funding this "dividend" payout, the oil royalties are also a chief source of revenue for the state government.

The Uses of Time

A related question involves the provision of expanded amounts (and substantial equality) of free time for democratic participation and for individual self-development and fulfillment in a more systemic vision.

Even with all its economic problems, the United States is so wealthy that if today its gross annual production were divided equally among all its citizens, each family of four would receive over $125,000. Allowing for only moderate growth, a conservative projection of actual twentieth-century trends suggests that this figure could well reach $200,000, then $400,000 and then substantially more by the end of the next century (all in today's dollars; more if inflation is assumed). Indeed, a straightforward projection of twentieth-century trends would yield over $500,000 for every four people (U.S. Census 1975, U.S. Council of Economic Advisers 1995). This assumes no change in the roughly forty-hour workweek. (The numbers would be much larger if, say, postwar Japanese trends were projected.)

An alternative possibility would be to maintain incomes, say, at the "average" $125,000 level (with adjustments for different family size, etc.) and over time slowly reduce what might be called the "necessary" workweek to twenty hours, then to ten hours, or even lower. (Another logical option would be to work longer hours and allocate a share of the production to the Third World.) Of course, in any of the options,

recycling and ecologically oriented planning would be necessary to reduce environmental costs.

The most interesting choice from the point of view of democratic
participation involves reducing the workweek in order to create greater
amounts of free time as a way to permit involvement in community
decision making. If democratic participation and personal liberty are
defined as necessary and fundamental requirements of a new system, the
time available must be fairly divided. Today some people work an
eighty-hour week and some are unemployed and without income, an
inevitable result of the haphazard functioning of the market. Planning is
needed to ensure not only that greater amounts of free time are available, but also that a reasonable degree of equality of free time is assured
to each individual.

More free time does not necessarily mean time spent not doing
productive work: If a portion of "necessary work" is required to meet
overall economic objectives, other time might be spent in small independent enterprises, worker-owned ventures, or cooperatives. A "dual"
conception of future economic life—one in which a portion of work is
defined as necessary for overall community goals, and another portion is
defined as totally "free"—is a commonsense, if all too little discussed,
possibility. Such an economic conception mirrors a dual moral emphasis
that gives equal weight to community, on the one hand, and to individual
independence, liberty, and fulfillment, on the other.

Also implicit in such structural conceptions is what might be called a
potential community-building cycle of relationships, in contrast to a common cycle in which economic inequality limits democratic participation,
which in turn weakens a politics of reform that might hope to achieve
positive movement toward greater equality. A community-building cycle
would aim to manage the community's inheritance so as to target economic activity that could sustain community as well as individual liberty.
Not only is the kind of planning that this requires premised upon non-
totalist objectives, but its specific goals are to produce greater individual
security and free time, which in turn are the conditions needed to sustain
liberty and real participation, and thus to ensure that planning itself can
be made increasingly democratic and accountable.

Egalitarian Culture and the Issue of Scale

An implicit aim of the potential elements of the alternative system
sketched so far is at least the partial development of a structural basis for
a more egalitarian culture. Questions of equality are not independent of

the culture that might potentially emerge from different institutional relationships, especially if these remove significant wealth from private to community control (and allocate the proceeds democratically); establish democratic control of local economic institutions; move toward increasing amounts of free time; attempt to build a more stable community (and potentially a healthier social environment for individual development); and nurture cooperative institutions. New structural underpinnings might also help establish the preconditions of a less materialist culture and facilitate a planning system to implement more rational ecological decisions.

A final element in a possible solution has been little discussed by either theoreticians or citizens: The United States now spans a continent. It includes roughly 260 million people. Does anyone really believe that "participatory democracy" can be meaningful in a nation that includes such a huge sweep of geography and such large numbers of people? (By way of comparison, the state of Oregon is bigger than the former West Germany.)

The visceral disgust many Americans now direct at Washington suggests that it is all but impossible to make a vast continent-scaled federal government responsive. The attack on big government, I believe, is not simply an attack on absolute size; it is an attack on the impossibility of responsiveness over huge distances involving large populations.

In towns and cities, and even in small states, far more people know each other; it is also much easier to learn directly, and with some confidence, the reputation of people who are not known personally. Organizing efforts by grass-roots groups that depend heavily upon individual contacts and person-to-person relationships are also easier in smaller scale units. In large geographic systems involving large numbers of people, what counts is the media — which means, as the saying goes, that "money talks." Indeed, the disproportionate advantages the rich enjoy in a highly unequal society are multiplied when large numbers and large areas are involved.

There is a further consideration, one that James Madison, the architect of the American Constitution, understood very well. Long before Karl Marx, Madison argued that the "principal political division" in society was between those who owned the "means of production" and those who did not. As a representative of the propertied group Madison worried that the "majority" would overwhelm the people he believed should guide the new republic. His checks-and-balances system was one method of slowing down the majority, but equally important (if less discussed) was his argument that large geographic scale gave the wealthy elites special advantages: the opposition could be divided and conquered.

Madison also recognized that large scale and the power it gave elites to break the people up into contending interests could be dangerous. Writing to his friend Thomas Jefferson when the nation was little more than a strip of colonies on the very edge of the ocean, Madison pointed out that if the nation grew "too extensive" then "a defensive concert may be rendered too difficult against the oppression of those entrusted with the administration" (1787). This, he predicted, was a recipe for tyranny.

It is uncomfortable to confront this argument head-on. It implies that if we wish to take the idea of a democracy seriously we must ultimately come to terms with the need for smaller scale units. The late William Appleman Williams argued that a large nation like the United States would be wise to consider the possibility of one day restructuring in terms of its regional units so that, say, ten or twelve groups of states might be brought together as the geographic elements of a longer term vision (Williams 1964). The United States would then comprise a confederation of these units. There would be much greater decentralization of authority, and at the same time the regional units would have to work together in matters of defense, foreign policy, ecological balance, and so on.

The fundamental question is whether large scale inevitably contradicts democratic values. If so, there is little choice but to take the need for smaller units seriously in any thoughtful system theory. Meaningful planning, administration, and the stewardship of a substantial share of community inheritance might also logically take place at the regional, subnational level. Regional units, too, would be the logical locus for larger-scale publicly owned enterprise.

As the federal government deadlock grows, a number of American states are now taking on increasingly important independent economic management functions. Some, like California and Texas, are regions unto themselves larger than many European nations. It is possible that this trend born of frustration and failure might one day have a silver lining in a new system.

NOTES

Portions of this essay are from Gar Alperovitz, "Speculative Theory and Regime Alternatives: Beyond Socialism and Capitalism," in Stephen L. Elkin and Karol Edward Soltan, eds., *The Constitution of Good Societies* (University Park, Pennsylvania: The Pennsylvania State University Press, 1996), 146–63. Copyright © 1996 by The Pennsylvania State University. Reproduced by permission of the publisher.

1. For a discussion of some proposals, see Williamson 1998.

REFERENCES

Alperovitz, Gar. 1994. Distributing Our Technological Inheritance. *Technology Review* 97, no. 8 (October).

Alperovitz, Gar, Thad Williamson, and Alex Campbell. 2000. Ecological Sustainability—Some Elements of Longer Term System Change. In Fred Gale and Michael M'Gonigle, eds., *Nature, Production, Power: The Theory and Practice of Ecological Political Economy,* forthcoming.

Bookchin, Murray. 1990. *Remaking Society.* Boston: South End Press.

Buber, Martin. 1950. *Paths in Utopia.* New York: Macmillan.

Collins, Chuck, Betsy Leonard-Wright, and Holly Sklar. 1999. *Shifting Fortunes: The Perils of the Growing American Wealth Gap.* Boston: United for a Fair Economy.

Council of Economic Advisers. 1995. *Economic Report of the President, 1995.* Washington: U.S. Goverment Printing Office.

Council on Budget and Policy Priorities. 1999. *Low Unemployment, Rising Wages Fuel Poverty Decline: Concerns Remain Amidst the Good News.* Washington, October 1.

Dahl, Robert A. 1996. Equality Versus Inequality. *PS: Political Science & Politics* 29, no. 4 (December).

Daly, Herman, and John Cobb. 1989. *For the Common Good.* Boston: Beacon Press.

Drucker, Peter. 1980. The Job as Property Right. *Wall Street Journal,* March 4.

Friedman, Milton. 1962. *Capitalism and Freedom.* Chicago: University of Chicago Press.

Goodman, Paul, and Percival Goodman. 1947, 1960. *Communitas.* New York: Random House.

Hayek, Friedrich. 1944, 1972. *The Road to Serfdom.* Chicago: University of Chicago Press. Quotation cited is from Hayek's foreword to the 1972 edition; de Tocqueville quotation is from *Democracy in America,* part 2, book 4, chapter 6.

House Ways and Means Committee. 1992. *1992 Green Book.* Washington: U.S. Government Printing Office.

Howard, Ted. 2000. Innovations in Ownership. Washington, DC: National Center for Economic and Security Alternatives, forthcoming.

Jefferson, Thomas. 1977. Letter to John Adams, 1813. Cited in C. B. Macpherson, *The Life and Times of Liberal Democracy.* New York: Oxford University Press.

———. [1781] 1954. *Notes on the State of Virginia.* Chapel Hill: University of North Carolina Press.

Jordan, Bill. 1985. *The State.* New York: Basil Blackwell.

Kirk, Russell. 1976, 1979. Ideology and Political Economy. vol. 96, *America.* Cited in George H. Nash, *The Conservative Intellectual Movement in America.* New York: Basic Books.

Madison, James. 1867. Letter to Thomas Jefferson, October 24, 1787. Reprinted in *Letters and Other Writings of James Madison.* Philadelphia: Lippincott.

Maritain, Jacques. 1985. A Society Without Money. *Review of Social Economy* 43, no. 1 (April).

Nakano, Dawn. 1994. *Community Economic Development: Findings of a Survey of the Field.* Washington: National Center for Economic Alternatives.

Rodriguez, Francisco. 1998. Essays on Redistribution, Development, and the State. Ph.D. dissertation, Harvard University.

Roemer, John E. 1998. Why the Poor Do Not Expropriate the Rich: An Old Argument in New Garb. *Journal of Public Economics* 70.

Simons, Henry C. 1948. *Economic Policy for a Free Society.* Chicago: University of Chicago Press.

Thurow, Lester C. 1980. *The Zero-Sum Society: Distribution and the Possibilities for Economic Change.* New York: Basic Books.

U.S. Bureau of the Census. 1975. *Historical Statistics of the United States, From Colonial Times to 1970.* Washington: U.S. Government Printing Office.

U.S. Bureau of the Census. 1994. *Statistical Abstract of the United States, 1994.* Washington: U.S. Government Printing Office.

U.S. Bureau of the Census. 1999a. *Money Income in the United States: 1998.* Current Population Report, P60–206. Washington: U.S. Government Printing Office.

U.S. Bureau of the Census. 1999b. *Poverty in the United States: 1998.* Current Population Report, P60–207. Washington: U.S. Government Printing Office.

Williams, William Appleman. 1964. *The Great Evasion.* Chicago: Quadrangle Books.

Williamson, Thad. 1998. *What Comes Next? Proposals for a Different Society.* Washington: National Center for Economic and Security Alternatives.

Winnick, Andrew J. 1989. *Toward Two Societies: The Changing Distribution of Income and Wealth in the U.S. since 1960.* New York: Praeger.

Wolff, Edward N. 1999. A Scholar Who Concentrates . . . on Concentrations of Wealth. *Too Much* (winter).

CHAPTER 2

The Case for the Global Commons

Baylor Johnson and Faye Duchin

Extreme Views about the Commons

Garrett Hardin's article "The Tragedy of the Commons" (1968) is probably the best known and most influential work in a tradition, dating back to Lloyd's lectures of 1832 (Cox 1985), that has treated common property as the cause of resource degradation, and privatization as the solution. Hardin and others have suggested that, in the words of Baxter, "The problem of the commons is the primary source of our environmental and conservation difficulties" (1974, 35).

Common-property institutions have received considerable attention in the quarter century since Hardin's article,[1] and it is now widely recognized that the "Tragedy of the Commons" involved an unfortunate misunderstanding.[2] What Hardin called a "commons" is better described as an "open-access resource" — a resource that is available to all without regulations or limits — while common property is an institution designed to avoid the ravages of open access. Depletion of resources indicates that common property has not been established or that the institution has broken down. Well-functioning commons can provide adequate protection for the resources they manage, just as private ownership is compatible with destruction, deliberate or inadvertent, of the resources under its control.[3] While the indictment of the commons on the basis of Hardin's arguments is now widely recognized as an error, the confusion unfortunately persists.[4]

Most scholars who have studied common property believe it is capable of protecting resources in its established and traditional settings (e.g., Bromley 1989, 1992; Ostrom 1990, 1994; Quiggin 1993). Quiggin (1993) argues that common property is generally more egalitarian than private-property alternatives in similar settings, and Jodha (1992) provides empirical evidence for the egalitarian effects of common property in India. The article "Whose Common Future?" by the staff of the *Ecologist* provides an even more enthusiastic endorsement of the commons (1993).

It is, however, an open question whether common property can be successfully extended to new settings. Hanna (1990), McGinnis and Ostrom (1993), Quiggin (1988), Sandler (1992), Stone (1993), and Swaney (1990) have all explored requirements for "scaling up" common-property institutions to protect regional or global resources.

Our objective in this paper is to clarify the nature of common property: what it is, under what conditions individuals find it in their interest to manage property in this way, what benefits accrue to commoners and their communities from this property form. We also contribute to the task of assessing what scaled-up forms of common property can offer for protection of regional and global environmental resources.

What Is Common Property?

The term *commons* calls to mind a physical entity. As used here, however, *commons, common property,* and *CPI* (for common-property institution) refer not to a place or thing but to a social institution for managing activities that affect a physical entity. We shall use the term *CPR* (for common-pool resource or common-property resource) to refer to the physical resource managed by the CPI.[5]

Common property is "owned" in common in the sense that users jointly determine who shall use it and how. But the shares harvested from the CPR are privately owned and typically gathered by the users' own efforts. Common property is often associated with natural resources like grazing areas, woodlots, rangelands, and local fisheries, but human artifacts like irrigation systems can also be managed in this way. Property includes anything that can be owned and used up or degraded by use. Some kinds of resources have often become common property while others are typically private or state property.

We shall show later that there are good reasons why common property is employed more frequently in socially and technically simpler societies, but it is by no means confined to these. Common property can be a useful institution in developed societies. Ostrom describes large water districts in southern California in which water is managed as common property by its appropriators,[6] and many irrigation facilities in developed countries are managed as common property. The common areas of condominiums are typically the common property of all residents, and the facilities of private clubs may also be the common property of the clubs' members. Nearly all of us have direct experience with common-property management through our families, which usually treat the household and its furnishings, and sometimes automobiles, as common property of family members.

Source and Flow

A CPI governs appropriation of a flow of goods from a source (e.g., grass from a pasture, water from an aquifer, or the uses of a commons room) by a defined group of users, or commoners. In contrast to what economists call public goods,[7] appropriation from the resources managed as common property subtracts from what is left for others.

The flow is fugitive in the sense that no user has a property right to a particular unit until it has been appropriated (Ciriancy-Wantrup 1985, 221). Even when commoners have a guaranteed share of the flow prior to capture, as in the aquifers studied by Ostrom (1990, chap. 4; 1994, chap. 13), they do not have prior rights to particular units of the flow.

It is a common, but not an essential characteristic that the flow may also be fugitive in the sense of unpredictable, that is, its location is variable from day to day or season to season, as with fish or wild fruit. This is generally true of fisheries and of the best grass or water in open, arid plains, but not of grass in the alpine meadows studied by Stevenson (1991) or water in the aquifers studied by Ostrom (1990).

Rules and Duties

A common-property institution needs at least four kinds of rules. These are clear understandings shared by the commoners but not necessarily in the form of a document or formal statement (Runge 1981).

1. Rules determine who is entitled to use the CPR and specify how this right is gained or lost. Such rules are the first, essential step to convert an open-access resource into a common-property resource.
2. Rules govern appropriation from the CPR (e.g., timing and means) and may govern obligations regarding maintenance or provision of the source. Appropriation may be limited through inputs, such as the number of animals pastured or the time, duration, or sequence of the harvesting activities of commoners — or outputs, such as the amount of firewood gathered or water pumped.

Some common-pool resources, like an ocean fishery, require no upkeep beyond avoidance of overexploitation.[8] In other cases, like fertilized pastures, common rooms, or irrigation facilities, the common-property institution must rely on rules to make sure the necessary activities are provided. There may also be rules governing attendance at meetings, holding of offices, etc.

3. To minimize free-rider problems, rules ensure that compliance with the foregoing rules is monitored and that failures of compliance are sanctioned. Procedures are needed for resolving conflicts that arise concerning compliance and sanctioning.

The expectation that violators will be detected and sanctioned will tend to enhance compliance. Acting as a monitor can itself affect compliance, insofar as it strengthens or weakens one's belief that others are conforming to the rules (Ostrom 1990, 95–97). Mild sanctioning for occasional violations provides the institution with additional flexibility: individuals are given the room to maneuver in special circumstances without the necessity of foreseeing and codifying all such circumstances in advance (Ostrom 1990, 186). The effectiveness of sanctions in commons is also enhanced when they can be supplemented by informal sanctions outside the formal commons procedures.[9]

4. A commons must have metarules about changing the operating rules given above. In particular, appropriation rules may change frequently in response to natural variations. The other rules must also be revisable as needed, however; to avoid conflict, procedures for making these changes must be established and recognized.

A common-property institution defined in this way involves self-governance by the commoners. This feature distinguishes common property from, say, a state-property resource where individuals appropriate a flow according to rules but have no formal say in making the rules. Though broad participation in governance by commoners is important to the success of commons, the governance structure need not be entirely democratic. Frequently "elders," or those with a larger stake, hold more power than other commoners. The delegation of decision making to representatives also occurs.

Rights

In some commons, users can sell or give their rights to others or hire someone else to exercise these rights. Stevenson (1991, 102), for example, describes common-property alpine pastures where rights may be rented or bought, and Ostrom (1990, 153) describes a fishery in which some wealthier commoners pay others to exercise their fishing rights.

In the simplest case every commoner has an equal right to take from the commons, but rights to appropriate and obligations to contribute to creation and maintenance of the CPR may also be unequal. The number of animals one has a right to graze in a common pasture, for example, could be determined by the number one has wintered over, the area of one's private land, or some other criterion. Contributions to maintenance of CPR might in turn be set according to the number of animals grazed.[10]

Common Property and the Alternatives

Common Property and Open-Access Resources

Common property differs from open-access resources by limiting access to the CPR to a defined group of users and by governing users' appropriations from the CPR through a system of rules backed by enforcement and sanctions. While most commons generally exclude outsiders, one can conceive of instances in which everyone (in a particular universe) might be a commoner. In this case all the burden of protection would fall on use rules.[11]

Common Property and Corporate Property

Ownership of property confers a bundle of socially sanctioned rights.[12] In modern societies ownership of private property generally entails the right to use property, to forbid or allow others to use it, and to exhaust or destroy the property; the right to transfer ownership of the property to others by gift, bequest, or trade (including sale); the right to the proceeds of transfer (if any), that is, private ownership of whatever is taken in trade.

In for-profit corporations (henceforth corporations) the shareholders delegate these rights to the corporation whose officers and employees exercise them on behalf of the owners. However, the right to proceeds devolves upon shareholders, not the employees. The benefits received by the owners are almost universally in cash, not in kind.

By contrast, the owners of common property typically own the "source" and the "flow" in different senses. They jointly "own" the right to use the common pool resource and to determine who else uses it and in what way, and they individually own the units of flow that they harvest from the CPR and the rights of use, transfer, and proceeds of this flow.

While corporate owners typically employ others to exercise their rights and produce a stream of cash benefits for them, commoners typically use their common property to produce benefits for themselves. Even in cases in which commoners employ others to exercise their rights to the commons, the individual commoners manage the appropriative process, contribute resources that are vital to it, and receive an individual stream of benefits in kind. Commoners act more like entrepreneurs than like corporate shareholders.

The rights of transfer and proceeds of a CPR are more difficult to describe because common-property institutions are extremely varied in their details and most CPRs have arisen outside the framework of modern, Western property rights. Despite this caveat, we believe that most common-property institutions have not possessed the rights of transfer and proceeds; in traditional societies, lacking a large and complex market structure, sale of the CPR would be impracticable if not inconceivable.[13] Commoners generally regard the CPR as a resource held in trust for future generations, not a commodity to be marketed when alternative investments exceed the discounted future benefits of the commons.

As traditional commons have come within the orbit of expanding markets (not least in the enclosure movement in early modern Britain), they have often been transferred from traditional to new owners. Sometimes the traditional commoners may have freely chosen as a group to transfer ownership of the CPR in return for compensation. But outright seizure, deliberate fraud, and cultural misunderstanding seem to have been more common. In sum, the exercise of rights to transfer and proceeds of traditional CPRs appears rare.

The not-for-profit corporation (NFP) is like the for-profit corporation in that rights to use and transfer of property are exercised by corporate officers and employees, not for their own benefit, but on behalf of the corporation. NFPs differ from corporations, however, in a crucial respect: NFPs have no shareholders, and consequently no individual or group of individuals holds the right to proceeds from the transfer of assets. The Pope, for example, cannot sell the Vatican and keep the money for himself, nor can he divide and distribute the whole of the Church's assets to the faithful. In this, NFPs resemble the de facto status of most traditional commons.

Conditions Favoring Commons

Several circumstances favor adoption of common property as an institution.[14] They tend to occur more frequently in socially and technologically simpler societies than in complex ones.

Difficulties of Exclusion

Property is likely to be used in common when it is technologically or socially difficult to exclude individuals from the resource in question. The costs of a bureaucracy to define, record, enforce, and adjudicate disputes of title to extensive private-property claims may be unaffordable or unjustified. The technical means of dividing the property into private holdings (barbed wire, for instance) may be unaffordable or unavailable. Though less developed societies are more likely to lack affordable social and technological means of privatizing resources, the need to weigh the costs and benefits of privatization in light of available social and technological means is always present. This is especially true for large regional and global environmental resources today.

Need for Secure Access to Vital Resources

A second factor favoring the adoption of common property is the need for secure access to unpredictable resources, for example, those whose abundance and spatial location varies considerably and unforeseeably. In such circumstances exclusive possession of private territory may lead to an alternation of surpluses and deficits, whereas common access to a larger territory provides greater security to all commoners, albeit perhaps at a consistently modest average return. This is the case, for instance, of a herder or gatherer restricted to one location in arid country where the rains fall in different places in different years.

The importance of this factor declines as social and technological growth provide alternative access to vital resources. Drilled wells can provide access to water for drinking and irrigation even in dry years. Storage and transportation facilities can provide access to surplus food from other years or other places. Bank loans and social security schemes can tide one over years when one's own resources are inadequate.

The need for secure access in variable conditions provides a reason for leaving some resources in common. However, as societies develop socially and technologically, alternative solutions may become available.

Efficient Use of Resources

Private ownership in cases of unpredictable variations may entail not only insecurity but also inefficient use of local resources: surpluses go unused, while those in deficit are likely to overexploit and degrade their property, decreasing its long-term productivity.[15]

In summary: in some cases, common-property rights can be less costly to establish and enforce, provide greater security to the ensemble of rights holders, and permit more efficient utilization of resources than would private- or state-property rights.[16]

Evaluation of Proposals for Commons

Local commons have often been successful for managing small-scale resources. Here we consider the potential for adopting the institution of common property to protect regional or global environmental resources.

Local Commons

In addition to the benefits to individual property owners just described, common property provides certain positive externalities to commoners as a group, and in some cases to their larger community. Common property can provide at least three public benefits to commoners or the local community: better resource protection than open-access, greater economic equality than private property, and development of skills and attitudes conducive to democratic governance of the larger community.

Resource Protection
CPRs such as forests, fisheries, and grazing lands usually tend to be left in a relatively natural state, while private property tends to be devoted to more intensive, monocultural uses. For this reason, common-property management may be able to promote greater biological diversity and put less stress on the environment.

Insofar as detailed local knowledge is important to successful management of resources, common-property management may be preferable to state management. The latter will almost inevitably tend to be bureaucratic and formulaic, while the former will enlist the self-interested involvement of knowledgeable locals.

While noting the strengths of common property, a realistic appraisal must also record its limitations in terms of ecological preservation. Common property will tend to preserve what commoners want to preserve, not necessarily what ecologists or environmental preservationists would favor. Commoners are interested in making a living from their resource, and this can involve practices that destroy an existing ecosystem.[17]

The claim has been made (e.g., in *Whose Common Future?* [1993]) that common property will be preserved as a legacy to future generations more frequently than private property. It is true that commoners may wish to prolong the security the commons provides and bequeath it and their way of life to their children. The same, however, may be true of private property as in the case of the family farm.

In order to prevent the intentional conversion of common property to other uses, a commons could be converted legally into a not-for-profit corporation by stripping the rights of sale and proceeds. But the same could be done for parcels of private property, were it desirable and politically feasible. In any case, other methods of achieving the same end are already well understood. It is possible, for instance, to buy development rights for private property through an easement that limits use rights but leaves the rights of sale and proceeds with the owner.

Equality

It is often claimed that local commons promote greater economic equality than private ownership of these resources.[18] Quiggin (1993) provides a theoretical argument while Jodha (1992) offers empirical evidence accumulated in Indian villages.

In Quiggin's analysis the primary attraction of common property is its ability to capture economies of scale and make them available to all commoners rather than reserving them for those wealthy enough to capture these advantages for themselves. By contrast:

> if scale economies are important and common property systems are unavailable, factor returns will be higher for well-endowed households, and income will be distributed more unequally than endowments. (1129)

Those who have greater ability to capture economies of scale will reap higher returns and tend over time to accumulate even greater advantages.

He also argues that the operation of a commons will further encourage equality. Inequality among commoners tends to produce divergent interests; those with greater wealth, for instance, will tend to favor more capital-intensive management policies. In the interests of reducing potentially divisive disagreements, the institution will tend to reduce differences, including economic inequalities.[19]

The conversion of a commons to private or state property is seldom accomplished in a way that adequately compensates all commoners for their losses; for familiar reasons involving the distribution of power and influence, it will seldom be the poor who come off best (Bromley 1989; Jodha 1992). The effects of inadequate compensation are, of course, intensified as the other factors just described come into play.[20]

Of course, an institution tending to promote equality can coexist with considerable inequality, and common property often does so. It is no panacea for inequality (Quiggin 1993). Furthermore, common property tends to promote equality among commoners only, ignoring those excluded from the commons.

Democratic Social Capital

Insofar as common property is managed by more or less democratic procedures, participation in a commons provides practice in self-governance skills such as participation in public meetings, public speaking, weighing of arguments, negotiation, compromise, and estimating and taking stock of the costs and benefits of various policies. Further, a successful commons develops particular attitudes and inclinations on the part of participants: commoners learn that groups of self-interested individuals can cooperate to produce benefits for their members; that free riding can be detected and kept in bounds; that friends and neighbors can, at least in suitably arranged circumstances, be trusted; that forbearance can lead to benefits. In sum, the commoner may be expected to acquire a suitably cautious faith in the benefits of cooperation, a working knowledge of the conditions required for such cooperation, and a set of practical skills necessary for self-interested individuals to cooperate successfully.

The importance of these skills and attitudes has been stressed by Robert Putnam (1994), who studied the regional governments of Italy, newly created in the early 1970s after a century of highly centralized national governance. He found the most successful new governments in regions characterized by strong civic traditions of cooperative institutions, and the least successful in areas lacking such institutions. These patterns were in turn related to the institutional history in the period prior to unification. The south was for centuries governed from the center, with clients depending for benefits on their standing with particular, powerful patrons. By contrast, many regions in the north experienced local, often semidemocratic forms of governance, together with cooperative associations including artisan guilds, singing clubs, and labor unions.

Putnam believes that the preexistence of this social capital may be necessary for building larger and more formal structures like regional governments. Common-property institutions appear to be especially suited to providing the skills and attitudes that constitute the social capital of democracy.

Global Commons

The emergence of CPIs is favored by the difficulty of exclusion, need for secure access, and the requirement of efficient use of resources. Large-scale CPIs are most likely to be workable and successful for resources with some or all of these characteristics.

Consider as an example the atmosphere, which supports life and serves as a sink for gaseous emissions. All nations require secure access, and exclusion is impractical and unthinkable. One way to avoid drastic degradation of this open-access resource is through international agreements to monitor and limit emissions and enforce compliance with these limits — essentially the creation of a global CPI for the atmosphere.

But should a CPI be favored over other alternatives? We shall address this question by examining the potential to realize at the global level the benefits that were identified at the local level, that is, resource protection, greater economic equality, and development of civic society.

Consider three alternatives for managing a regional fishery: through open access, monopoly by one state, or access restricted by and to a few states that conserve the resource. The first option is likely to lead to overexploitation, leaving everyone worse off; while the second and third produce benefits, the third distributes them more widely.

A commons for the atmosphere is a different kind of case. Presumably no one can be excluded from use, so the burden of protection falls entirely on restrictions governing use. Safeguarding the atmosphere is an outcome that no nation can achieve alone, and the cost per nation to reach a given pattern of concentrations of gases falls as more nations limit their emissions. There are also benefits from research, monitoring, and enforcement that allow for scale economies.

But can global and regional commons work? The transaction costs of creating and operating a global commons whose members are individuals appear daunting. Regional and global commons will need to rely on existing structures of governance, with the first layer of commoners consisting of nations. Each of these can, in turn, provide its own rules for distributing benefits and responsibilities.[21]

Can the prospect of large-scale CPIs increase the disposition of countries to cooperate for the common good? Successful collaboration between nations for environmental protection at regional and global levels might increase trust and teach diplomatic skills, but there are numerous political obstacles, and early failures would be discouraging. Some conclusions can be drawn on the basis of the attributes examined in this paper.

A major challenge to protection of the global environment is convincing the most influential nations that their stake is large enough to justify the investments that protection will require.[22] It is important to proceed by incremental steps rather than to expect to create an ambitious structure at the outset. Small steps reduce initial costs, build confidence, and permit refinement of structures in the light of experience.

Sandler (1992) identified two obstacles to collective action on greenhouse gases (GHGs). First, the costs of limiting emissions (which he contrasts with the much smaller costs for banning CFCs) are significant. Second, nations have different interests, since some will be clear losers, while others have less at stake or might even benefit, for example, from increased rainfall. Given the high costs and uncertainty about consequences, there is at present no set of intensely felt needs among potential key actors, and further research may even reduce their stake. Sandler suggests that it may be easier for key players to initiate action before enough is known to clearly identify more of the winners and losers.

Despite the absence of agreement among key actors as to their interests, international research on global environmental problems has begun. Collaboration in this research may itself serve as an early step toward building a CPI for the global atmosphere by building trust and confirming that at least some key actors have an adequate stake in limiting GHG emissions to formulate rules for doing so.

Among the possible early steps is Christopher Stone's (1993) proposal to create a trust fund from taxes or fines on activities like ocean dumping and GHG emissions and use the proceeds for environmental research and remediation. The sums that could be collected would no doubt be modest compared to potential claims on them, and obtaining agreement to such a scheme seems a formidable challenge. It would be easy to dismiss the proposal. In the light of the theory of common property, however, this proposal seems stronger: such a trust fund could be a modest first step that commits none of the commoners irrevocably to further action. Providing it runs smoothly and generates benefits, it might encourage the consideration of other steps.

An environmental research agenda could backfire if it reveals that significant actors have divergent interests, but this is unlikely to be true across the full range of problems. Ecological changes tend to have multiple, interlocking effects. In addition, the nations of the world become more interdependent daily. It seems unlikely that any major nation would fail to have a direct stake in some global environmental problems and an indirect stake in others through the fates of political allies and trading partners.[23]

Such research could be expected to provide an improved basis for monitoring that would be needed for expansion of the common-property institution. Prominent among the outstanding research questions are: How can a global commons be structured so that monitors and sanctioners have incentives to do their work rigorously but without favoritism? What sanctions are feasible, and who will apply them?[24]

Conclusion

For too long the self-governing commons has been a maligned and misunderstood institution while in fact it is often a robust protector of environmental resources and a significant source of social benefits as well. Local commons can continue to provide these benefits if not undermined from the outside. In this era, community initiative is extolled in political settings as different as development-oriented NGOs and the U.S. Congress. Casebooks that distinguish the commons from open-access resources and provide guidelines and examples for building local commons could stimulate new experiments.

The CPI probably has benefits to offer at the regional and global levels as well. Indeed, the creation of a CPI may be the only way to protect some truly global resources such as the atmosphere. On the basis of our knowledge about the benefits and requirements of common property, it is time to begin the systematic evaluation of alternative schemes to protect specific, large-scale environmental resources as common-pool resources. In the process, we will need to develop a vastly generalized cost-benefit framework for comparing the advantages and disadvantages of different management regimes. The best approach is to build confidence by starting with the easiest cases.

NOTES

1. See, for example, Berkes 1989, Bromley et al. 1992, McCay and Acheson 1987, and Ostrom 1990, 1994. An online bibliography is maintained by the International Association for the Study of Common Property at <www.indiana.edu /~iascp>. The influence of this research has been wide enough to reach Garrett Hardin, who recently acknowledged the distinction between open-access and limited-access commons. See Hardin (1998).

2. Ciriacy-Wantrup and Bishop (1975) first diagnosed the mistake.

3. Clark (1973) offered an early discussion of the conditions leading to destruction of resources under private ownership.

4. The article on common land in *The New Palgrave* distinguishes commons from open access regimes, declaring, "With the notable exception of some village greens, commons do not represent areas which are owned by nobody, nor areas which are owned by everybody, nor even by everybody within a given locality."

But five pages later the entry on common property rights treats commons as open access resources: "In a common property, there is no limitation or delineation of its use rights to any private party. No one has the right to exclude others from using it and all are free to compete for its use. Hence there are no exclusive use rights, no rights to be transferred, and in the limiting case, no net income can be derived from using the common property."

5. This section draws on Stevenson 1991, Bromley et al. 1992, and Ostrom 1990.

6. Ostrom 1990, esp. chap. 4.

7. A public good is defined by economists as being both "nonexclusive," meaning that it is available to all, and also "nonrival," meaning that its use by one person does not diminish its usefulness to others.

8. Historically, open ocean fisheries have required no maintenance, but pollution and destruction of inshore spawning sites, for instance, are increasingly reducing fish populations. Commoners alone cannot resolve these problems.

9. This condition is frequently met in small, tightly knit communities. Runge (1986) puts it well: "In a village economy, the benefits possible from free riding in the short term may be more than offset by the costs imposed on those who break the rules. Recognized interdependencies make the costs of reputation loss high, much like losing one's credit rating in a developed economy." Arguably something like this is present on the international scene, where nations often use informal sanctions like trade restrictions, withdrawal of ambassadors, and opposition to a rival's international interests in order to punish other nations whose actions are not sufficiently restrained by international laws or treaties.

10. For examples of differential rights and duties, see Stevenson 1991, chap. 4, esp. 105 ff., 126.

11. For a somewhat different treatment, see Quiggin 1988.

12. For a fuller account of property rights, see Honoré 1961.

13. The right to transfer the CPR itself is not to be confused with the right to transfer membership in the common property institution.

14. This account draws on Runge 1986.

15. Jodha (1992) states, "the transfer of submarginal CPR lands to crop cultivation through their privatization is tantamount to a step towards long-term unsustainability for land-based activities in dry regions."

16. Quiggin 1993 provides an alternative view in which the advantage of common property is its capture of economies of scale.

17. Fernandez (1987) relates incidents in which common pastures had been nationalized by the Spanish government and planted in forests. Villagers set fire to the forests in order to keep the areas free for illegal grazing.

18. McCay (1987) describes how memories of enclosure of the commons in the Old World induced commitment to open access in the United States as a way of establishing greater economic equality. She describes conflict in New England in the late nineteenth century over new capital-intensive and labor-intensive fishing technologies. Small-scale fishermen explicitly cited adverse effects on the distribution of income and on community in arguing that the new technologies should be banned (206).

19. In agricultural communities in which common property plays a part, an individual's holdings are often fragmented into small, dispersed parcels. If, for instance, the holdings lie at both the head and the tail of an irrigation work, a

commoner will tend to oppose policies that systematically benefit one over the other. This kind of equalization may be more or less actively encouraged by the common property institution.

Wade (1987) observes that holdings in south Indian villages are typically scattered in small parcels, partly to diffuse risk and partly because of inheritance practices: a landowner with a plot close to one irrigation outlet may have another plot close to the tail end of a block fed from another outlet. This practice helps build consensus regarding rules and joint regulation (220).

20. Jodha (1992) studied the loss or decline of CPRs (due to degradation, privatization, and state appropriation) in eighty-two villages across India and argues that pauperization and economic inequality have increased as a result (17).

21. This structure corresponds to the "nesting principle" identified by Ostrom as characteristic of "robust" commons, that is, commons that endure, protect the CPR, and evolve in ways consistent with the original purpose and design of the institution. According to Ostrom: "Appropriation, provision, monitoring, enforcement, conflict resolution, and governance activities are organized in multiple layers of nested enterprises" that allow these activities to be undertaken at appropriate levels of group size, governance responsibility, and so on (1992, 23).

22. This need corresponds to one of a number of conditions necessary to the successful emergence of CPIs. The most important of these are as follows:

1. The commons must address "intensely felt needs that could not be met by individual responses" (Wade 1992, 222).
2. There must exist a group of important actors who have a sufficient incentive to bear the transaction costs of organizing others (Wade 1992).
3. It should be possible to create the CPI in incremental steps with low initial costs, which produce demonstrable benefits encouraging further steps (Ostrom 1990).
4. Commoners must share, or establish, norms of reciprocity and trust (Ostrom 1990).
5. Operational rules for the commons must have similar effects on most commoners, in particular on key actors (Ostrom 1990).

23. If global warming occurs, its effects can be expected to reverberate through many of the world's ecosystems. Short of global warming, scientists anticipate substantial effects of increasing greenhouse gas emissions on climate and ecosystems. Even if the buildup of atmospheric CO_2 is balanced by more extensive cloud cover, insolation and rainfall patterns will be affected.

24. McGinnis and Ostrom 1993 uses the design principles for "robust" common property institutions developed in Ostrom 1990 to speculate about which organizations might do the sanctioning and with what degree of success.

REFERENCES

Baxter, W. 1974. *People or Penguins: The Case for Optimal Pollution.* New York and London: Columbia University Press.

Berkes, F., ed. 1989. *Common Property Resources: Ecology and Community-based Sustainable Development.* London: Belhaven.

Bromley, D. W. 1989. Property Relations and Economic Development: The Other Land Reform. *World Development* 17, no. 6: 867–77.

Bromley, Daniel W., et al., eds. 1992. *Making the Commons Work: Theory, Practice and Policy.* San Francisco: ICS Press.

Ciriacy-Wantrup, S. V. 1985. Economics and Policies of Resource Conservation. In R. C. Bishop and S. O. Andersen, eds., *Natural Resource Economics: Selected Papers.* Boulder and London: Westview Press.

Ciriacy-Wantrup, S. V., and R. C. Bishop. 1985. "Common Property" as a Concept in Natural Resources Policy. In R. C. Bishop and S. O. Andersen, eds., *Natural Resource Economics: Selected Papers.* Boulder and London: Westview Press.

Clark, C. 1973. Profit Maximization and the Extinction of Animal Species. *Journal of Political Economy* 81:950–51.

Cox, S. J. B. 1985. No Tragedy on the Commons. *Environmental Ethics* 7 (spring): 49–61.

Eatwell, J., M. Milgate, and P. Newman, eds. 1989. *The New Palgrave.* London: Macmillan. New York: Stockton Press.

The Ecologist. 1993. *Whose Common Future? Reclaiming the Commons.* Philadelphia: New Society Publishers.

Fernandez, J. W. 1987. The Call to the Commons: Decline and Recommitment in Asturias, Spain. In McCay and Acheson 1987, 266–89.

Hanna, S. S. 1990. The Eighteenth Century English Commons: A Model for Ocean Management. *Ocean and Shoreline Management* 14:155–72.

Hardin, G. 1968. The Tragedy of the Commons. *Science* 162:1243–48.

Hardin. G. 1998. Extensions of "The Tragedy of the Commons," *Science* 280: 682–83.

Honoré, A. M. 1961. Ownership. In A. G. Guest, ed., *Oxford Essays in Jurisprudence,* 107–47. Oxford: Clarendon Press.

Jodha, N. S. 1992. *Common Property Resources: A Missing Dimension of Development Strategies.* Washington, DC: The World Bank.

Martin, F. 1989. Common Pool Resources and Collective Action: A Bibliography. Bloomington: Indiana University Workshop in Political Theory and Policy Analysis.

McCay, B. 1987. The Culture of the Commoners: Historical Observations on Old and New World Fisheries. In McCay and Acheson 1987, 195–216.

McCay, B. J., and J. M. Acheson, eds. 1987. *The Question of the Commons: The Culture and Ecology of Communal Resources.* Tucson: University of Arizona Press.

McGinnis, M., and E. Ostrom. 1993. Design Principles for Local and Global

Commons. In *Proceedings of a Conference on Linking Local and Global Commons,* 16–65. Cambridge: Harvard University Center for International Affairs; Bloomington: Indiana University Workshop in Political Theory and Policy Analysis.

Ostrom, E. 1990. *Governing the Commons: The Evolution of Institutions for Collective Action.* Cambridge and New York: Cambridge University Press.

———. 1994. *Rules, Games and Common Pool Resources.* Ann Arbor: University of Michigan Press.

Quiggin, J. 1988. Private and Common Property Rights in the Economics of the Environment. *Journal of Economic Issues* 22, no. 4: 1071–87.

———. 1993. Common Property, Equality, and Development. *World Development* 21, no. 7: 1123–38.

Runge, C. F. 1981. Common Property Externalities: Isolation, Assurance and Depletion in a Traditional Grazing Context. *Amer. J. of Agr. Econ.* 63, no. 4: 595–606.

———. 1986. Common Property and Collective Action in Economic Development. *World Development* 14, no. 5: 623–35.

Sandler, T. 1992. After the Cold War, Secure the Global Commons. *Challenge* 35, no. 4: 16–23.

Stevenson, G. G. 1991. *Common Property Economics: A General Theory and Land Use Applications.* Cambridge and New York: Cambridge University Press.

Stone, Christopher. 1993. *The Gnat Is Older than Man: Global Environment and Human Agenda.* Princeton, NJ: Princeton University Press.

Swaney, J. A. 1990. Common Property, Reciprocity, and Community. *Journal of Economic Issues* 4, no. 2: 451–62.

Wade, R. 1987. Common Property Resource Management in South Indian Villages. In Bromley 1992, 207–28.

CHAPTER 3

Development Connections:
The Hedgerow Model

Neva R. Goodwin

In economic thinking, development is a teleologic process; it aims to accomplish changes that will bring the state of the world closer to some preferred state. Different development actors and agents hold different visions of the preferred state — the goal. For development to achieve its objectives, the process must be well matched to the goal.

One version of the development process will be described in this essay and given the name *hedgerow model of development.* This model is intended to be a good match for a particular goal that I will refer to as SAEJAS (socially and environmentally just and sustainable) development. Before setting out the model, it will be useful to explain what is meant by this development goal.

The goal of SAEJAS development departs from the common (though not always explicit) equation of "development" with "growth in GNP or GDP." Such growth may be an important aspect of development, but it is a means, not an end in itself — to be valued only when it is an effective means to ultimate goals. The final goal embedded in SAEJAS development is distilled from many sources, including the *Human Development Reports* of the UNDP, the 1987 report of the World Commission on Environment and Development, and work by theorists such as David Seckler, Amartya Sen, and Paul Streeten. Drawing on these sources, the goal of SAEJAS development may be analyzed into three statements: (1) Development is the use of economic means to enhance people's choices and improve human well-being; (2) Development must be especially concerned with the people who now have the poorest choice set and the most unsatisfactory quality of life; and (3) Achievements in development must not imperil the range of choices or the well-being of people in the future.

SAEJAS development differs from the standard economic focus on output growth, which has been relatively insensitive to goals (2) and (3).

SAEJAS development can include, but is not limited to, market institutions and market-oriented development. It must also recognize possible tensions between the goals of poverty alleviation and environmental preservation. It is thus broader than the concept of environmentally sustainable development.

"Unsustainable" development can occur for a variety of reasons. The best-known examples are on the physical side, where apparent successes may impose environmental strains that, in the long run, make things worse; or when new technologies may, for a variety of reasons, fail after the initial introduction. Unsustainable development on the social side is equally tragic, when gains for the poor may be reversed by powerful people who find that their interests lie elsewhere; actions that are believed, or claimed, to be taken on behalf of the poor may turn out, in fact, to help only the elite; or the social coalitions necessary to maintain the development thrust may fall apart, or may not have existed to begin with.

What does it take to achieve development that is both socially and environmentally just, and also socially and environmentally sustainable? The following propositions, which form the basis for the hedgerow model, are a distillation from myriad experiences and writings (far beyond the number of references that can be included in this essay).

1. Effective development usually must involve both the elite and the most needy within any particular society — these two groups being seen not as polar types but as the opposite ends of a spectrum that runs continuously between them.
2. The form of that involvement must include connections that allow for the free exchange of information between the two ends of the spectrum.
3. These connections must also facilitate flows of power and physical resources. It is sometimes assumed that these must be asymmetrical flows, going primarily *from* those who have the greatest access to power and other resources, *to* those who have least access. However, within this overall context, under certain circumstances there is development value in flows that are equalized by the market — where the poor either pay for what they get, or sell what they make at a market price.
4. All of these flows have the best chance of occurring when the connections are made via intermediaries — social entities who generally have less access to resources than the elite, but more than the most needy.

Not all development practitioners, at all times, would have agreed with these propositions. Indeed, since World War II, when *development* first came into wide use as a term and a concept, the theory has been peculiarly fashion-ridden, tending to lurch from one extreme to another (Meyer 1995). The top-down extreme has either emphasized planning (whether by a central government or by foreign development agencies) or else focused on big projects to build up infrastructure and other types of constructed capital: for example, big dams for hydroelectric power, or huge irrigation schemes. At other times the fashionable theories have stressed a bottom-up approach, often based upon efforts to satisfy such basic needs as nutrition, sanitation, primary education, and basic health services. Also near this pole are examples of grass-roots institutional development that emphasize small businesses and local empowerment. The propositions set forth above, on what is required for SAEJAS development, start from the assumption that successful efforts will not focus exclusively upon either one of society's poles, but must recognize that these poles are connected — and how they are connected.

The Hedgerow Model

The hedgerow model, sketched out in figure 3.1, identifies (as a first approximation) four levels of actors in society, defined in terms that indicate what the development process may mean to them. The resource-rich are grouped together as the "trunks" of the trees, which together make up a hedgerow. The resource-poor (families and individuals) are seen as the "leaves" (those who in other models are sometimes referred to as the "grassroots"),[1] while the intertwining "twigs" and "branches" are the intermediary groups that can carry resources of many kinds in both directions, between the trunks and leaves.

It should be noted that this is not a formal model as that term is generally used in modern economic parlance, where it generally refers to a formula for the mathematical or logical manipulation of symbols. Rather, the hedgerow model is offered as a more generalized way of understanding relationships and flows among the individuals and groups who are involved with development. Its function is to provide an image of how things work, one that gives a context for understanding particular events. As the development hedgerow is here conceived, it is composed of a number of trees. It is easier to start by contemplating individual trees (without, it is to be hoped, losing sight of the whole forest), and the second section of this essay will give descriptions of three such trees. For now, just to give the general idea, we will very briefly cite a few examples.

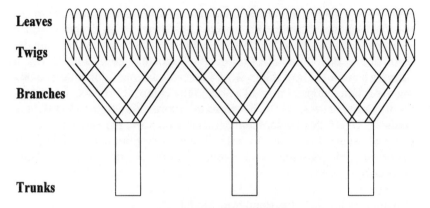

Leaves

Twigs

Branches

Trunks

Fig. 3.1.   The hedgerow model

A development hedgerow might include an international aid tree, where the trunk sends up funding from bilateral or multilateral donors to support the flow of resources, including information, through the branches (for example, international NGOs) to the twigs (which could be local NGOs, or other organized community groups) and then to the leaves — the ultimate recipients.

Other well-known examples for this model include the development trees that have been built around suppliers of microcredit, such as the Grameen Bank, or Women's World Banking (WWB). The latter can be modeled as a major branch that conduits loan funds from commercial banks, while the participating banks are bundled together as the trunk. WWB offers a partial guarantee for credit that goes to its fifty-plus local affiliates in about forty countries. As is often the case when a hedgerow model is scrutinized, it turns out to be necessary to make subdivisions within our original four rough divisions. The WWB affiliates are best viewed as (smaller) branches; the Indian affiliate, for example, is an umbrella organization of more than 100 NGOs that work with thousands of tiny thrift and credit cooperatives. Each of the latter is composed of small groups of poor, rural women (the leaves) who are the ultimate recipients of microloans. The NGOs (twigs) and the WWB and its affiliates (branches) are intermediaries that link what are commonly thought of as grass-roots women's savings groups with the banking system (Mehra et al. 1995, 20).

The examples just cited are of existing development efforts. This essay will not propose some wholly new way of doing development; instead, what it does offer that I believe to be novel — and, I hope, useful—is a way of understanding and talking about a particular approach to development. The novelty lies, first, in an emphasis on a clearly spelled-out goal (SAEJAS development); second, on relating the form of the development effort to the particular goal; and, third, in offering a model of how things work that gives a context for conceptualizing the relationships of myriad actors in the complex process of development, and for guessing which actions are more likely to lead toward the goals of SAEJAS development. To build on this, the last part of the essay will suggest ways in which development practitioners and theorists may more self-consciously, or intentionally, make practical use of the theoretical model.

The Intermediaries in the Hedgerow Model

Given the goal of SAEJAS development, the question that the hedgerow model attempts to answer is: *What are the best ways to mobilize and deploy the resources needed for bettering the condition of the poor—in the present and in the future—given the concentration of these resources in the hands of an elite minority?* This question gives focus and concreteness to a commonsense, already proven idea of how development can work—an approach whose outstanding characteristic is *the creation of a network that constructively connects the elite portions of a society with those who have the least access to power and other resources.*

In figure 3.1 this network is schematized as numerous intermediaries who channel flows of resources and information between leaves and trunks. These are divided into two types: branches (including mid-level governments, smaller corporations, and international NGOs), and twigs (community organizations, local governments, microenterprises, delivery NGOs, "participatory appraisal" type systems, etc.). This conceptualization is rather arbitrary, intended to divide the universe of groups intermediate between the resource-rich and the resource-poor in a way that indicates the proximity of the intermediate groups to one pole or the other.[2]

A classification of development intermediaries should take account of other factors besides the issues of identification and point of view. One factor would be physical proximity; another would be size. Consider, for example, a comparison between a local government and an international NGO. The former listens to many constituencies and probably hears most clearly the voices of the local elites, while the latter might have a less equivocal commitment to the welfare of the poorest of the poor. Nevertheless, both in scale and in geographic location, in the context of the hedgerow model it will usually make sense to think of the local government as among the twigs that are contiguous to the leaves, and the international NGO as a branch closer to the trunk.

Some other, more general points may be made about the intermediaries. They may have a special role to play with regard to information, for the intermediaries are sometimes able to piece together a worldview that can include portions, at least, of the worldviews of the two extremes. They can often act as interpreters, putting the knowledge and values that come from one extreme into language that is comprehensible at the other. This ability is also important for the creation of trust between the more widely separated extremes.

Figure 3.1 should be understood as suggesting that there is likely to be a plurality of intermediaries in most connections between the trunks and the leaves. Often the reason for this is a simple matter of scale. The elite deal in resources at a very large scale. For example, it is difficult for the World Bank to offer funds for development in amounts smaller than multimillions of dollars. If the poor are to be the final beneficiaries of a World Bank program, a series of intermediaries is usually required to break down the original loan or grant into sufficiently small portions.

All of the branches and twigs could be understood as channels, or potential relationships, in that they represent opportunities for things to flow—*in both directions.* What are the things that might flow along these channels? The major categories are: information (including ideas, values, and goals); power (i.e., the ability to influence events), along with a related though not identical resource—access, or connections; financial resources; material resources; and services.

Some asymmetry is expected in these flows. There is, by definition, a concentration of power as well as material and financial resources at the bottom of the picture—in the trunks of the trees. For SAEJAS development to occur, on the whole more of such resources must move up than down. However, when we think of the different kinds of capital that are relevant to the development process, to the familiar categories of financial and constructed capital, we must add natural, human, and social capital. Among these there is a requirement for information (related to human capital) to flow approximately equally in both directions. Also, social capital—the willingness and ability to cooperate for mutual ends—usually depends on trust, on the expectation and the reality of honest and responsible behavior, and on the ability to perceive and to value the needs and goals of others. This, too, is a valuable resource; when it can reach in all directions through the development tree, the development process is greatly facilitated.

With that said, it is usually necessary that the elite (those who control a disproportionate share of their society's resources) more or less voluntarily agree to the ways in which the resources they control are deployed. This is because power, listed as one of the resources necessary for development, permeates the allocation and use of nearly all the others (e.g., power results from the ownership of financial and human capital; it also helps people to gain more of these resources). When the sources of power are lined up with ownership or other control over most resources, it is hard for those in greatest need of development to force the elite to hand over their advantages. A common advantage of the nonelite is their superiority in numbers: this can have the effect of force, in cases of armed revolution or in democratic voting. However, the force of numbers in a revolution is often countered by the better education and equipment of the elite (and armed revolution, in any case, rarely achieves development objectives); while the democratic advantage of numbers can be outweighed by the elite's enormously greater ability to persuade voters of positions they favor (especially through access to media). Hence it is useful, sometimes requisite, to have the acquiescence of the elite for many (though not all) development scenarios.

What the Hedgerow Model Is Not

As a model of flows that travel a considerable social distance, the hedgerow model is not about flows that take place within a restricted part of its scope. For example, consider the demand for education, credit, housing, technology or know-how, and so forth that exists at the grassroots or leaves level of society. Some of these demands are filled by closed-loop interactions among what the hedgerow model identifies as the leaves and the twigs: for example, self-help groups organized to pool savings and provide small loans (such as the ROSCAs—rotating savings and credit associations; see Bouman 1995). Important though such activities often are, they are not what this model is designed to depict.

Aside from restricted flows at the leaf-and-twig end (such as the ROSCAs), the hedgerow model is also not about flows that are restricted to the trunks and branches—such as export assistance given by the government to agribusinesses, or the relationship between the defense department and its major suppliers.

It is important to mention another subject that is not the focus of this model, namely, patron-client relationships. One could draw a schema of a patronage system in India or Russia that would look very much like figure 3.1. What, then, distinguishes the hedgerow model from a patron-client system, when the latter also channels information, power, services, and material and financial resources between the resource-rich and the resource-poor? The difference is that, *as a model of how development can occur, the hedgerow model is about activities that enhance the common good.* In a patronage system, patrons and clients are expected to act for themselves and their families (with some reciprocal regard for the welfare of the patron or client with whom they are interacting). These actions, and the system in which they are embedded, often externalize enormous costs to the rest of society. Within a hedgerow system the common good is more broadly defined, so that there is less "external" area onto which to push costs.[3]

Finally, as mentioned earlier, this is a different kind of model from the mathematical or logical formulas common in modern economics. The function of the hedgerow model is to aid in conceptualizing the relationships of myriad actors in the complex process of development, and in providing a basis on which to judge which actions are more likely (given the actors and their relationships) to lead toward the SAEJAS goals.

Examples

The hedgerow model is intended to suggest a rich network of channels, many of them co-interacting so that resources from several different trunks may be carried via numerous branches and twigs—some of them acting in concert, while some may be quite unaware that others are working toward the same ends. In order to make this concept more concrete, three examples will be given. It should be noted that each of these examples will be described as a single, or at most a double, tree. A hedgerow, of course, is composed of many trees, whose branches, twigs, and leaves are so closely interwoven that it is nearly impossible to tell where one begins and another leaves off. However, any attempt at a full hedgerow model, though useful to have in mind, would be far too complex to depict. Only at the end of this section will we return to consider how a view of the integrated hedgerow may create a useful context for dealing with the individual trees.

Example 1: The Agricultural Extension Tree

Our first example will be a familiar one. It will be presented in a simplified and generalized form that is probably a reasonably close representation of how it has usually been seen by the actors identified with the trunks. The story will be enlivened by caveats and complications to this view.

In an agricultural extension tree (see fig. 3.2) the trunks are government departments, major research agencies, and universities. The

Leaves: Farmers

Twigs: Extension agents

Branches: CGIAR system, universities, other research sites

Trunks: Funding from governments, private sector, and foundations

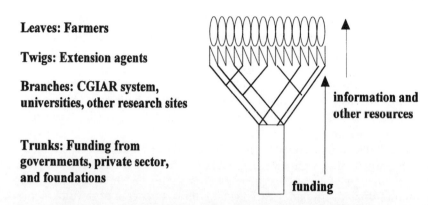

information and other resources

funding

Fig. 3.2.   The agricultural extension tree (simple version)

branches include regional or county extension agencies, and the twigs are the local extension agents.[4] The flows consist of money and information, which essentially move in one direction. The farmers — the ultimate recipients — receive information from the extension agents, who are trained and fed new knowledge by work coming from universities, branches of the Consultative Group on International Agricultural Research (CGIAR), and other research sites (in the United States, a major role is played by the land-grant colleges). The money to support the research and the extension services comes from governments, the private sector, and foundations.

That is the simple model of agricultural extension, which in the 1960s and 1970s was applied worldwide to promote the Green Revolution. A more realistic model — not shown here — would be somewhat more complicated. Agricultural extension in the United States, for example, arose from a complex network of farmers' associations, local agricultural societies and publications, correspondence courses, and the Grange and Farmer's Alliance movements originating in the second half of the nineteenth century. Land-grant colleges were established in the United States by the Morrill Act of 1858, which also established an extension role for the U.S. Department of Agriculture. But only with the Smith-Lever Act of 1914 did the USDA emerge as the coordinator of a systematic agricultural education and extension system including the land-grant colleges and county extension agents (Scott 1970). One might say that the U.S. extension system grew from leaves, twigs, and branches, and only in its more recent history has it been primarily characterized by flows that now originate in the trunks.

In addition, the role of the private sector in modern agricultural extension is significant. Private sector funding is related to the expectation that both the research and the extension activities will result in the promotion of increased input use by farmers. The branches and twigs may therefore include individuals hired by the private sector to interact with both the extension agents and the farmers to promote hybrid seeds, fertilizers, pesticides, herbicides, farm machinery, and other commercial products. There is also a reverse flow of money, from the farmers to the private sector (with credit institutions likely playing an intermediary role), to pay for these inputs. Also, even in the simple model there is often a money flow from the farmers in partial if not full payment for extension services.

In the view of some critics, the political power of agribusinesses has captured the modern extension system, reorienting it primarily to promote the fertilizers, seeds, pesticides, and agricultural machinery that large agribusinesses supply (Hightower 1978). Thus the needs of the trunks have come to overshadow those of the leaves. On an international scale, this has led to the heavy promotion of "modernized" agricultural sectors, and the neglect of the needs, and potential information inputs, of small farmers (Johnston and Clark 1982).

An alternative approach to agricultural extension would give primacy to the needs of small farmers and would include, among the twigs, individuals who carry out participatory rural appraisal. The important change resulting from this introduction is that the information flow now becomes two-way, with farmers' observations, as well as their needs and preferences, feeding back into the research loop. In ideal circumstances this affects the goals prescribed by the funding sources. This reorientation of flows and objectives requires new extension institutions and different kinds of training for agricultural professionals (Pretty and Chambers 1993 and this vol.). An extensive literature has emerged on "participatory research," with support for the proposition that much of developing nation agriculture is ill-served by the highly centralized, one-way flow model promoted by the CGIAR system and international development agencies such as the World Bank (see, e.g., Sumberg and Okali 1997).

Example 2: A Supply-Demand Tree

Here we will retell a story provided by Judith Tendler and Monica Alves Amorim, about a development activity initiated by the state of Ceará in Brazil. Figure 3.3 schematizes this activity, illustrating the important role of two intermediary bodies: the State Department of Industry and

Leaves: Unemployed workers

Twigs: Small and informal firms (especially SJA); small firm associations and local governments

Branches: State Dept. of Industry and Commerce (SIC) & Brazilian Small Enterprise Assistance Service (SEBRAE)

Trunk: Ceará governments (demand for goods and services)

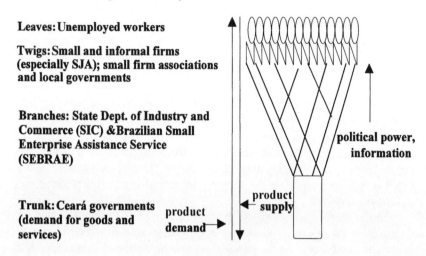

political power, information

product demand

product supply

Fig. 3.3.   A supply-demand tree

Commerce (SIC) and the Brazilian Small Enterprise Assistance Service (SEBRAE) (the latter being a semipublic technical assistance agency). Both of these organizations had initially been set up to render assistance to small firms, principally in the areas of credit, management training, and marketing.

Consistent with this supply-driven approach, the technicians of SIC and SEBRAE tended to characterize the problems afflicting their clients as generic to small firms — lack of access to credit, limited technical and managerial capacity, and difficulties in marketing. All this is typical of small-enterprise (SE) programs in many countries, despite a growing literature showing how the needs of firms differ markedly from one sector or subsector to another.

In the the 1980s, the government of the state of Ceará, faced with massive rural unemployment caused by a drought, "redirected some of its customary purchases — school furniture, repair and reconstruction services for public buildings, small metal grain silos — from large firms outside the state or their distributors to small firms located in the drought-stricken area" (Tendler and Amorim 1996, 412). Thus the government directed its demand toward small enterprises (twigs — some of which, however, due to the success of this development activity, grew beyond microenterprise status). These enterprises, in expanding to supply the required goods and services, employed many of the people in need.

The point of the article from which this example is taken is that (to put it in the terms of the models under consideration) a supply-demand tree in which the leaves are at the supply end may be most effective when the trunk and branches put more emphasis on directing demand to the suppliers rather than focusing on the supply-end problems. In the more common variant of this model — what the authors refer to as the "supply-driven approach" — the flow from the trunk upward, via such branches as SIC and SEBRAE in their earlier roles, is a flow of information and credit — once again, essentially a one-way street. The unusual aspects of the Ceará situation included the fact that there was relatively little in the way of subsidy flowing up from the trunk; the major flow was a demand for goods and services. Moreover, unlike some government purchasing arrangements, the suppliers were held to high quality standards. For example,

> in the case of school furniture, each item had a metal plate with the producer's name and the number of the contract. If an item proved defective, it was returned to the producer for repair or replacement; if that producer had closed down in the interim, the association of producers to which he had belonged was contractually responsible. (Tendler and Amorim 1996, 413)

Some degree of responsibility on the part of the supplier is often assumed in transactions involving private actors, but may be missing in government contracts that are part of a development agenda. The responsibility insisted on in this case achieved a number of ends, including making the flows more equal; that is, the government gets what it pays for. A practical result of the pressure to maintain quality was that the suppliers organized to request, from local government, training programs to upgrade workers' skills. In this process the government actors, including technical advisers, were in various ways brought to the firm site (rather than a classroom) and were turned into partners with the suppliers, dealing with problems as they arose. This helped the support agencies to understand the actual needs of the small enterprises. This impetus against standardization is one of the characteristics that the authors of this study believe to be especially relevant in causing demand-driven assistance to be, in a number of respects, superior to supply-driven assistance.

Example 3: An Energy Tree

In 1995 the Rockefeller Brothers Fund (RBF) convened a conference to address the needs of some two billion people who still rely on kerosene, fuel wood, and batteries for light and power. The importance of rural electrification for these households — 70 per cent of the population in the developing world — includes considerations of health risks from smoke and fumes, the work and school disadvantages of inadequate indoors light, and the impetus to rural-urban migration. As the RBF report on the conference states the problem:

> Household solar power systems represent a clean, climate-friendly alternative for rural electrification. . . . Solar photovoltaic units are cost-effective relative to other available energy sources, far cheaper than grid extension, and profitable for companies to provide. Model projects in several Asian countries and the Caribbean have shown that demand for these systems is high and that rural households can afford them if financing is available.
>
> Why, then, aren't private markets rushing to take advantage of the huge opportunity represented by the millions of developing world households that need and could buy these systems? (Northrop et al. 1995, 1)

The answer to this question that emerged during the conference is a good start for a description of the flows that are required if an appropriate energy tree (see fig. 3.4) is to take its essential place as part of the development hedgerow:

> Participants at the October 1995 conference analyzed the "market chain" that would be needed to deliver solar energy from producer, to distributor, to rural consumer. Currently missing from this chain, the conference report argues, are the kinds of financing mechanisms — opportunities for investment in the industry, working capital for manufacturers and distributors, and credit for purchasers — that facilitate the manufacture and sale of automobiles (for example) in the industrialized North. (Executive Summary, Northrop et al. 1995)

Focusing on the need to develop market infrastructures to handle the required capital flows, the conference considered the opportunities for developing mechanisms for financing at each of the three levels mentioned above (industry investment, working capital for manufacturers and distributors, and credit for purchaser).

Those who are unfamiliar with this issue may, perhaps, be surprised by the idea that the level nearest the leaves — purchaser credit — is an appropriate location for a symmetrical, market-based, two-way flow, rather than a one-way, aid-type flow; the question could be raised, Is

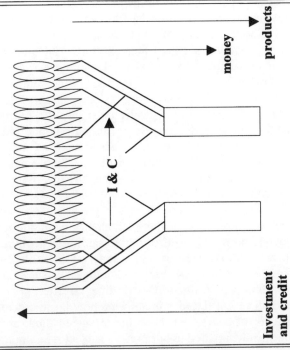

PRODUCT SIDE

Twigs: Local retailers

Branches: In-country wholesale, assemblers and distributors

Trunk: Photovoltaic module manufacturers

money

products

FINANCIAL SERVICES SIDE

Leaves: Rural people in need of a clean, affordable energy source

Twigs: Village credit facilities; local banks product retailers

Branches: Leasing companies, such as finance companies or regional or national banks; investment banks to securitize loan portfolios; investment retailers such as EEAF

Trunk: Investors, such as pension funds, insurance companies, and endowments of foundations and other public purpose institutions

Investment and credit (I & C)

I & C

Fig. 3.4.   A (projected) two-trunk energy tree

this properly considered a development activity? In answer, the conference report first confronts the reality that the amount of funding needed to achieve reasonable energy access for the more than one-third of the world's population now lacking it could not be achieved through international aid, even if all the direct aid funds likely to be available in the foreseeable future were devoted to this single task. It then presents the following argument:

> The need for purchaser credit becomes clear when one compares the purchase of a solar home system (at $350–700) by a rural household in the developing South with the purchase of an automobile by a household in the industrialized North. Both purchases represent costs equal to approximately 50 weeks of income. In the case of the car purchase, a well-established financial infrastructure links customers to manufacturers to capital markets, and a wide array of financing choices is available from banks, leasing companies and dealers. But in the SHS [solar home system] market, financing is unavailable, and a customer typically must pay the full price up front. Imagine the negative effects on the automobile industry if every customer had to pay the full cash price. And imagine the positive effects on the SHS industry if the same financing options available to car purchasers were available to solar home system buyers. (Northrop et al. 1995, 8)

The primary obstacles to achieving such financing options appear to be issues — or perceptions — about affordability and creditworthiness. Regarding the former, efforts need to be made to publicize the real cost comparison between ever-cheaper SHS technologies versus energy grid extensions to rural areas. Fortunately, regarding the latter, great strides have been made in recent decades in showing how far microcredit can extend. The leader, of course, has been the Grameen Bank in Bangladesh. More specifically targeted to our present subject is Sudimara Solar, an operation in Indonesia that both provides customer financing and distributes SHS products. It was cited as already servicing 5,000 purchasers of solar homes. In spite of a 100 percent payback rate from customers, Sudimara is frustrated by the unwillingness of Indonesian banks to pick up the credit business. "In addition to being reluctant to provide credit to individual solar purchasers, banks have generally also been unwilling to provide working capital to the SHS industry" (Northrop et al. 1995, 8).

Some organizations are beginning to step into this breach. Environmental Enterprises Assistance Fund (EEAF) is a Washington, DC-based, for-profit company that "retails" investments in renewable energy investment opportunities, including "off-the-grid" SHS companies. A variety of sources have supported EEAF, including grants from USAID, PRI (program related investments) from foundations such as MacArthur, and investments from the Swiss government and the Inter-American Bank. Several years ago the founder of EEAF wrote:

> The World Bank and its sister regional development banks . . . make energy loans to governments in very large sums — typically several hundreds of millions of dollars — and these are then handled by state-run utilities. Dishing these funds out to a wide variety of small-scale power projects is simply not within the institutional capability of these organizations.[5]

Happily, the World Bank is now actively seeking ways to do exactly what the hedgerow model suggests — to find partners that can subdivide loans into progressively smaller packages.[6] Other possible sources at the trunk of the financial services side of the energy tree include insurance companies, which "are now more interested in financing solar energy because they recognize that fossil fuel-caused climate change is having a negative impact on their core insurance businesses" (Northrop et al. 1995, 10).

Reflections

The approach that has been put forward in this essay is intended to assist in understanding specific development activities within a broader context. The broadest context for which we will reach is that which places any particular development tree within a hedgerow composed of the whole set of such trees that represent processes simultaneously aiming for the same SAEJAS goal, of socially and environmentally just and sustainable development. Before making what will be, in any case, only a first step toward conceptualizing this larger context, we will briefly reflect on our examples to show how the models depicted here can be useful in raising essential questions and clarifying our understanding of what is actually taking place in a given development activity.

How Is a Development Tree Assembled?

We will consider first the question What are the circumstances that allow the formation of a development tree, especially when it includes actors (such as private businesses) that are not necessarily development-oriented?

One obvious answer has to do with a convergence of interests. Private, for-profit interests are more likely to coincide with the common good when there is an important development-related need that could conceivably be expressed as effective demand (i.e., desire to purchase that is backed up by the ability to purchase). No market system has yet been devised that can distinguish between need and want. The distinction that markets are assumed to be good at making is that between effective demand and ineffective demand (the latter being wants that exceed the purchasing power of those left wanting). Markets respond only to effective demand, regardless of the social value of the goods being demanded, and will not supply goods or services (such as health care in poor areas) that may be urgently needed but for which the demand is not backed up by purchasing power. One interesting aspect of the SHS (solar home systems) case is that it illustrates a wide category of circumstances in which markets fail to respond even when the demand is potentially effective. Specifically, the possibility that solar energy systems could be leased or purchased (on credit) by third-world villagers has largely remained invisible to entrepreneurs, because of the absence of several significant pieces of market infrastructure.

Thus, if the market were working perfectly, figure 3.4 would depict an already existing market structure — and we would not call it a "development tree" because it would no longer be about a way of filling important, previously unmet needs, or of increasing the economic potential to fill those needs. In such a well-working-market scenario, there would be no role for the specifically development-oriented actors who are now involved (such as public-purpose organizations who make program-related investments). Like the first world market for automobiles, to which a comparison was made in example 3, the profit-driven market system would provide credit for purchasers, working capital for manufacturers and distributors, and credible financing opportunities to attract investors into this industry.

Another Look at What Activities Should Be Considered "Development"

There is more to learn from the comparison of solar home systems and automobiles. The auto industry has in several countries played a significant role as an engine of societywide economic growth as well as private profit. Conceivably, SHS production could play a similar role, providing jobs and income and fostering the development of market infrastructure. Another similarity is that both products provide important services, with transportation just a little lower than energy on a list of contemporary human needs.

However, at this time in history we cannot help but be aware of a critical difference. SHSs are environmentally benign, in that they have far less adverse impact than virtually all realistic alternatives — while automobiles have very severe negative environmental impacts. In many countries the automobile industry has received very large direct or indirect subsidies. It has, at the same time, produced massive negative externalities — costs in terms of climate change, health, accidents, removal of land from other uses, and so on, that are not borne by those who profit from making and selling cars. Thus, in terms of total social benefit, the theory of externalities (and pricing theory, as regards subsidies) suggests that in many parts of the world there is a significant overproduction of automobiles. At the same time, SHSs appear to be massively underproduced, relative both to the potential effective demand and to their social utility.

This is why an "automobile tree" might not qualify as part of our hedgerow model, even if someone were to draw a figure, similar to figure 3.4, showing how automobiles reach the final user at the end of a process whereby resources are concentrated and then progressively subdivided.[7] However, the comparison has allowed us to sharpen our understanding of when it is that private, for-profit firms are rightfully included in a hedgerow-type model: it is *when they produce a good or service that genuinely and sustainably improves human well-being, especially for those who are least well-off.*

Part of this definition refers us to a set of contentious questions: should we assume that the output of all firms is socially useful? If we think that some firms produce socially harmful products, and that, among the rest, there are different degrees of usefulness, should society treat these in some way differently? Without getting into what products should be allowed to be advertised by what media, or how, for example, tobacco production or marketing should be regulated, we may note that "development" is generally accepted to be a more value-laden concept than simple "market functioning." If we accept the goals for SAEJAS development that were set out in the beginning of this essay, then we can — indeed must — notice the differences among industries and among firms, with regard to what they produce, how, and with what impact on the people for whom development is especially intended.[8]

Where a Hedgerow Model Can Go Wrong

There will be some readers who will recognize the hedgerow model as a picture of how they have always assumed development should be done. It is hoped that, even to such old hands, it is useful to have these ideas spelled out. For those who have never made this approach conscious, as well as for those who have, it may also be useful to note why this approach can sometimes fail:

1. The goals of SAEJAS development will not be met if *the leaves are inappropriately identified* — for example, when development efforts are directed toward groups who are relatively well able to fend for themselves, while those in greatest need are ignored.
2. Another common problem is that *the goals are improperly defined.* A common reason for this to occur is that the leaves (the presumed beneficiaries) were not consulted, and their values were not reflected in the design of goals.
3. It may also happen that *the twigs cannot make adequate contact with the leaves.* This could result from insufficient recognition of cultural or other characteristics of the leaves. As a simple example, male agricultural extension agents will likely fail to make contact with female farmers when there are cultural inhibitions about communication between women and unrelated men. Another cause for this type of failure is that the people who are slightly better off than the most needy also have their own urgent needs, and may have the ability as well as the motivation to give priority to their own needs. Thus, identification of those who can play the role of twigs is a nontrivial task. There is often a role here for committed professionals (e.g., anthropologists, sociologists, NGO personnel). It is crucial for the latter to understand the leaves and twigs in terms that include gender, ethnicity, and culture, along with simple economic interest.
4. *The resources flowing upward from the trunk may stop at the branches or the twigs.* Some use of resources by the intermediaries is inevitable and justifiable. In most successful development stories the resources devoted to the intermediaries are used to mobilize other resources — of information, skill, organizational capacity, and so forth — which then continue to flow upward to the leaves. Development failures occur when the intermediaries simply keep the resources — especially funding — while performing actions that have little or no development impact, but can persuade the donor that the funds are well spent.

There is no single solution to these problems, but they can often be ameliorated — perhaps even prevented — if development practitioners learn what is now known, and what is teachable, about how to identify different groups in a given society and how to compare their needs; how to listen to people who are different from oneself, or how to find an intermediate listener who can communicate with both sides so as to learn about others' values and priorities; and how to offer knowledge and concepts that are useful to the recipients and are acceptable (both in content and in form of delivery) within their existing worldviews.[9]

The Whole Tree

An important element in each of the examples selected for this essay has been the presence of what we might call an *arboreal entrepreneur.* This is comparable to a business entrepreneur, whose role is that of "opportunity-spotter, resource-completer, and gap-filler."[10] In order to see the gaps and to know what it takes to complete the list of necessary resources, the entrepreneur must be able to see the world in larger than usual frames. The arboreal entrepreneur, similarly, is someone who perceives the whole potential development tree, ideally even before it exists (although it often serves well enough to have the image unfold organically, as the various parts of the tree come into the picture) and who takes some responsibility for ensuring that the right branches and twigs connect constructively with the trunk and with the correctly identified leaves.

Looking for arboreal entrepreneurs, we may consider our oldest example, the agricultural extension trees, whose development extends well back into the nineteenth century. The evolution of agricultural research and education systems in the United States has depended on many such entrepreneurs, starting with wealthy farmers such as George Washington and Thomas Jefferson, and Southern agrarian reformers such as Edward Ruffin of Virginia, who promoted agricultural innovation both at the leaf level (through correspondence with other farmers) and at the trunk level (through government institutions). Numerous innovators and proselytizers helped to spread improved agricultural methods through a twig network of agricultural associations throughout the East Coast and the South, and then to the expanding homestead agriculture of the Midwest and West.

The originators of the Morill Act of 1862, the Hatch Act of 1887, and the Smith-Lever Act of 1914 sought to expand this effort by creating the branch level network of land-grant colleges and experiment stations that would come to full fruition in the decades after World War I.[11] Extension agents were the key to completing the essential connections in this system; their training and placement was promoted by individuals such as Kenyon Butterfield, director of Michigan's Agricultural Institute system at the turn of the century. Agricultural leaders like Butterfield had most of the tree clear in their minds, and they organized the necessary political support to institutionalize the extension network as a federal-state partnership.

On the international level, the extension model was applied to global agricultural development starting in the 1960s and 1970s. When, one by one, the major agricultural research institutes in the global CGIAR system were set up, they were seen as adding a necessary piece to what was by then a fairly well-understood tree. Early assessments of the CGIAR system recognized that it was failing to reach the truly resource-poor farmers, and a mid-course correction was instituted by Norman Borlaug and other pioneers of the Green Revolution who emphasized the role of extension trees in bringing high-yielding technologies to the village level. Since then, social and ecological critiques of the Green Revolution have given rise to a new generation of arboreal entrepreneurs who are promoting farmer participation as a counterbalance to domination by corporate-oriented trunks. Thus in a sense the modern "Farmer First" movement[12] is completing the circle that began with initiatives by individual farmers two centuries ago.

In our third example, of the energy tree, the overview role was played by a foundation, the Rockefeller Brothers Fund. In our second example the promoter was the governor of Ceará. Unfortunately, while the Ceará state government was proud of what had been achieved, it failed to capitalize in development terms on the critical element in its most dramatic success, in the district of Sao Joao do Aruaru (SJA). SJA is cited as "the classic case of a small-firm cluster or industrial district" (Tendler and Amorim 1996, 415). The state government used the SJA success in a large public relations effort to show how well it had responded to the drought crisis. This publicity unhappily "contributed to spoiling the possibility for replication, making it politically difficult to grant assistance to only a few *municípios* at a time" (421.) The various state actors who responded to pressure for premature diffusion either were not committed to the SAEJAS development goal, or did not understand the importance of concentrating demand, or lacked enough power to withstand the political pressures.

It would be interesting to examine a large array of development projects, to assess their success in terms of SAEJAS development, and to see which of the successful and unsuccessful projects were assisted by an arboreal entrepreneur. (I have not performed this exercise; however, some relevant data may be found in a variety of places, including Tendler 1993a, 1993b; World Bank 1994; Serageldin 1995.) My hypothesis is that successful projects are more likely than unsuccessful ones to include an active arboreal entrepreneur—but that even in the successful projects this role often remains unfilled. There are doubtless cases where the less rare talents are sufficient: where all of the necessary links can be made by individuals who perceive their own bridging roles without necessarily having a picture of the whole system. However, a more efficient use of development resources seems likely where there is an actor who possesses such an overview. Thus one of the results that may be hoped for from this essay is to validate this role and make it self-conscious — and also, perhaps, more common.

An outstanding arboreal entrepreneur, the founder of Synergos Institute, makes a distinction between the personal linkages that are created between any two types of actors (leaves and twigs, twigs and branches, etc.) and the dynamic process undertaken by an arboreal entrepreneur, who must perform the following functions:

- make sure that the ultimate recipients (the leaves) are recognized by all the other actors and that they are assisted to discover and define their goals;
- find allies who share the SAEJAS values and/or some part of the project goal;
- identify the gaps in the relevant portion of the development hedgerow (which are the missing twigs or branches?);
- identify the self-interest of each group (where do the different interests overlap?); and
- ensure that the different players are aware of one another. (In the most consciously applied version this means creating a safe space where people of different views can meet repeatedly, with a convener.)[13]

In many instances it may be easier for an arboreal entrepreneur to identify and check off these functions if he or she actually attempts to sketch in a development tree like the examples in the second section. In order to draw such a picture, it will be necessary to ask oneself:

- What are the things — material or immaterial — that are flowing between the trunk and leaves?
- Is the content as well as the direction of the flows such as to promote socially and environmentally just and sustainable development?
- Are all of the necessary players in place? That is, are the people and groups in the positions of twigs, branches, and trunk the right ones for the activity modeled in this tree? Are there any missing or inappropriate actors, so that one or more of the flows are interrupted or diverted before achieving the intended goals?

Such an exercise is not only relevant for the "arboreal entrepreneur"; any actor who is involved in a development tree could benefit from working (alone, or with other participants in the process) to identify the leaves, the twigs, the branches, and the trunk. Each one could benefit from knowing the answer to two further questions:

- Where do I, and my activities, fit into this picture?
- How does the tree that models the development activity in which I am engaged fit into the hedgerow (the larger picture of development for this region or country)?

The Whole Hedgerow

The last question introduces the final, most inclusive level of context that we will consider. Figure 3.1, you may recall, showed a plurality of trunks supporting a network of interlacing branches, connecting to another network of twigs, which interact with the leaves. In figure 3.4 we saw a case where one tree (the SHS products tree) absolutely requires close interaction with another (the financial services tree) if it is to thrive at all.[14] Going beyond the SHS example of complementary pairs of products and financial services, what other trees are required as complements if any individual project is to participate in full-scale SAEJAS development?

One thinks immediately of education: a system that usually (though not in every case) requires a concentrated source of resources and a network of branches and twigs for the transmission of material goods (schools, desks, books, etc.), as well as teaching (the transmission of knowledge and ways of thinking), if it is to spread through a whole society and assist the most disadvantaged as well as the more comfortable members. Every society needs at least one fully developed education tree; many have more than one. Another universally important tree has to do with basic life-support — the tree that provides the social safety net (see article by Molly Anderson and John Cook in this volume).

Note that, according to the terminology we have used, education trees and life-support trees would both be called *development trees* only when they represent a way of filling important, *previously unmet* needs, or of *increasing* the economic potential to fill those needs. When they are part of an established system whose effect is not growing, they are still very good things — they just don't fall into the category of *development*.

A job for the future is to fill out the description of some less obvious trees. These might include some that deal with the process of democracy, theoretically osmosing power up from the trunks where it tends to collect (in particular places in central governments, or along with concentrations of wealth, etc.), and recycling it back toward the leaves from whence much of it was originally drawn. Others would have to do with such subjects as rights over land or water (these might have twin trunks to deal with the treatment of externalities), or the provision of a variety of kinds of health services. Many more could be imagined.

Who are the hedgerow-minders who see, and cultivate, the largest context for development, and who provide encouragement and support for arboreal entrepreneurs? The world probably has not many individuals or institutions in this category. Obviously, the UNDP (United Nations Development Programme) should be one — and, indeed, its annual *Human Development Reports* give some good overviews of how the world's hedgerows are progressing. On a national level the rare agency head may take such a view, but more commonly each agency sees only its own cone of responsibility and ignores the synergies that may be useful, and in many cases are essential, if development is to take hold justly and sustainably.

Do we need research institutes or NGOs that will identify the thriving and the ailing development trees in a particular context, and prioritize the actions that will most effectively address the health of the whole hedgerow? Is such an approach needed for industrialized as well as for third world countries? Can the job of hedgerow-minder be filled by the UN and its various agencies, or does it also require new kinds of national-level institutions such as Gar Alperovitz proposes in his essay in this volume? The questions that emerge when we come to the most general level of the hedgerow model are, evidently, more about policy than about facts. They take us beyond the scope of this essay and must, at this stage, be left as open questions, pending further grounding in conceptualizing and understanding the trees that make up the hedgerow.

Such a conclusion could provoke a reader to ask: In that case, why was this essay not simply about development trees? Why bring up the hedgerow at all? The answer is that, just as each development tree provides a context for the activities taking place at its various, interrelated sites, the hedgerow provides a context for the trees. We are better off asking questions about it than not thinking about it at all.

NOTES

The model offered in this essay draws heavily upon insights from a number of people and institutions. I have benefited greatly from the observations and experiences afforded by my relationship with the International Center for Research on

Women, Winrock International Institute for Agricultural Development, the Environmental Enterprises Assistance Fund, and the Rockefeller Brothers Fund. In addition to many individuals in those institutions, I owe a special debt for my education in this area to Peggy Dulany, president of Synergos Institute, and Roberto Mizrahe, president of South North Development Initiative. The essay has also received extremely helpful editorial and substantive input from Jonathan Harris and Peter Riggs.

1. This metaphor should not be taken too literally; any attempt to do so would run into objections that the trunk is not, in fact, a tree's main store of resources. However, it does not hurt to remind ourselves that, within our metaphor, while water and minerals are, indeed, channeled upward through the trunk, photosynthesis, the capturing of essential energy, comes through the leaves.

2. This arbitrary division can be self-validating if used as a classification scheme: for example, if an entity claiming to be a community organization in fact has a closer identification with the interests and the point of view of the resource-rich than of the resource-poor, we might be inclined to say, "this is not a true community organization — it should be classified as a branch, not a twig." However, these terms are simply descriptive. They are not value judgments.

3. This is not to say that a hedgerow system is by definition concerned with the good of "the whole system," however defined (as all of humanity, the total ecosystem, throughout all time, etc.). The hedgerow models that will be described in this essay are most often defined on a national or somewhat smaller than national level. Actors in these arenas may see nothing wrong with externalizing costs onto other nations. In the example of Ceará, discussed below, the benefit to workers in that state was to some degree offset by loss of jobs in other areas from which Ceará had previously purchased school furniture, silos, etc.

4. Among the many ways of complicating this simple picture, one would be to acknowledge that in some contexts (the following quotation refers specifically to Latin America) "most of the organizations engaging in extension prefer to deal with groups or group leaders rather than individual farmers in order to achieve the most impact with their scarce resources and elicit greater levels of participation from their clients" (Carroll 1992, 53) Thus a second level of twigs would need to be defined — group leaders — who mediate between the local extension agents and the farmers.

5. Franklin Tugwell, "Energy for Development: Institutions, Incentives, and the Misallocation of Resources," in Goodwin 1996, 243. This article gives an excellent overview of the needs and the problems addressed in the "double energy tree" described here.

6. Good examples may be found in the World Bank's support for the Participatory Provincial Partnership project in Tra Vinh Province in southern Vietnam, where the Bank's Country Director for Vietnam is attempting to explicitly tie big infrastructure projects (the Bank's expertise) to the welfare of the poor, reaching out to both the private sector and NGOs (e.g., Oxfam) in intermediary roles.

7. This does not rule out the possibility that there might be some circumstances where the other development advantages of automobile production

might outweigh the environmental disadvantages, such that an "automobile tree" could be drawn to describe a reasonable development scenario. In general, however, it increasingly appears that it is more beneficial to search for viable transportation alternatives than to continue subsidizing automobile industries.

8. Some of the issues raised here will be developed in *It's Legal But It Ain't Right: Highly Capitalized Anti-Social Activities* (ed. Nikos Passaf, in manuscript; this is projected as vol. 4 in the University of Michigan Press series Evolving Values for a Capitalist World).

9. A good discussion of the professional retraining that this approach requires may be found in Pretty and Chambers 1993.

10. This definition was offered by Harvey Liebenstein in conversation (1982).

11. See Scott 1970 for a detailed and fascinating account of the early evolution of the U.S. extension system.

12. For more extensive discussion of the "Farmer First" movement, see Pretty and Chambers 1993 and this volume.

13. Conversation with Peggy Dulany, August 1997.

14. Given the outcome of the agricultural extension tree — that is, the spread of modern agricultural techniques, with a concomitant demand on the part of farmers for purchased inputs — it should also ideally be drawn with a twinned financial services tree to be complete.

REFERENCES

Bouman, F. J. A. 1996. Rotating and Accumulating Savings and Credit Associations: A Development Perspective. In *World Development* 23, no. 3.

Carroll, Thomas F. 1992. *Intermediary NGOs: The Supporting Link in Grassroots Development.* West Hartford, CT: Kumarian Press.

Clark, John. 1995. The State, Popular Participation, and the Voluntary Sector. In *World Development* 23, no. 4: 593–602.

Goodwin, Neva R., ed. 1996. *As If the Future Mattered: Translating Social and Economic Theory into Human Behavior.* Ann Arbor: University of Michigan Press. (Vol. 1 in the series Evolving Values for a Capitalist World, of which the present book is vol. 3.)

Gupta, Geeta Rao, and Ellen Weiss. 1993. *Women and AIDS: Developing a New Health Strategy.* ICRW Policy Series, no. 1. Washington, DC: International Center for Research on Women.

Johnston, Bruce F., and William C. Clark. 1982. *Redesigning Rural Development: A Strategic Perspective.* Baltimore: Johns Hopkins University Press.

Mehra, Rekha, Annelies Drost-Maasry, and Ruba Rahman. 1995. *Financing Poor Women: The Record, the Prospects.* Washington, DC: International Center for Research on Women.

Meyer, Carrie A. 1995. Opportunism and NGOs: Entrepreneurship and Green North-South Transfers. In *World Development* 23, no. 8: 1277–90.

Northrop, Michael F., Peter W. Riggs, and Frances A. Raymond. 1995. *Selling Solar: Financing Household Solar Energy in the Developing World*. Pocantico Paper no. 2; the Rockefeller Brothers Fund, New York, NY.

Pretty, Jules N., and Robert Chambers. 1993. *Towards a Learning Paradigm: New Professionalism and Institutions for Agriculture*. London: Institute for Development Studies Discussion Paper no. 334.

Saito, Katrina A., and Daphne Spurling. 1992. *Development Agricultural Extension for Women Farmers*. Washington, DC: World Bank.

Scott, Roy V. 1970. *The Reluctant Farmer: The Rise of Agricultural Extension to 1914*. Chicago: University of Illinois Press.

Seckler, David. 1996. Economic Regimes, Strategic Investments, and Entrepreneurial Enterprises: Notes toward a Theory of Economic Development. In Neva R. Goodwin, ed., *As If the Future Mattered: Translating Social and Economic Theory into Human Behavior*. Ann Arbor: University of Michigan Press, 1996.

Sen, Amartya. 1993. Capability and Well-Being. In Martha C. Nussbaum and Amartya Sen, eds., *The Quality of Life*. Oxford: Clarendon Press.

Serageldin, Ismail. 1995. *Nurturing Development: Aid and Cooperation in Today's Changing World*. Washington, DC: World Bank.

Streeten, Paul. 1981. *First Things First: Meeting Basic Needs in the Developing Countries*. New York: Oxford University Press.

———. 1995. *Thinking about Development*. New York and Cambridge: Cambridge University Press.

Sumberg, James, and Christine Okali. 1997. *Farmers' Experiments: Creating Local Knowledge*. London and Colorado: Lynne Rienner Publishers.

Tendler, Judith. 1993a. *New Lessons from Old Projects: The Workings of Rural Development in Northeast Brazil*. Washington, DC: World Bank Operations Evaluation Department.

———. 1993b. Tales of Dissemination in Small-Farm Agriculture: Lessons for Institution Builders. In *World Development* 21, no. 10: 1567–82.

Tendler, Judith, and Monica Alves Amorim. 1996. Small Firms and Their Helpers: Lessons on Demand. In *World Development* 24, no. 3: 407–26.

Thompson, John. 1995. Participatory Approaches in Governmental Bureaucracies: Facilitating the Process of Institutional Change. In *World Development* 24, no. 3: 1521–54.

United Nations Development Programme. 1990–1998. *Human Development Report*. New York and Oxford: Oxford University Press.

Uphoff, Norman. 1992. *Learning from Gal Oya: Possibilities for Participatory Development and Post-Newtonian Social Science*. Ithaca: Cornell University Press.

Uvin, Peter. 1995. Fighting Hunger at the Grassroots: Paths to Scaling Up. In *World Development* 23, no. 6: 927–40.

World Bank. 1994. *The World Bank and Participation*. Washington, DC: World Bank publication.

World Commission on Environment and Development. 1987. *Our Common Future*. Oxford University Press. 1987.

CHAPTER 4

Wealth, Poverty, and Sustainable Development

David Barkin

Two Paths Diverge: One to Wealth, the Other to Poverty

Stereotypical accounts of the modernization process in rural Latin America describe the march of progress in glowing terms. The conventional analysis of agricultural development commends and rewards the small community of farmers that uses aggressive and innovative packages to modernize rural production. In contrast, poor farmers, said to be confined by inherited ethnic and social mores and a lack of knowledge and capital, destroy or waste the productive potential of their natural heritage and continue to cultivate traditional crops in inappropriate regions with outmoded techniques and unimproved seeds.

Around the world, poor people are accused of causing the declining quality of their surroundings. These allegations are then used to justify policies that further threaten the viability of traditional social groups and productive systems: their inability to modernize is identified as the cause of the social and economic backwardness in rural areas. Even in the more enlightened societies, blaming the victims for their own plight and the lack of collective progress is a common phenomenon.

This popular perception that the poor are the cause of rural environmental problems is not only misleading, it is alarmingly wrong. Whereas the conventional debate bemoans the fate of millions born into poverty and focuses on the paucity of resources that can be mustered to attack the symptoms of deprivation that persist in the midst of affluence, this paper focuses on the unprecedented accumulation of wealth that has increased the ranks and exacerbated the plight of the poor. The reorganization of the control and use of space and resources, engendered by the intensification of rural production, is violating the basic tenets of nature and threatening the viability of rural communities. The poor do not despoil the land because of their callous waste of resources, but rather for the lack of an equitable distribution of available social wealth

77

and the ruthless way in which the rich and powerful defend their control. The disparity in social and productive systems prevalent throughout Latin America is leading to disaster. With the deteriorating employment situation, and the discrimination against small-scale rural producers, it is no wonder that environmental degradation is proceeding apace.

In the alternative view presented here, the world system is one of increasing duality, polarized between rich and poor — nations, regions, communities, and individuals. A small number of nations dominate the global power structure, guiding production and determining welfare levels. The other less privileged nations compete among themselves to offer lucrative conditions that will entice the corporate and financial powers to locate within their boundaries. Similarly, regions and communities within nations engage in self-destructive forms of bargaining — compromising the welfare of their workers and the building of their own infrastructure — in an attempt to outbid each other for the fruits of global growth. This dynamic is not conducive to promoting sustainable development. The regions unable to attract investment suffer the ignoble fate of losers in a permanent economic olympics, condemned to oblivion on the world stage.

Official development theory seeks the solutions to poverty in market-led structural changes. But this strategy raises two important questions that are at the core of this essay. First, is a new era of growth in its current mode either possible or desirable given environmental limitations? Second, given the historical record, is there demonstrated evidence that new levels of growth will provide for greater economic (and therefore political and social) equity among diverse groups of nations, regions, communities, and people?

This article proceeds from the assumption that the answer to both these questions is *no*. A market-driven strategy will not bridge the chasm between rich and poor. Instead, we propose an approach that recognizes the limits of natural resources and capital expansion, one that addresses the issues of poverty and sustainability by offering a program of rural development for those presently excluded, a program that eventually would also ameliorate conditions in the rest of society. Both the increasing number of poor people and the accumulating environmental problems require solutions that are less market-dependent; that take into account the redundancy of large portions of the population in the current framework for production and economic growth; and that provide for these people by creating a system in which communities can survive without complete integration into the global marketplace.

When given the chance and access to resources, the poor are usually willing to engage in direct actions to protect and improve the environment. From this perspective, then, an alternative development model requires new ways to encourage the direct participation of peasant and indigenous communities in a program of job creation in rural areas to increase incomes and improve living standards. By proposing policies that encourage and safeguard rural producers in their efforts to become once again vibrant and viable social and productive actors, this essay proposes to contribute to an awareness of the deliberate steps needed to promote sustainability.

We go on to examine the importance of sustainability, and the possibilities of implementing approaches that move us in a new direction, as well as the obstacles to such progress. Overcoming these obstacles requires more than well-intentioned policies; it requires a new coordination of social forces, a move toward broad-based democratic participation in all aspects of life, within each country and in the concert of nations. Strategies to face these challenges must respond to the dual concerns of insulating these communities from further encroachment and assuring their viability.

Among the many questions raised by this discussion, some of the more important ones might be grouped into the following areas:

- What is the relationship between poverty and environmental degradation?
- Can the obstacles to sustainability be overcome by raising national per capita income levels?
- Can policies directed toward poverty eradication also contribute to reducing pressures on the environment?
- Are wealthier people around the world confronting the problems of sustainability responsibly? What is their level of responsibility to support environmental protection and conservation in areas inhabited by the poor?[1]

Sustainability is not possible in rural Latin America as long as the expansion of capital is enlarging the ranks of the poor and impeding their access to the resources needed for mere survival. Profound changes are required to facilitate a strategy of sustainable development. A new form of development is outlined based on a structure of local autonomy that allows people to rebuild their rural societies and produce goods and services in a sustainable fashion while expanding the environmental stewardship services they have always provided.

Wealth, Poverty, and Environmental Degradation

Background to the Current Crisis

Rural poverty has its roots in the profound inequalities that characterize our societies: in a social structure that displays a disdain for things rural and in the exercise of economic and political power that appropriates other peoples' goods and even their rights for private enrichment. The environmental problems of rural Latin America today reflect this heritage of polarized political development. In this section we identify the major forces that are driving this process of simultaneous rural development and rural impoverishment, and discuss some of its manifestations.

Although the process differed greatly from country to country, and even within each country, the results have been remarkably similar. The colonization of Latin America gave rise to a never-ending series of displacements, appropriation, and expropriation. As successive waves of colonizers and neocolonizers laid claim to the most highly productive lands, the use of land evolved from its historical vocation, producing basic products for human and social survival, to the present emphasis on producing crops that promise a profit to the owners. For more than 500 years, the first peoples of the Americas and their successors have been forced to seek refuge in ever more marginal conditions, in ever more fragile ecosystems.

Haciendas and plantations were but two of the variety of organizations that launched a process of productive specialization and intensification that continues to wreak human impoverishment and environmental havoc (Wolf 1982). Productive systems from the Old World displaced indigenous farming methods in efforts to open areas to exploitation and to produce and extract goods for the overseas markets: the minerals and precious metals, the tropical hardwoods, strange animals, and the wealth of exotic fruits and vegetables. Small but powerful groups of landowners centralized control over the land and became influential in shaping or actually controlling national governments.

By the mid–twentieth century, state and corporate resources were mobilized to forge what soon would be known as the Green Revolution. Displacing agronomists who had been working in the peasant tradition, technical staffs introduced agrochemicals, machinery, and nonrenewable energy sources to increase productivity. Responding to the neo-Malthusian specter, policymakers urged the multilateral financial and development institutions (e.g., FAO, IBRD, IMF) to expand the reach of the Green Revolution. Insisting on the need to extract ever greater volumes from commercial farms, development practitioners focused their efforts to promote agricultural development on those social groups best prepared to respond: those integrated into modern institutional settings, including the elitist political structures and the credit system.

These agribusiness elites enjoyed ready access to credit and control of the most fertile lands, which allowed them to employ the most modern technologies to raise productivity and select the most valuable crops. With machines to reshape the earth, equipment to channel water, and agrochemicals to control pests and compensate for the decline in soil quality, they were able to raise the bounty of the land. Guided by an optimistic vision of the powers of technology in which nothing seemed beyond their reach, they unleashed the productive potential of high-yielding germ plasm, forged in the new biotechnology laboratories, to produce valuable commercial products for local markets or export. Even when they sowed the more traditional staples of the local diet, they were often able to realize record levels of productivity. Similarly, modern commercial enterprises in livestock, fishing, and forestry significantly raised output, going beyond the Green Revolution package of mechanical and chemical inputs, to incorporate rapidly the newest advances in biotechnology. Finally, the social and political structure facilitated their access to the distribution channels and thus allowed them profits that eluded other groups.

Profligate use of water, energy, and agrochemicals by agribusiness has been a logical response to the incentives created by ill-considered development policies that stimulated output with subsidized prices for key agricultural inputs. In the name of progress, and to counter the perceived Malthusian threat, they reshaped the whole hemisphere: making the deserts bloom, clearing the tropical rain forests, denuding the mountains, and filling in the wetlands.

Little thought was given to the long-term impact of the new "input package" on the soil, or on other dimensions of the physical environment, such as water quality. The health risks to workers and consumers were addressed only belatedly and partially. No importance was attached to the objection that such advances would further impoverish the majority of farmers for whom credit was rarely available; scarce human and institutional resources for research and technical assistance were channeled away from traditional farming groups.

The human toll continues to be extraordinary. Throughout Latin America, agrarian communities have been displaced from valuable lands and forced into inappropriate settings, banished to regions of most difficult access, with the poorest or most unsuitable lands and the most precarious availability of water. Lured or trapped into untenable regions and employments, they find it difficult or even prohibitive to continue the important tasks of soil and water conservation and management that were an integral part of their ancestors' normal practice. They have no choice but to devastate their own environments in their desperate struggle to survive.[2]

Even when they possess tillable land, poor farmers are mired in a morass of bureaucratic restrictions. Without access to credit, they cannot choose to cultivate valuable commercial products or modern varieties of their traditional crops. With deteriorating terms of trade, many small farmers have no alternative but to seek employment elsewhere and frequently are forced to sell, transfer, or simply abandon their lands. This creates new waves of migrants who search for new places to colonize and survive, frequently in areas with fragile ecosystems that are unsuited for such settlements.

The accelerated expansion of the modern segment of rural society is, therefore, occasioning the broader range and increased severity of environmental problems observed in recent decades. Workers are poisoned in the fields, while their families suffer from the effects of chemical and organic contamination in their communities. Peasants suffer intolerable working conditions as laborers or challenge militarized states in their struggle for some measure of dignity. Although strains on the environment have been accumulating for decades, their rhythm and intensity have quickened so much as to now represent a great threat to the viability of uncountable species of flora and fauna, as well as to human society itself. The outcry of citizen groups and organized environmentalists is testimony to this phenomenon.

An Inadequate Policy Response

In response to the devastation, many in the entrepreneurial sector are now obliged to "rationalize" their use of scarce resources. After having reshaped nature, they must now turn to protecting their investment. Some react to the controls placed on imported products by the richer nations, using chemicals more sparingly or changing to less harmful formulations. Efforts by Latin American countries themselves to promulgate an adequate set of protective regulations have also prompted some producers to modify their practices, but in many places bureaucratic distortions make it difficult to mount an effective enforcement structure. Others respond to new policies that removed subsidies from all manner of products, using resources more carefully or changing techniques to reduce costs or increase productivity. For this sector, a combination of enlightened self-interest and market and administrative mechanisms, reinforced by appropriate social supervision, can be expected to lead to a progressive reduction in the environmental damage, in regions already occupied by the commercial sector.

But while such tentative steps toward environmental protection in production and policy strategies are moves in the right direction that should be encouraged, few steps have been taken to protect the endangered populations that inhabit the environments in question. Moreover, the crucial policy link addressing correlations between expropriations of the environment and the exploitation of people remains the domain of the grass roots: NGOs, women's groups, some environmental groups, workers' rights organizations, and the direct producers themselves. In spite of the ample experience demonstrating how sustainable development fits into a broader picture of economic justice, human rights and cultural diversity (such as a growing movement that confronts environmental racism), the climate for rural development policy-making continues to reinforce the social processes penalizing the poor. Official analyses blaming the victims for their own dilemmas, combined with devastating critiques of government institutions created to support the underclasses, reinforce the developing consensus that the "free" market produces a much more efficient use of resources and a higher rate of economic growth.

Modern production systems continue to expand, challenging peasant and indigenous claims to productive lands and valuable resources. Official institutions, domestic and international, promote new strategies to reward the commercial farmers for their contributions to national development, assuring them continuing privileged access to the most valuable resources in the modernizing society: land and natural resources, technology, credit and marketing channels. Poverty is accentuated by the voraciousness of this expansion that frequently condemns certain regions and the people who live there to devastation. In the new policy arena, the struggle of the poor is all the more difficult; marginal groups at best can only attempt to claim a small proportion of official budgets for their efforts; they now look to the worldwide nongovernmental community for understanding and support or must resort to various forms of resistance to advance their claims. Even when massive reforms forced a redistribution of land to peasant and indigenous groups, as in Mexico, Bolivia, and Nicaragua, the complementary financial and technical resources to help the new owners to take full advantage of the opportunities were invariably channeled to other uses.

The Dynamics of Rural Poverty

Underlying all of these factors, rural poverty is the historical consequence of existing systems of economic organization that continue to discriminate against these direct producers. When compared to producers in other sectors, they are not endowed with comparable amounts of accumulated capital that would raise the productivity of land and labor. Even more distressing, however, the evolving organization of agricultural production in the Third World places rural producers at a disadvantage not only with regard to people in other sectors, but also in their struggle to compete against farmers in other parts of the world; they lack access to the technical, financial, and institutional systems of support that protected these farmers during different historical periods from threatening competitive processes.

These fundamental problems can be most easily examined by identifying some of the principal causes of rural poverty, which will then enable us to develop guidelines for an alternative strategy of sustainable rural development.

Discriminatory Macroeconomic and Sectoral Policies

Today, as in the colonial regimes of a past era, production and export taxes, complex systems for controlling foreign exchange and trade (overvalued exchange rates and protected tariffs for industrial products), and price controls on various commodities are among the most common tools used to extract surplus from rural producers. In the post–World War II period, new techniques for fiscal and monetary regulation were added to the toolbox, leading to transfers from rural communities to finance industrialization through the banking system, and systems of wage control through commodity regulatory mechanisms. The high costs and arbitrary impacts of these programs left the crops produced by the rural poor (and sometimes those of wealthier producers) seriously "disprotected."

Other facets of the public policy agenda have the contradictory effects of increasing output while exacerbating the social inequalities that characterize most rural societies in the Third World. The Green Revolution led to significant productivity increases for those groups able to gain access to the technical know-how, finance the input package, and use the infrastructure. Similarly, public investment in irrigation and colonization schemes to expand the productive frontiers generally promoted large-scale commercial agriculture amenable to mechanization (Barkin 1972; Hecht 1985). Such programs not only have devastating effects on the environment, but also are socially destructive. Local populations are relocated or even exterminated, while the fragile and complex ecosystems soon become unproductive, even for the new colonizers. Small-scale traditional producers are displaced from their historic missions, while the new systems contribute to the wealth of a small group that rarely has to account for the environmental damage it occasions.[3]

A different agenda would be required to counter the persistent bias. Investments would be channeled to agroecology and technologies or infrastructure that directly increase productivity on a small scale of the popular foods produced by the peasantry or their environmental priorities, such as microscale projects for land and water management (Altieri 1987). It is not merely a coincidence that such policies are also conducive to creating sustainable development systems, as we shall see in the last section.

Inadequate and Polarized Land Tenure Systems
Inequality of access to land and insecure tenure arrangements are major obstacles to maintaining or improving environmental quality. Land ownership in much of the Third World remains highly concentrated in spite of numerous attempts at land reform. Throughout Latin America, the increased number of small farms (growing at a rate of 2.2 percent per annum during the post–World War II period) and shrinking plot sizes created a peasantry that is being pushed and pulled "away from being primarily farm producers and toward increasing integration into the labour market" as larger farms continue to command most of the land, and a greater share of other rural resources (de Janvry et al. 1989, 406–7).

Inadequate property rights exacerbate the discriminatory impact of scarce and high-cost credit and discourage local initiatives to engage in soil and water conservation tasks. These problems become even more serious when the lack of clear titles and defined rules for access affect "the commons," that is, resources that are generally available to many people (production units). The "tragedy" of overuse in such cases is so familiar as to have spawned its own group of scholars, as well as a series of proposals that would contribute to approaches for sustainable development (McCay and Acheson 1990; Olson 1990; Ostrom 1990, 1993).

Ironically, land reforms also can have pernicious effects on the ability of recipients to improve their conditions and protect the environment. In many situations, the regulations limit or even prohibit various kinds of land transactions (e.g., renting or leasing) and limit the beneficiaries to seeking credit from government banks, thus excluding them from the commercial banking system. The application of these restrictions by inefficient and corrupt government bureaucracies further stratifies a system of privilege that has placed a brake on social mobility and agricultural improvements. Unfortunately, the headlong race to undo the errors of the past with new legislation by "freeing" up the land for use in its most productive form by titling ownership and encouraging rural communities to associate with private capital may only further exacerbate existing problems, if the peasantry does not have independent access to capital markets and technical assistance to assure it of an ability to negotiate effectively with potential investors.[4]

Antipeasant Bias in Development Institutions
The antipeasant bias among development agencies, and within rural institutions, is particularly egregious. Resources are systematically denied for "peasant" approaches to problem solving and social organization. Peasants are considered to be backward and incapable of incorporating innovations into their productive systems. The economic effects of this bias are especially troublesome, because they lead directly to a decline in the value of peasant resources dedicated to rural activities. This is evident in the differential manner in which peasant and commercial product prices are manipulated by regulatory agencies, and in the different types of decisions about the import of basic commodities that negatively impact small-scale and rain-fed agricultural zones more often than the larger, irrigated farming sectors. As a result, many of the scale-neutral innovations of the Green Revolution and biotechnology have been transformed into mechanisms for further social polarization, in spite of the best intentions of their inventors.

The emergence of NGOs as a mechanism for challenging this bias on a global scale and within local bureaucracies is a particularly notable feature of institutional change that is directly related to the broadening of alternative strategies for rural development (to which we will return).

Unequal Distribution of Income and Political Power
Related to the previous topics, but worthy of separate mention, the system of regional or provincial bosses (caciques) is frequently a major obstacle in progress for poor people in rural areas. (In rare cases, a powerful patriarchal leader may retain control in a poor region by ensuring that resources are equitably distributed and that social and political problems are resolved with local resources, if at all possible.) The various forms that bossism takes are too numerous to be listed here, but the effects are remarkably similar, and reminiscent of the stories told about manorial lords in the Middle Ages. A power hierarchy, sometimes tied to political parties, which extends from the state into local communities, often plays a determining role in the availability and distribution of desperately needed aid packages, work projects, and welfare programs.

Inappropriate Employment Policies
Although population growth figures are generally declining, they are still above the growth of the productive labor force. Throughout the Third World, one of the most serious problems facing planners is the creation of remunerative employment. Traditionally an important source of livelihood, agricultural employment has been declining precipitously in recent decades.

The trends are striking. Between 1960 and 1980, peasants as a proportion of the economically active population in rural Latin America increased from 60 to 65 percent of the total, yet the total agricultural labor force declined from almost one-half of the total to less than one-third in this period (de Janvry et al. 1989, 399–402). This change reflects the incorporation of new laborsaving technologies into commercial agricultural sectors, leading to a falling share of labor in this area while stranding workers in the peasant sector for want of better alternatives.

The opening of economies to international competition complicates matters in two ways. First, traditional productive activities are becoming unprofitable as imported consumer goods displace locally produced goods and the former producers themselves find it more profitable to import than to produce. Second, foreign investment offers new technologies and raises the scale and capital intensity of production, reducing the rate of job creation below social needs.

Pressures against Local Cultural Institutions

As peasant farmers have been transformed into "proletarianized" workers, they have all the responsibilities of such groups, with none of the privileges that might come from having a steady income in return for productive work (Barkin 1985). This individualization of the labor force is notable in many rural communities where inherited systems of mutual self-help and voluntary labor to construct projects of collective interest are rapidly disappearing without adequate replacements. The authority of the traditional community is being eroded and substituted for by new forms of authoritarian imposition.

The long-term process of pushing indigenous groups to increasingly marginal lands is one of the most important factors contributing to the loss of cultural identity in the Third World. In many cases, the new settlers have no access to or ignore inherited information about how to manage the ecosystems they have invaded. This is further compounded by official commitments to technological approaches from the temperate zones, which are rarely suited to the newly colonized areas, often in the tropics. In many of these cases, as we shall see, it becomes necessary to generate a new type of appropriate knowledge so that the settler populations can be sensitized to sustainable approaches to productive survival.

Migration and the Feminization of Poverty

Women's role in rural society has changed dramatically in recent decades. With the proletarianization of the labor force and the greater difficulty of satisfying social needs with on-farm and rural community production, the typical family has had to develop complex survival strategies that involve migration and greater participation in the wage-labor force. Even while more women are wage laborers and migrating, there is also a worldwide tendency toward more rural households being headed by women. Throughout the world increasing numbers of women are now being assigned the full burden of providing for the basic subsistence needs and other income needs for their families. Moreover, these new duties have not led to the end of discriminatory practices that limit women's access to education or economic opportunities.

As the environment is degraded, life in the rural sector has become more difficult, making women's tasks more difficult. With deforestation, the search for firewood requires longer treks and often sacrifices younger trees on steeper slopes; similarly, the task of assuring water supplies is also becoming more arduous. Such an overload of burdens affects household nutrition, as family farm plots where fruits and vegetables were cultivated and small farm animals reared on household and garden wastes are frequently renounced because of the press of other activities.

The Urban Factor and Rural Poverty

Urbanization in the Third World is creating networks of densely settled areas, fed largely by rural migrants. Increasingly, rural families count on the cities or even international migration for their very subsistence. As the urban areas expand, they make enormous demands for resources and for places to deposit their wastes, without any corresponding improvement in their ability to address the problems of the majority of poor people (Hardoy, Mitlin, and Satterthwaite 1992).

In this complex interweaving of rural and urban, peasant and proletarian, the urban/rural dichotomy of former epochs is not helpful. Off-farm income is now an integral part of rural incomes, and the technical and other skills acquired in these employments could contribute to diversifying the economic base of rural areas. Conversely, rural populations and experience also have a great deal of potential to contribute to improving the urban experience. Throughout the Third World, the important differences in productivity and incomes between industry and agriculture have formed a barrier to a more balanced urban development program that would include a much more diverse land use pattern. For example, the possibility of food production in reserved urban areas as part of a response to growing unemployment might lower transport costs and provide employment opportunities.

The Internationalization of Capital

Expanding Trade and the Growth of Transnational Corporations

The international economy insinuates itself into every aspect of life. Its growing influence on seemingly independent and isolated rural communities is poorly understood in analyses of rural change and virtually nonexistent in discussions of sustainability. International expansion, however, has transformed the dual economy into a global phenomenon, systematically creating structures that further polarize society and accelerate processes that threaten social welfare and the environment.[5]

For centuries, the expansion of the world market has left its mark on local societies and their ecosystems (e.g., Wolf 1982). Endless waves of "boom and bust" characterized this process in Latin America and throughout the Third World. Many of the earliest producers and merchants who introduced new crops and created new markets for existing products became immensely rich. Lured by promises of vast markets and personal enrichment, successive waves of producers imitated the initial success stories, planting cotton, grains, tropical fruits, coffee, chile, and myriad other products, but on a smaller scale and with fewer resources than their forerunners. The longer the process continued, the greater the number of people who failed in their attempts to produce and market the products profitably.[6]

On a global scale, Raul Prebisch identified this problem early in the post–World War II period and summarized the concerns of an important group of Latin Americans who observed a secular decline in the terms of trade of raw materials and food crops in relation to industrialized products.[7] His admonition still haunts us: long-term relative prices of many commodities produced in the Third World, especially for those produced by the poorest, are still systematically declining.

In many countries of the Third World, external pressures and domestic policies prevent farmers in poor communities from cultivating the crops that supply people with their basic food needs. The effects of this process have been devastating: low productivity and deteriorating environmental conditions make it difficult for workers and peasants to compete with producers from abroad who are better financed, enjoy greater institutional support for training workers, have ready access to technological innovation, and can depend on integrated marketing systems for distributing their merchandise. As a result, throughout the developing world basic foodstuffs are being imported and rural families impoverished

(Barkin, Batt, and Dewalt 1990). The loss of food self-sufficiency magnifies the impact of international competition, forcing significant numbers of people to migrate in search of income with which to buy food.

In contrast, agribusiness interests are occupying the best lands, planting export products, and transforming vast regions into pastures. This tendency is often celebrated in the institutional circles of development bankers and neoliberal multilateral research organizations, a reflection of the success of years of arduous labor to persuade or coerce governments around the world to restructure production to take advantage of the gains from specialization in international trade.

A cornerstone of this new world order is the push toward felling the barriers to international trade. The broadening of the GATT framework in the new World Trade Organization (WTO) and the consolidation of regional trading blocs (e.g., EU and NAFTA) are symptomatic of the rapid changes that are affecting national economies. Local producers everywhere are threatened by the discipline imposed by the specter of imports.

Transnational corporations are thriving in this new regime. Their move south is part of a global strategy to exploit abundant supplies of raw materials, to lower costs of production, and to guarantee access to emerging markets. Although they create new jobs, the gains are rarely sufficient to counterbalance the massive displacement of people from traditional industries and rural pursuits. In most of Latin America, national economic adjustment has reduced employment or shifted people into part-time and low-income jobs with a generalized fall in living standards and social welfare indicators. The result is a rapid and profound transformation of these societies into specialized production systems and off-shore assembly and procurement centers.

These trends are common to all primary producers. National fisheries and deep sea fishing are plagued by problems of overharvesting while coastal ecosystems are menaced by contamination; commercial demands lead governments to transfer rights from traditional fishing communities. Foresters face competition from imported wood products, even while they must intensify their cutting beyond the capacity of the woods to support the new levels of extraction (Place 1993).

Small and medium-sized industrial producers, like peasant and indigenous communities, must compete in their local markets with similar products imported from other parts of the world. Producers transform themselves into merchants, finding it easier and more profitable to import basic consumer goods from the global marketplace than to forge a modern competitive industrial facility. The obstacles they face range from inadequate technological information and advice, to expensive, limited credit and serious bureaucratic hurdles.

The debt crisis of the 1980s created yet another opportunity for the financial community to accelerate the pace of internationalization. Structural adjustment programs (SAPs) not only dismantled the complex structure of government regulation and direct public sector intervention in the economy, but also lowered the real wages of workers and limited the autonomy of peasants and other independent workers. The SAPs were structured to "correct" the excesses of the past. By opening local economies, they unraveled a highly protected industrial apparatus created during the period of import-substituting industrialization to promote the production of capital goods as well as consumer goods.

The multilateral development community (World Bank, International Monetary Fund, regional development banks) joined with the private international financial community and some national development agencies to enforce these shock programs. In their view, costly subsidy programs and direct government intervention had produced economic structures ill-suited to the realities of these countries. Throughout the Third World, private initiative had been stymied by a regulatory morass and inadequate incentive systems. Although these distorted systems often benefited a small elite, they rarely contributed to thrusting these societies onto a path of dynamic economic growth.

The movement toward freer international trade was joined by a process of regional integration. Market mechanisms replaced bureaucratic councils, allowing greater freedom for capital and guiding investment decisions by entrepreneurial groups. Competition among financial groups surged as they took advantage of the opportunities offered by the international economy to create new industries and modernize old ones, to bring new technologies to bear to solve old problems, and to reposition the society and its people to confront the challenges of international competition. The development community began to finance the institutional and productive changes that were needed to push dozens of countries around the world into the world market. The new approach to national economic management created the conditions for private producers (often foreign corporations) to profit handsomely by attending to the demands of the international marketplace and a new group of very prosperous local consumers who are the principal local beneficiaries of the new strategy.

The Failings of the Global Marketplace

The perceived benefits of globalization were accompanied by a range of problems created or exacerbated by the expanding global market. By strengthening local capital markets (especially for trading securities), internationalization opened a new avenue by which speculative movements of capital could now more readily influence productive decisions. Latin America quickly felt the destabilizing effects of capital movements: international financiers imposed narrow strictures on the ability of national governments to promote broad-based sustainable development. These strictures exacted particularly heavy costs from workers and peasants.

The high-profile NAFTA, GATT, and WTO negotiations also made us aware of the heavy burden that international trade and regional integration are placing on the environment. Specialization is accelerating with the internationalization of the global economy, hastening the pace of ecosystem degradation and destruction. By creating new opportunities for investment and profit and accelerating the dynamics of internationalization, the new institutional arrangements are further polarizing nations in both North and South; the greater concentration of wealth and the spread of poverty is making the task of controlling and reversing environmental damage increasingly difficult.

This problem has sparked a heated continuing debate about the trade-off between improvements in economic welfare for a few generated by increases in trade and investment, on the one hand, and the widespread decline in living standards for workers and peasants who can't find productive employment, on the other. Environmentalists point to the heavy costs that this trade will occasion in terms of contamination from transport and wastes of the production process and a more rapid use of natural resources, especially energy. Other critics go further, objecting to the rapid dissemination of an unattainable and unsustainable model of development based on increasing consumption as the basis for propagating improvements in human welfare.

Just as serious, the increased economic activity produced by globalization is coming at a time when national governments are shedding traditional functions and sacrificing parts of their revenue base to attract new investment; they are devolving responsibilities to regional (state or provincial) and local administrations that are unprepared to confront the challenge; their lack of technical personnel and modern administrative systems sharpens the problems occasioned by their narrow revenue base. This heightens the cause for concern about deteriorating environments and greater polarization as international traders reap the benefits of the new opening in the international system.[8]

The political power of transnational corporations often enables them to negotiate subsidies or exemptions from various kinds of public service charges (including local taxes, municipal infrastructure fees, and energy tariffs) that lead to technological choices that are not in the best interests of the country or of the planet as a whole. These programs frequently bring about an increase in the capital and energy intensity of production, and they absolve the new installations from contributing to the substantial public investments in public services required to assure production.

International expansion also increases the intensity of natural resource extraction, with dire consequences for the environment. Many production arrangements are short-term, with the time horizon limited to the period required to amortize the investment (frequently less than five years). As a result, investors have a strong incentive to raise the intensity of the extraction of value, a problem that is becoming particularly acute in the plantation and monocropping areas of the Third World. The increased intensity of extraction by one region often leads to impoverishment in others, as traditional methods of husbanding the forests or the coastal areas prove too costly to allow most groups to compete in national and international markets. These specialized production systems, whether they are located in agriculture, mining, forestry, oceans, or urban areas, are frequently accused of being among the most notorious violators of even the most minimal norms of environmental responsibility.

The Separation of Consumption and Production

Affluence and the accumulation of wealth represent a serious threat to the sustainability of the global system. Consumption patterns in the richer countries are shaped by a productive apparatus that only thrives by generating new demands for goods in order to continue growing, rather than by attempting to define a socially desirable package of individual and collective goods that would satisfy basic needs. At present, creative energies are directed toward increasing the volume of goods with a concomitant rise in the use of energy and other natural resources, often sacrificing society's capacity to meet its larger social goals.

With a growing consciousness of the impending environmental crisis, pressures are growing for more responsible production technologies and consumption patterns. In select cases, resources are being used more efficiently and greater attention is being directed toward reducing and recycling waste streams.[9] Initial steps have been taken and further advances are foreseeable in this regard, but the underlying problem of the imperative for further growth on the basis of increased consumption of a more diverse basket of goods and services means that more resources and energy will be required to assure economic growth. This creates an unsustainable model that affluent societies are still unprepared to contain, much less reverse.

There is a fundamental contradiction in a system that promotes an increasing separation between consumption and production. Urbanization certainly contributes to this separation. In the urban areas, people lose their perspective on the relationship between consumption and the processes of production. Throughout society, even as people are acquiring a greater consciousness of the need to care for the environment, the growing complexity of production processes and the characteristics of urban consumption lead them to lose touch with the intrinsic relationship between environmental well-being and human welfare.

With changing settlement patterns and important migratory flows uprooting people from their communities, there is a widespread breakdown of the relationship between cultural traditions and practices that, through the generations, perfected and transmitted mechanisms to protect environments and species. The plethora of case studies examining the rapid displacement of inherited wisdom by productive solutions offers ample evidence of the complexity of these mechanisms. The pressures of social and productive reorganization, however, have now gone far beyond the capacity of many of these societies to adapt, with the result that many of them are witnessing or actually participating in accelerated processes of environmental deterioration. We now need to examine the contributions that new technologies and adaptations of old ones might make to enhance deteriorated landscapes and productive systems; as our understanding of traditional knowledge systems advances, it may be possible to cross-fertilize particular social systems with environmental management approaches from other societies.

The Economic Analysis of the "Problem"

Like the field of development itself, many of the leading international institutions reacting to the challenges created by the demand for "sustainability" have adopted the analytical framework and the tools of economics to help them design their responses. As a result, a great deal of intellectual effort and considerable expenditure have been devoted to quantifying the problems of environmental degradation and formalizing the questions into economic models that offer ways of placing prices on resources and assigning costs to pollutants and processes of degradation.[10]

For many of the multilateral agencies facing the problem of "sustainable development," the economists' toolbox offers a comforting set of analytical instruments. Varying in degree of sophistication, their approaches explain that heightening environmental problems in the developing world are the logical result of choices by policymakers and citizens. Economists argue that, under the circumstances of poverty and capital scarcity, they would expect people with economic and political power to allocate resources to promote investment, thereby increasing the rate of growth in the short run so as to have more resources available later on. According to this line of reasoning, environmental quality is a relatively luxurious commodity, one that can be better appreciated when people have met their basic subsistence needs.

The "Environmental Kuznets Curve" is a heuristic device used to justify this line of thought. Some research has identified a tendency for wealthier nations to allocate an increasing proportion of their national income to improving the environment. (The results are similar to those derived by the economist after whom the curve is named, which showed, on the basis of a cross-section analysis of the most affluent nations, that the distribution of income became more egalitarian as countries became richer. The original Kuznets hypothesis itself is controversial, since recent data does not indicate a similar trend in presently developing nations.)[11] Thus, we find some economists interested in environmental issues arguing, for example, that the North American Free Trade Agreement (NAFTA) will contribute to improving the environment by raising the rate of economic growth and stimulating demand for a cleaner environment[12] (Grossman and Krueger 1993).

In a similar vein, neoclassical economists offer a series of analytical conclusions and policy prescriptions on the basis of their understanding of the way in which markets function. Larry Summers, the chief economist of the World Bank at the time (later the Deputy Secretary of the United States Treasury in charge of international economic policy, and appointed Secretary of the Treasury in 1999), offered a vivid example of this line of reasoning when he asked whether "the World Bank [should not] be encouraging more migration of the dirty industries to the LDCs?" He explained that "a given amount of health-impairing pollution should be done in the country with the lowest cost, which will be the country of the lowest wages." Furthermore, he pointed out that "the demand for a clean environment for aesthetic and health reasons is likely to have very high income-elasticity"; since people in these countries have high infant mortality rates, they need not worry about diseases provoked by contamination that only manifest themselves in older people (*Economist,* Feb. 8, 1992; Foster 1993).

Poor people contribute to environmental degradation, we are told, because of the urgency of their current needs for survival. In technical terms, they discount the future highly, placing more value on products available in the near term at the expense of activities that will only bear fruit in the future. Thus, they must make an explicit trade-off, accepting long-term environmental degradation (by ignoring or underinvesting in such activities as soil and water conservation and reforestation projects, which would only lead to increased output five or more years hence) to meet their immediate needs for food and shelter (such a line of thinking was attributed to Indira Gandhi in Leonard 1989, 4). Economists suggest that these priorities will change with economic growth, not only because producers themselves have more resources and the greater availability of capital will reduce the social discount rate, but also because their governments will be better equipped to face the problems.[13] Thus, "only after poor farmers increase their incomes can they turn their attention to reducing soil erosion and other long-term environmental problems" (Leonard 1989, 4).[14]

Population growth is another culprit in environmental degradation, according to those using models of rational choice behavior. Their models have integrated this "given" into a disarmingly simple quantitative relationship now widely known as the *IPAT* formula (for $I = PAT$), which links environmental impact (I) to population size (P), affluence (A), and technological advance (T) (Meadows et al. 1992, 100–103; Ehrlich and Ehrlich 1991). When discussing problems of the developing world, analysts adopting this perspective emphasize the high rates of fertility among women in poor societies and environmentally sensitive areas to support their call for stricter measures to limit population growth. Their policy prescriptions often assume that childbearing is an unplanned or culturally obsolete result of social organization; it seems inconceivable that in many poor societies children are virtually the only insurance that a couple can acquire to provide for periods of extreme hardship or old age. Rather than admitting that population growth is frequently a symptom of the failure to incorporate poor people into remunerative activities, these analysts dismiss those groups choosing to have more children as irrational, people who have to become more responsible. Policymakers intervene with appropriate family planning, female literacy, or social welfare strategies, then more coercive measures, should the first approach fail.

The task of how to identify and assign prices to many resources and waste flows has become a high priority for economists. Economists also participate in the political arena, advocating alternative mechanisms for translating these prices into real charges to be borne by producers and consumers. These costs, they argue, would promote a more careful use of scarce resources and a more responsible attitude toward the generation and disposal of wastes. Decisions about how to express these issues in financial terms, however, are not simple technical questions; rather, they involve complex questions about the distribution of resources and benefits among different social classes and among generations, about control over resources now and in the future, about the role of technology in society. In short, the technical debates among economists mask fundamental questions about the present functioning and future evolution of society.

The technical discussions among economists beg some important questions about how their results are to be used. Once the decision is made about what to charge people for their use of resources and for the costs they impose on society from their damage to the environment, the question arises of how to distribute these funds. If a significant system of "green taxes" was initiated, it could provide a source of revenues to help finance the enormous expenditures needed to reverse the damage inflicted by a long history of our carefree misuse of nature. The monies might also be used to compensate communities for the mining of their resources, or to pay for the investments required to replace the resources with new productive activities that will guarantee gainful employment in the future. The institutional reforms required by this approach involve a major reordering of political and social priorities, a theme to which we must return frequently.

A Popular Response

Confronting the official defense of the necessity to accelerate the internationalization of capital, nongovernmental organizations, representing the diverse interests of "civil society" throughout the world, have begun to play a crucial role in offering alternative models of sustainable development. NGO international secretariats have been active in mobilizing national and local groups throughout the world to oppose the structural adjustment programs (SAPs) since their "invention" in the 1970s, because of the disproportionately heavy burden they imposed on the most vulnerable groups throughout the developing world. These organizing efforts continue to be especially effective because they are not limited to the sectoral interests of environmental groups, or others interested in human rights, women's problems, labor, or peasants. Rather, they share a common analysis that identifies inequality as one of the major problems and therefore broad-based democratic participation as the overarching strategy and principle for political action (Barkin 1994; Gregory 1992; Johnson and Cooperrider 1991; Livernash 1992; Cruz and Repetto 1992; Mumme 1993).

Although the World Bank acknowledged NGOs' existence as early as 1975, substantive NGO participation only began after a Consensus Document was drawn up in 1987 "agreeing on the necessity of drawing upon the knowledge and experience of Southern NGOs and grassroots organizations." The NGO Working Group brings together a wide variety of national and local organizations that have been attempting to coordinate their efforts; its members have gradually become more vocal in demanding a greater role in the design and implementation of Bank-financed projects. The group is collaborating in studies to analyze the SAPs in detail and confront the program-planning and operations staffs with their critiques; the Bank now recognizes, albeit grudgingly, that these organizations can be effective in ensuring the design and implementation of many development-assistance programs.

An institutional base is being built for moving beyond the dichotomy between inward- and outward-oriented growth. The systematic organizing of grassroots groups throughout the world, together with the growing recognition of the failure of market solutions to provide answers to all the problems, is creating a new framework in which advocates of popular participation in the promotion of sustainable development can not only take a major place in the debates but can also participate in the design and implementation of national development programs. Of course, this does not resolve the more intractable problems of the conflicts of interest among social groups within each country and region, which constitute the major barrier to sustainable development.

New Strategies for Rural Sustainable Development: Popular Participation, Food Self-Sufficiency, and Environmental Regeneration

> Certain societies, traumatised by political, economic and ecological shocks, need catalysers to regain their organizational and creative capabilities.
>
> Ben Abdallah and Engelhard (1993)

Sustainability

Sustainable development has become a powerful and controversial theme, creating seemingly impossible goals for policymakers and development practitioners. Virtually everyone now couches proposals for change in terms of their contribution to "sustainability." There is a widespread acknowledgment that present levels of per-capita resource consumption in the richer countries cannot possibly be generalized to people living in the rest of the world; many argue that present levels of consumption cannot be maintained, even for those groups who now enjoy high levels of material consumption. In this new discourse, resources encompass not just inherited natural capital, including raw materials (such as soil, subsoil products, good quality air and water, forests, oceans, and wetlands), but also the earth's capacity to absorb the wastes created by our productive systems; of course, the analysis of resources also includes considerations about the quality of the built environments in which we live and work. (An excellent introduction to the underlying discussion can be found in Wilson 1992.)

The concern for sustainability has become global, reflecting a widespread fear of deterioration in the quality of life. Existing productive systems and consumption patterns threaten the continuity of the existing social organization. The inequitable and undemocratic nature of current patterns of development raises the specter of the unraveling of present social, political, and productive systems. A different structure, more attuned to the earth's possibilities for supporting and reproducing life, must replace them.

To address questions of sustainability, then, is to confront the fundamental dilemmas facing the development community today. While the trickle-down approaches to economic progress enrich a few and stimulate growth in "modern" economies and "modern" sectors within traditional societies, they do not address most people's needs; moreover, they have contributed to depleting the world's store of natural wealth and to a deterioration in the quality of our natural environment.

The search for sustainability involves a dual strategy: on the one hand, it must unleash the bonds that restrain people from strengthening their own organizations, or creating new ones, to use their relatively meager resources to search for an alternative and autonomous resolution to their problems. On the other hand, a sustainable development strategy must contribute to the forging of a new social pact, cemented in the recognition that the eradication of poverty and the democratic incorporation of the disenfranchised into a more diverse productive structure are essential.

Sustainability is not "simply" a matter of the environment, economic justice, and development. It is also about people and our survival as individuals and cultures. It is, most significantly, a question of whether and how diverse groups of people will continue to survive. In fact, the burgeoning literature about the move toward sustainability celebrates the many groups who have successfully adapted their cultural heritages, unique forms of social and productive organization, and specific ways of relating to their natural environments.

Sustainability, then, is about the struggle for diversity in all its dimensions. International campaigns to conserve germ plasm, to protect endangered species, and to create reserves of the biosphere are multiplying in reaction to the mounting offensive, while communities and their hard-pressed members struggle against powerful external forces to defend their individuality, their rights, and their ability to survive. The concern for biodiversity, in its broadest sense, encompasses not only threatened flora and fauna, but also the survivability of these human communities, as stewards of the natural environment and as producers.

Internationalization has stymied this movement toward diversity. The powerful economic groups that shape the world economy (transnational corporations and financial institutions, and influential local powers, among others) are striving to break down these individual or regional traits, molding us into more homogenous and tractable social groups. They would position us to support the existing structure of inequality and to engage in productive employment; and, for those lucky enough to enjoy high enough incomes, to become consumers.

Sustainability is a process rather than a set of well-specified goals. It involves modifying processes in nature, the economy, and society. It has become more fashionable as people have discovered that increasing production or even national wealth does not guarantee improved living standards; but the challenges of environmental protection are perhaps the most immediate force making the discussion so important. There are fundamental ethical questions about the sustainability of a global structure that perpetuates high degrees of international inequality while leaving rural communities with little chance of satisfying even the most basic of their needs. These overall questions go far beyond the scope of this paper, which addresses strategies to promote a greater degree of sustainability in rural development. But for an effort to be successful it will also contribute to modifications in national development programs conducive to greater popular participation in their design and implementation.

In contrast to generalized theories about the development process and sophisticated models of economic growth, the literature on sustainable development offers a mixture of high ethical principles, manuals for practical organization and implementation, and very concrete case studies of successes and failures. In this section we offer a rapid overview of some general approaches and solutions that might be suitable for various regions and problems. Rather than attempt to be comprehensive, this discussion is meant to convey the flavor of the discussion and the directions for future work. More than anything else, it is meant to reinforce the growing conviction that sustainable development may be an idea whose time has come; its implementation requires challenging not only the self-interest of the wealthy minority, but also the consumption package that is defining our quality of life. This is the real challenge we face today.

A strategy to promote sustainability must focus on the importance of local participation and control over the way in which people live and work. The question of local or regional autonomy is an important part of any discussion of national and international integration. The issues of autonomy versus cooperation and coordination are very much related to others having to do with self-sufficiency versus international specialization. The analysis of the previous sections places strategies for sustainability at the opposite end of the spectrum from the prescriptions of the neoliberal reforms. However, most advocates of sustainability recognize that the choices are not this simple: industrial products and technologies will not (and should not) be rejected simply because they involve hierarchical control and alienated work. The response must be more reflective; it must confront the realities of an urbanized global society. In what follows we will briefly review some possible strategies to promote sustainable development in different contexts.

Food Self-Sufficiency: The Relationship between Production and Consumption

The first issue that must be dealt with squarely is that of self-sufficiency versus integration into the global trading system, with its tendency toward specialization based on monocropping systems. Sustainability need not be tantamount to autarchy, although it is conducive to a much lower degree of specialization in all areas of production and social organization.

Food self-sufficiency is a controversial objective that cogently raises the question of autonomy. Although development practitioners are virtually unanimous in rejecting calls for an extreme position, Mexico's commitment to such a program in 1980 was widely applauded. Today the discussion is more complex, for there is general agreement on two contradictory factors in the debate:

1. On the one hand, local production of basic commodities which can be produced more efficiently elsewhere is a luxury few societies can afford, if and only if the resources not dedicated to the production of these traded goods can find productive employment elsewhere.
2. On the other hand, there are probably few exceptions to the observation that greater local production of such commodities contributes to higher nutritional standards and better health indices. In the context of today's societies, in which inequality is the rule and the forces discriminating against the rural poor legion, a greater degree of autonomy in the provision of the material basis

for an adequate standard of living is likely to be an important part of any program of regional sustainability. It will contribute to creating more productive jobs and an interest in better stewardship over natural resources than any other single productive strategy.

There are many parts of the world in which a strategy of food self-sufficiency would constitute a wasteful luxury. It would involve the diversion of resources from other uses that could be more productive in contributing to the availability of goods for trading. But even in circumstances in which wholesale importation of basic commodities is advisable, people concerned with sustainable development raise questions about modifying local diets so that they are more attuned to the productive possibilities of their regions; in the current scene, the tendency to substitute imported products for traditional foods is particularly troublesome.[15]

Food self-sufficiency, however, is only part of a broader strategy of productive diversification whose tenets are very much a part of the sustainability movement. The principles of greater self-reliance are fundamental for the whole range of products and services of which a society would like to assure itself. Historically, rural denizens never have been "just" farmers, or "just" anything else, for that matter. Rather, rural communities have been characterized by the diversity of the productive activities in which they engaged to assure their subsistence. It was only the aberration of transferring models of large-scale commercial agriculture to development thinking in the Third World that misled many into ignoring the multifaceted nature of traditional rural productive systems. Sustainable development strategies directly face this problem, attempting to reintroduce this diversity, as they grapple with problems of appropriate scales of operation and product mix.

Popular Participation, Social Justice, and Autonomy

Sustainability is about direct participation. If there is one constant in the diverse literature in the area, it is the recognition that the movement has emerged from the grass roots; intermediate level NGOs can only claim legitimacy to the extent that they can speak for the extraordinary proliferation of community groups and civic organizations that are beginning to demand an increasing role in the national policy debate.

These demands and the responses from official agencies on the multilateral and national levels are quite instructive. There is a generalized agreement among practitioners that sustainable development policies cannot be designed or implemented from above.[16] To be successful they require the direct participation of the intended beneficiaries and others who might be impacted. But there is also general agreement that this participation must involve more than a mere consultative role. For such an approach to work, it requires that the powerful become aware of the need to integrate people into real power structures in order to confront the major problems of our day. This entails a redistribution of both political and economic power (Boyce 1994; Goodland and Daly 1993).

In this formulation, sustainability is not simply about environmental preservation. It is about the active participation of people in the understanding of the dynamics of natural systems and the redesign of productive systems that will allow them to be productive while conserving the planet's ability to host uncounted future generations. It is an approach to the problem of *empowerment,* another word that has also become popular. The literature on sustainability provides many examples of the ways in which people can and do "act in solidarity with each other when the state isn't watching" to solve common problems and initiate creative experiments for social innovation (Friedmann 1992, 168–71; also see Ostrom 1990, 1993). The lifework of Albert Hirschman offers countless examples of the ways in which the NGOs and other grassroots groups have been successful in exerting pressure to modify development projects as part of their own (local) perception of development priorities.[17] Interestingly enough, however, under special circumstances, the state itself may (be forced to) play a creative role in encouraging or "liberating" creative participatory energies to promote programs of local development and social justice that also contribute to moving the society in the direction of sustainability (Alves Amorim 1994; Tendler 1993).

Lest we become too sanguine, much of the literature shows how and why the state does not operate to "empower" the downtrodden. The difficult juncture of the late 1980s forced the Mexican government to finance grassroots development schemes through local mobilization in communities dispersed throughout the country; the Solidarity program was highly regarded by the international press and development community as an effective welfare (and vote-getting) program, but did little to create permanent productive opportunities for the participants, who were rarely able to continue once the official programs were terminated. Colombia's later copy of the program promises to offer no more opportunities for the poor. In his pathbreaking examination of problems of soil erosion, Piers Blaikie goes further to explain that market signals generally push government into programs that benefit the rich, and that much productivity-enhancing research is misguided. His most general proposition is one that neatly encapsulates much of the criticism of development experience of the past half-century: "the emphasis is upon particular commodities isolated from social, economic and environmental context" (1985, chap. 2).

A program focusing on sustainability must also deal with poverty. There is a widespread recognition that poverty and environmental destruction go hand in hand, although less thought has been directed toward the enormous environmental problems occasioned by the present consumption standards of the affluent throughout the world. In the coming period, economic progress itself will depend on involving the grassroots groups to help the affluent find ways to control their consumption and in the organization of development programs that offer material progress for the poor and better stewardship of the planet's resources.

A Strategy of Democratic Participation for Rural Diversification and Productive Improvement

Sustainable development is an approach to productive reorganization that encompasses the combined experiences of local groups throughout the world. The techniques for implementation vary greatly among regions and ecosystems. A single common denominator pervades this work: the need for effective democratic participation in the design and implementation of projects (its centrality is evident in the titles of some the excellent writing on the subject: Ben Abdallah and Engelhard 1993; Calderon et al. 1992; Machado et al. 1993; Nuñez 1993). Another lesson from recent experience is the importance of creating networks to support and defend this work; without the mutual reinforcement that the international grouping of NGOs provides, the individual units would not be as effective in obtaining funds for their projects, technical assistance for their implementation, and political support against intransigent or incredulous local and national politicians and institutions (Arruda 1993; Friedmann and Rangan 1993). The successes are due, however, not just to the tenacity and sacrifice of committed organizational workers and local participants, but also to the forging of a support structure, nationally and internationally, of workers, peasants, scholars, and activists, who are willing to mobilize to support the spontaneous or well-organized efforts of individual groups throughout the world that promote projects of democratic participation for sustainable development. Organizations are forming, alliances being recast, experiences reevaluated; in Latin America one of the most promising is the RIAD (Red Interamericana de Agriculturas y Democracia 1993) with headquarters in Chile.

Sustainable development, however, is not an approach that will be accepted simply because "its time has come." The opening of the multilateral development community to the NGOs and other grassroots groups, including the long-term commitment of organizations like the Inter-American Foundation in the United States, the IICA in Costa Rica, and numerous foundations from western Europe to support such efforts, is not just a token gesture by powerful agencies to the powerless; rather, it reflects the recognition that these base-level groups have been effectively mobilizing people and resources to achieve measurable improvements in living standards while contributing noticeably to protect the environment. Such victories signal the beginning, not the end of a process.

Sustainable development, in the final analysis, involves a political struggle for control over the productive apparatus. It requires a redefinition of not only what and how we produce but also of who will be allowed to produce and for what ends. For organizations involved in projects of sustainable development in rural areas, the conflict will center around control of mechanisms of local political and economic power, and the use of resources. The struggle to assure a greater voice in the process for peasants, indigenous populations, women, and other underprivileged groups will not assure that their decisions will lead to sustainable development. But such broad-based democratic participation will create the basis for a more equitable distribution of wealth, one of the first prerequisites for forging a strategy of sustainable development.

The Varieties of Sustainable Development

The Regions that Get Left Behind

International economic integration will not affect all peoples equally. In the case of the NAFTA, for example, large segments of the Mexican population will remain in the backwaters of international progress. To some degree, these people are in regions that have a unique opportunity to take advantage of their status as marginal. Many of these regions are peopled with groups of indigenous origin who still treasure much of the experience that has been passed down through the generations; recent research in the Third World on ethnobotany, ethnobiology, agrobiology, and agroforestry is attempting to capture some of this wisdom. This work is showing that the productive potential of traditional agriculture is many times what is currently obtained, that there are cultural factors preventing the full application of this knowledge (including, of course, the prevalent disdain for indigenous culture, except as a consumption good for tourists and eccentric intellectuals), and that some of our discoveries about these systems are transferable among cultures, as well as useful in improving cultivation systems used by "modern" farmers. Finally, as we conduct more research on these native cultural practices, we are learning that the native practitioners have begun to integrate more recent technological advances to improve productivity and reduce the amount of labor required in production.

In these regions the redevelopment of the "peasant economy" is both desirable and urgent. It is not simply a matter of rescuing ancient cultures, but rather of taking advantage of an important cultural and productive heritage to provide solutions to the problems of today and tomorrow. It is not a question of "reinventing" the peasant economy, but rather of joining with their own organizations to carve out political spaces that will allow them to exercise their autonomy, to define ways in which their organizations will guide production for themselves and for commerce with the rest of the society. Once again, the technocratic identification of productive mechanisms and the cataloging of systems of indigenous knowledge (which, for example, are now the order of the day among transnational corporations looking for new sources of germ plasm for their biotechnological advances) are not going to reverse the structure of discrimination, unless accompanied by effective political participation (Nuñez 1993).

These regions that get left behind will have many opportunities to explore ways in which to use their resource endowments in creative ways. Among the most important are projects administered by local community groups that begin to diversify their productive base, using sources of renewable energy, and evaluating the natural environment to develop new products or find new ways of adding value to traditional technologies and goods. Projects mentioned in the literature include the harnessing of solar, geothermal, and wind energy for food processing; improving the quality and increasing the output of artisan crafts (or marketing them so that they command better prices); and developing facilities for recreation and institutional arrangements to permit outsiders to gain an appreciation of indigenous cultures. The opportunities to seek out new ways of organizing the natural resources base are great, and the initiatives to implement such programs are gradually finding respondents interested in exploring this and other alternatives.

The Centers of Biodiversity

The world's scientific and environmental community has mobilized to identify and protect an increasing number of particularly valued areas. These "biosphere reserves" in the wilds and urban "heritage" centers are guardians of part of the ecosystem's natural and produced treasures. But they are also controversial battlefields where science and community are struggling for an operational definition of environmental protection and sustainability. The lines are drawn most clearly in the efforts to create nucleus areas in the designated biosphere reserves or national parks where people are not permitted to intrude; in some cases, the designation actually involves the removal of local inhabitants from the area in the name of the environment. On a more general level, the growing concern for protecting endangered species has led to conflicts between local populations that have traditionally coexisted with these species, exploiting them in sustainable ways, until the powerful forces of the market led to increased kill rates that threatened their very survival.

While there is no one generalized solution to the conflicting needs and goals of the groups involved in these regions, it does seem that the philosophical approach of "sustainability" offers some insights. One promising proposal suggests creating "peasant reserves of the biosphere" or "neighborhood restoration clubs" in which local communities are encouraged to continue living within a region, husbanding the resources. In exchange, the "outside world" would accept the obligation to ensure that the community was able to enjoy a socially acceptable quality of life with economic opportunities similar to those of other groups and full political participation at all levels. (One particularly interesting example of this approach is the attempt to create such a model in the Chimalapas region of southwestern Oaxaca in Mexico, an attempt that has overcome many political obstacles, but still has not been completely successful.)

Other approaches involve organizing local communities that formerly were engaged in predatory activities to participate in (or actually help design) protective activities as part of a strategy of productive diversification for community development. This could include but would not be limited to ecotourism. Ideally, this strategy would include sufficient activities of sustainable harvest and local production to ensure economic security.

Autonomous Development: A Strategy for Sustainability

Sustainable development is not consistent with the expansion of "modern" commercial agriculture. Commercialized rural development has brought in its wake the progressive marginality of peasant and indigenous populations. Global integration is creating opportunities for some, nightmares for many. Domestic production is adjusting to the signals of the international market, responding to the demands from abroad, and importing those goods that can be acquired more inexpensively elsewhere. Urban-industrial expansion has created poles of attraction for people and their activities that cannot be absorbed productively or healthfully. Urban slums and deteriorating neighborhoods house people seeking marginal jobs while local governments are overwhelmed by the impossible tasks of administering these burgeoning areas with inadequate budgets. At the same time, peasant communities are being dismembered, their residents forced to emigrate and abandon traditional production systems. They also cease to be stewards of the ecosystems of which they are a part.

In this juxtaposition of winners and losers, a new strategy for rural development must be considered: a strategy that revalues the contribution of traditional production strategies. In the present world economy, the vast majority of third world rural producers cannot compete on world markets with basic foodstuffs and many other primary products. The technology and financial power of agribusiness in the richer nations combine with the political necessity of exporting surpluses to drive down international prices, often below the real costs of production in the Third World (especially if these farmers were to receive a competitive wage). Unless insulated in some way, their traditional products only have ready markets within the narrow confines of communities that are suffering a similar fate.

Marginal rural producers offer an important promise: if encouraged to continue producing, they can support themselves and make significant contributions to the rest of society. In contrast, if prevailing rural policies in third world countries define efficiency by the criteria of the international market, based on the political and technological structure of the industrialized nations, peasants will be driven from their traditional planting programs, and food imports will begin to compete for scarce foreign exchange with capital goods and other national priorities, as has happened in many countries (Barkin, Batt, and DeWalt 1991).

The approach suggested by the search for sustainability and popular participation is to create mechanisms whereby peasants and indigenous communities find support to continue cultivating in their own regions. Even by the strictest criteria of neoclassical economics, this approach should not be dismissed as inefficient protectionism, since most of the resources involved in this process would have little or no opportunity cost for society as a whole.[18]

In effect, we are proposing the creation of autonomous local economies. By recognizing society's inability to eradicate the sharply stratified social structure that is the root of many of our current ills, we will be in a better position to design policies that recognize and take advantage of these differences to improve the welfare of groups in both sectors. A strategy that offers succor to rural communities, a means to make productive diversification possible, will make the management of growth easier in those areas that are developing links with the international economy. More important, such a strategy will offer an opportunity for the society to confront the challenges of environmental management and conservation in a meaningful way, with a group of people uniquely qualified for such activities.[19]

The call for a form of local autonomous development is not new. Unlike the present version of the dual economy that permeates all our societies, confronting rich and poor, the proposal calls for creating structures so that the segment of society that chooses to live in rural areas finds support from the rest of the nation to implement an alternative regional development program. The new variant starts from the inherited base of rural production, improving productivity by using the techniques of agroecology. It also involves incorporating new activities that build on the cultural and resource base of the community and the region for further development. It requires very site-specific responses to a general problem and therefore depends heavily on local involvement in design and implementation. While the broad outlines are widely discussed, the specifics require specific investment programs from direct producers and their partners.[20]

What is new is the introduction of an explicit strategy to strengthen the social and economic base for autonomous development. The strategy is based on recognizing the importance of marginal groups and local cultures, and encouraging these groups to create an alternative that offers better prospects for their own development. The key to the proposal is not a simple transfer of resources to compensate groups for their poverty, but rather an integrated set of productive projects that offer rural communities the opportunity to generate goods and services that will contribute to raising their living standards while also improving the environment in which they live.

NOTES

This document has benefited from the generous comments of many readers of the earlier printed or electronic versions. Particular thanks for their support and patience are due David Kaimowitz and Blanca Lemus. Neva Goodwin and Jonathan Harris have advised on this version.

1. Although the question of the relationship between population growth, poverty, and sustainability is commonly included in North America, in Latin America we take it for granted that population growth is not an independent variable.

2. Although frequently described as the "tragedy of the commons" (Hardin

1968), the process examined here is significantly different, because the dynamic underlying the problem of degradation is tied to the unequal access to resources and resulting polarization rather than to increasing population pressures. This fundamental difference underlies one of the contributions of the present analysis, deflecting the "blame" for environmental damage from the victims to the underlying processes.

3. There is an abundant literature both on the fierce struggles between agronomists working with peasants and those associated with modern farmers and on the second-generation effects of the Green Revolution on communities and social structures (e.g., Hewitt 1976; Barkin and Suárez 1983; Jennings 1988; Barraclough 1991).

4. This is a concern with the way in which Article 27 of the Mexican Constitution regulating the ejido system was modified to permit private land sales and the subdivision of commonly held land.

5. For a more complete discussion of the internationalization of capital and its impact on society see, for example, Froebel, Heinrichs, and Krey 1979; Barnett and Cavanagh 1994; and Barkin 1985.

6. The difficult adjustment process in markets for rural products is an example of the "cobweb model" in standard economic analysis. Because there is a lag in the supply process, important differences in supply and demand at prevailing prices often leads to unstable fluctuations in supply and significant changes in market prices that invariably affect the majority of smaller, less well capitalized producers more seriously than their more affluent competitors.

7. Clearly, the analysis in the text of the short-term cycles facing individual producers is considerably different than the long-term phenomena facing society as a whole, discussed by Prebisch (1950, 1959). His discussion of the terms of trade is based not only on the type of supply and demand analysis offered here, but also on the long-term price and income elasticities of these products as compared to the industrialized products. The argument is probably even more striking if the comparison were made with the behavior of services in international markets. Although northern neoclassical economists are quite critical of this argument, the empirical evidence assembled by southern analysts remains persuasive.

8. For excellent examples of these discussions see, among others, Low 1992; Arden-Clarke 1991, 1992; and Daly 1993.

9. The corporate community's attempt to forestall further public regulation of environmental matters led to the development of the ISO 14000 set of norms. Many analysts are skeptical that this approach will be sufficient to confront the problems raised in this article, because the individual firm approach begs many of the structural issues raised here.

10. An example of the spate of textbooks available from commercial publishers and international organizations to prepare technicians and professionals to construct these models and perform the environmental impact assessments required for many projects is Goodstein 1995. The World Bank has published several books oriented toward policy formulation that cover much the same ground: e.g., Pearce and Warford 1993.

11. For a review of evidence on the original Kuznets curve hypothesis, see Ackerman et al. 2000.

12. From a strictly technical standpoint, this analysis is seriously flawed: the authors make claims about dynamic processes on the basis of a quantitative description in comparative statics. The analysis of likely changes in both income distribution and environmental quality cannot be inferred from a simple description of what is transpiring in a broad range of countries at a single point in time. The analysis also does not address the complex distributional issue of who pays the costs for environmental improvements and which groups enjoy the benefits.

13. The *social discount rate* is a construct used by economists to examine the ways that societies evaluate the value of future increases in production and welfare in comparison with the present-day sacrifices required for growth. These calculations do not introduce differences of such benefits and costs among social groups; skilled practitioners are now trying to include environmental considerations in the process.

14. In fact, these claims contradict historical evidence that shows that peasant and indigenous societies invested a great deal of effort and social organizing skills in developing major systems for terracing, irrigation, and other methods that guaranteed the productivity of the land without compromising its long-term fertility. These systems have been compromised or dismembered as the exigencies of the market economy have forced people to abandon traditional methods for mobilizing labor to perform collective tasks.

15. The complexity of the task of ending hunger is widely recognized. But recent literature has stressed the social rather than the technical (or supply-based) origins of famine and hunger; Sen (1981, 1992) is a particularly effective exponent of this point, while others have gone into greater detail about the "social origins" of food strategies and crises (Barraclough 1991). The "modernization" of urban diets in Nigeria, by substituting wheat and rice for sorghum and millet, is an egregious case of creating dependency, reducing opportunities for peasant producers, and raising the social cost of feeding a nation (see Andrae and Beckman 1985).

16. This is the theme of Stiefel and Wolfe's book (1994), summarizing a broad range of experience about popular participation. They point to the "declining state capacity to provide services and reduce income inequalities," accompanied by an equal reduction in "public confidence in the legitimacy of its efforts." When joined with the processes of political democratization, it is not surprising that the international community is "looking to 'participation' as a means of making their development projects function better, helping people cope . . . [and] as an indispensable dimension of the environmental policies . . . that can no longer be evaded or postponed" (19).

17. In a recent book, Rodwin and Schön (1994) offer us the opportunity to explore Hirschman's singular contributions to development theory and practice. Emphasizing the importance of placing people at the center of the process, we have learned from Hirschman that to succeed these actors must become integrated into the larger processes of which they are a part.

18. This is a crucial element. Many analysts dismiss peasant producers as working on too small a scale and with too few resources to be efficient. While it is possible and even necessary to promote increased productivity, consistent with a strategy of sustainable production, as defined by agroecologists, the proposal to encourage them to remain as productive members of their communities should be implemented under existing conditions.

In much of Latin America, if peasants ceased to produce basic crops, the lands and inputs are not often simply transferable to other farmers for commercial output. The low opportunity costs of primary production in peasant and indigenous regions derives from the lack of alternative productive employment for the people and the lands in this sector. Although the people would generally have to seek income in the "informal sector," their contribution to national output would be meager. The difference between the social criteria for evaluating the cost of this style of production and the market valuation is based on the determination of the sacrifices society would make in undertaking one or the other option. The theoretical basis for this approach harks back to the initial essay of W. Arthur Lewis (1954) and subsequent developments that find their latest expression in the call for a "neostructuralist" approach to development for Latin America (Sunkel 1993).

19. Much of the literature on popular participation emphasizes the multifaceted contribution that the productive incorporation of marginal groups can make to society (Friedmann 1992; Friedmann and Rangan 1993; Stiefel and Wolfe 1994). While very little has been done on specific strategies for sustainability in poor rural communities, it is clear that much of the experience recounted by practitioners with grassroots groups (e.g., Glade and Reilly 1993) is consistent with the principles enunciated by theorists and analysts like Altieri (1987).

20. For the more general discussion, see Adelman 1984 and Barkin 1990, chap. 7. FUNDE (1994) offers a specific program for the reconversion of El Salvador based on the principles discussed in the section "New Strategies for Rural Sustainable Development" (in this essay). The proposals of groups like the IAF and RIAD offer specific examples of ongoing grassroots efforts to implement initiatives like those discussed in the text. The Centro de Ecologia y Desarrollo (Barkin 1999) is pursuing a program of regional development consistent with the proposed strategy.

REFERENCES

Ackerman, Frank, et al. 2000. *The Political Economy of Inequality.* New York: Island Press.

Adelman, I. 1984. Beyond Export-led Growth. *World Development* 12, no. 9: 937–49.

Altieri, Miguel A. 1987. *Agroecology: The Scientific Basis of Alternative Agriculture.* Boulder: Westview.

Alves Amorim, Monica. 1994. Lessons on Demand. *Technology Review* (MIT) (January): 30–36.

Andrae, Gunilla, and Bjorn Beckman. 1985. *The Wheat Trap*. London: Zed Books.

Arden-Clarke, Charles. 1991. The General Agreement on Tariffs and Trade, Environmental Protection and Sustainable Development. WWF discussion paper. Gland, Switzerland.

———. 1992. South-North Terms of Trade, Environmental Protection and Sustainable Development. *International Environmental Affairs* 4, no. 2 (spring): 122–37.

Arruda, Marcos. 1993. NGOs and the World Bank: Possibilities and Limits of Collaboration. Geneva: NGO Working Group. Mimeo, 17 pp.

Barkin, David. 1972. *Los Beneficiarios del Desarrollo Regional*. Mexico City: Sep-Setentas.

———. 1973. A Case Study of the Beneficiaries of Regional Development. *International Social Development Review* (United Nations) 4: 84–94.

———. 1985. Global Proletarianization. In S. Sanderson, ed., *The Americas in the New International Division of Labor*. New York: Holmes and Meier.

———. 1990. *Distorted Development: Mexico in the World Economy*. Boulder: Westview.

———. 1994. Las organizaciones no-gubernamentales ambientalistas en el foro internacional. In A. Glender and V. Lichtinger, eds. *La Diplomacia Ambiental: Mexico y la Conferencia de las Naciones Unidas sobre Medio Ambiente y Desarrollo*. Mexico: Secretaría de Relaciones Exteriores y Fondo de Cultura Economica.

———. 1999. The Economic Impacts of Ecotourism: Conflicts and Solutions in Highland Mexico." In P. Godde et al. eds., *Tourism and Development in Mountain Areas*. London: CAB International.

Barkin, David, R. Batt, and B. DeWalt. 1990. *Food Crops vs. Feed Crops: The Global Substitution of Grains in Production*. Boulder: Lynne Rienner.

Barnett, Richard J., and John Cavanagh. 1994. *Global Dreams: Imperial Corporations and the New World Order*. New York: Simon and Schuster.

Barraclough, Solon. 1991. *An End to Hunger? The Social Origins of Food Strategies*. London and Atlantic Highlands, NJ: Zed Press and UNRISD.

Ben Abdallah, Taoufik, and Phillippe Engelhard. 1993. The Urgency of Fighting Poverty for Democracy and the Environment. Occasional paper no. 5, UN Non-Governmental Liaison Service, Geneva.

Blaikie, P., and H. Brookfield, eds. 1987. *Land Degradation and Society*. London: Methuen.

Boyce, James. 1994. Inequality as a Cause of Environmental Degradation. *Ecological Economics* XI:1.

Calderon, Fernando, Manuel Chiriboga, and Diego Pieiro. 1992. *Modernización Democratica e Incluyente de la Agricultura en America Latina y el Caribe* (Serie Documentos de Programas No 28). San José, CR: IICA.

Cruz, Wilfrido, and Robert Repetto. 1992. *The Environmental Effects of Stabili-*

zation and Structural Programs: The Philippines Case. Washington, DC: World Resources Institute.

Daly, Herman E. 1993. The Perils of Free Trade. *Scientific American* 269, no. 5 (November): 50–57.

De Janvry, A., E. Sadoulet, and L. W. Young. 1989. Land and Labour in Latin American Agriculture from the 1950s to the 1980s. *Journal of Peasant Studies* 16, no. 3 (April): 396–424.

Foster, John Bellamy. 1993. 'Let Them Eat Pollution': Capitalism and the World Environment. *Monthly Review* 44, no. 8 (January): 10–20.

Friedmann, John. 1992. *Empowerment: The Politics of Alternative Development.* New York: Basil Blackwell.

Friedmann, John, and Haripriya Rangan. 1993. *In Defense of Livelihood: Comparative Studies on Environmental Action.* West Hartford, CT: Kumarian Press.

Frobel, F., J. Heinrichs, and O. Kreye. 1979. *The New International Division of Labour.* Cambridge: Cambridge University Press.

Fundacion Nacional para el Desarrollo (FUNDE). 1994. Bases para la construcción de un nuevo Proyeto Económico Nacional para El Salvador. San Salvador. Mimeo.

Glade, William, and Charles Reilley, eds. 1993. *Inquiry at the Grassroots: An Inter-American Foundation Reader.* Arlington, VA: Inter-American Foundation.

Goodland, Robert, and Herman Daly. 1993. Why Northern Income Growth Is Not the Solution to Southern Poverty. *Ecological Economics* 8:85–101.

Goodstein, Eban S. 1995. *Economics and the Environment.* Englewood Cliffs, NJ: Prentice-Hall.

Gregory, Michael. 1992. Environmental, Sustainable Development, Public Participation, and the NAFTA: A Retrospective. *Journal of Environmental Law and Litigation* 7:99–174.

Grossman, Gene M., and Alan B. Krueger. 1993. Environmental Impacts of a North American Free Trade Agreement. In Peter M. Garber, ed., *The Mexico-US Free Trade Agreement,* 13–56. Cambridge: MIT Press.

Hardin, Garrett. 1968. The Tragedy of the Commons. *Science* 162 (Dec. 13): 1243–48.

Hardoy, Jorge, Diana Mitlin, and David Satterthwaite. 1992. *Environmental Problems in Third World Cities.* London: Earthscan Publications.

Hecht, Susanna B. 1985. Environment, Development and Politics: Capital Accumulation and the Livestock Sector in Eastern Amazonia. *World Development* 13, no. 6 (June): 663–84.

Hewitt de Alcontara, Cynthia. 1976. *Modernizing Mexican Agriculture.* Geneva: United Nations Research Institute for Social Development.

Hirschman, Albert O. 1958. *A Strategy of Economic Development.* New Haven, CT: Yale University Press.

Jennings, Bruce. 1988. *Foundations of International Agricultural Research.* Boulder: Westview.

Johnson, Pamela, and David Cooperrider. 1991. The Global Integrity Ethic: Defining Global Social Change Organizations and the Organizing Principles Which Make Transnational Organizing Possible. *Associations Transnationales* (Belgium) 2:90–109.

Leonard, H. J., ed. 1989. *Environment and the Poor: Development strategies for a common agenda.* New Brunswick, NJ: Transaction Books for the Overseas Development Council.

Lewis, W. Arthur. 1954. Economic Development with Unlimited Supplies of Labour. Republished in A. N. Agarwala and S. P. Singh, eds., *Economics of Underdevelopment.* New York: Oxford, 1963.

Livernash, Robert. 1992. The Growing Influence of NGOs in the Developing World. *Environment* 34, no. 5 (June): 11–20, 41–43 (adapted from World Resources Institute, *World Resources, 1992–93,* New York: Oxford University Press, chap. 14: 217–34).

Low, Patrick, ed. 1992. *International Trade and the Environment.* World Bank Discussion Paper no. 159. Washington, DC: World Bank.

Machado, A., L. C. Castillo, and I. Suarez. 1993. *Democracia con campesinos, campesinos sin Democracia.* Bogotá, Colombia: Ministerio de Agriculture, Fondo DRI, IICA and Universidad del Valle.

McCay, Bonnie, and James Acheson, eds. 1987. *The Question of the Commons: The Culture and Ecology of Communal Resources.* Tucson: University of Arizona Press.

Mumme, Stephen. 1993. Environmentalists, NAFTA, and North American Environmental Management. *Journal of Environment and Development* 2:1.

Nuñez, Oscar. 1993. Desarrollo Sostenible y Economía Campesina. Managua: Centro Para la Promoción, la Investigación y el Desarrollo Rural y Social (CIPRES). Mimeo.

Olson, Paul A., ed. 1990. *The Struggle for the Land.* Lincoln: University of Nebraska.

Ostrom, Elinor. 1990. *Governing the Commons: The Evolution of Institutions for Collective Action.* Cambridge: Cambridge University Press.

———. 1993. *Institutional Incentives and Sustainable Development: Infrastructure Policies in Perspective. Theoretical Lenses on Public Policy.* Boulder: Westview Press.

Pearce, David, and Jeremy Warford, eds. 1993. *World Without End: Economics, Environment and Sustainable Development.* New York: Oxford University Press for the World Bank.

Place, Susan, ed. 1993. *Tropical Rainforests: Latin American Nature and Society in Transition.* Wilmington, DE: Scholarly Resources.

Prebisch, Raul. 1950. *The Economic Development of Latin America and Its Principal Problems.* New York: United Nations, ECLA.

———. 1959. Commercial Policy in the Underdeveloped Countries. *American Economic Review* 49 (May): 251–73.

Red Interamericana de Agriculturas y Democracia (RIAD). 1993. *Qu es la agricultura sustentable?* Mexico: Grupo de Estudios Ambientales y RIAD.

Rodwin, Lloyd, and Donald A. Schön, eds. 1994. *Rethinking the Development Experience: Essays Provoked by the Work of Albert O. Hirschman.* Washington, DC, and Boston, MA: Brookings and Lincoln.

Sen, Amartya. 1981. *Poverty and Famines.* New York: Oxford University Press.

———. 1992. *Inequality Reexamined.* Cambridge: Harvard University Press.

Stiefel, Matthias, and Marshall Wolfe. 1994. *A Voice for the Excluded: Popular Participation in Development: Utopia or Necessity?* London and Atlantic Highlands, NJ: Zed Books and UNRISD.

Sunkel, Osvaldo. 1993. *Development from Within: Toward a Neostructuralist Approach for Latin America.* Boulder: Lynne Rienner.

Tendler, Judith. 1993. Tales of Dissemination in Small-Farm Agriculture: Lessons for Institution Builders. *World Development* 21, no. 10 (October): 1567–82.

Wilson, Edward O. 1992. *The Diversity of Life.* Cambridge: Harvard University Press.

Wolf, Eric. 1982. *Europe and the People without History.* Berkeley: University of California Press.

CHAPTER 5

Free Trade or Sustainable Trade? An Ecological Economics Perspective

Jonathan M. Harris

Free Trade—The Conventional Wisdom

Free trade, as a theoretical ideal as well as a policy goal, until recently has been virtually unassailable in economics. It is part of a holy trinity of concepts embodied in traditional economic thought as essential for improvement in human welfare: economic growth, technological progress, and free trade. From the perspective of the emerging discipline of ecological economics, all three of these articles of faith have been challenged. Continuous economic growth, as Herman Daly and others have argued (Daly 1991, 1996), is inherently in conflict with the limited resource base and waste absorption capacity of the environment. Technological progress, viewed by most economists simply as a means of increasing output per unit input, can be faulted on the same general grounds: ecological economics emphasizes the unintended consequences and environmentally disruptive impacts of technological innovations such as intensive agriculture, large-scale power production, nuclear energy, and automotive technology. It is not surprising, therefore, that theorists whose emphasis is on the negative ecological impacts of economic activity should also have developed a critique of the theory and practice of free trade.[1]

The words *free trade* carry a powerful ideological freight both in the economic and political arenas. To be opposed to free trade is to court the label *protectionist,* which, like *Luddite* applied to opponents of technological innovations, clearly invites intellectual scorn and moral opprobrium.[2] But free trade in practice is simply the international application of an unregulated free-market system. In modern economic policy discussion of domestic issues, an unequivocal defense of unregulated free markets is generally seen as an extreme position. Yet many who would never endorse a thoroughgoing laissez-faire doctrine in domestic policy unhesitatingly sing the praises of international free trade. As we move toward an increasingly integrated global economy, this odd dichotomy in policy analysis requires some further examination.

What is the theoretical basis of economists' enthusiasm for free trade? The formal model of free trade, deriving from David Ricardo's theory of comparative advantage, predicts mutual benefits from trade in the form of greater efficiency in production and higher overall consumption. In this model, some groups may lose as a result of trade, in particular those whose incomes are linked to import-competing industries. But overall national gains, including increased incomes in export industries and lower prices for raw materials and consumer goods, will necessarily exceed losses. This result can be proved rigorously, but only given certain assumptions. Criticisms of the free-trade model may therefore be of two kinds. One approach is based on criticism of the model's assumptions as unrealistic. A broader critique focuses on inherent limitations of the model, such as its short-term equilibrium framework and its use of consumption gains as the sole measure of social welfare.

The conclusion that free trade will necessarily bring net gains to trading nations is dependent on some quite sweeping assumptions. These include perfect competition in all factor and product markets, full employment in all trading nations, labor mobility between industries in all nations, "well-behaved" production functions showing diminishing returns to scale in all industries, and immobility of capital across national frontiers. In the real world, of course, none of these assumptions holds true. The case for free trade must then rest on the assertion that real-world conditions do not deviate sufficiently from the model's assumptions to alter the main conclusion. Limitations of the standard model are evident in a number of areas. Imperfect competition (monopoly or oligopoly) in international trade can create a situation in which one country can use strategic trade policies to improve its position at the expense of others. Structural unemployment and labor immobility can lead to income declines in import-competing industries without offsetting increases in export industries. Industries with increasing returns to scale, such as aircraft construction, or those characterized by rapid innovation, such as computers, can seize benefits and impoverish competitors through systematic government subsidies. Mobility of capital across frontiers can lead to substantial job losses and increased inequality in high-wage industrial nations competing with low-wage trade partners.[3] Possibilities such as these have been acknowledged by economists (see, e.g., Krugman 1990, 1994), but in general have not led to rejection either of the free-trade model or of free trade as a policy goal.

When we consider the impacts of trade on the environment and on natural resources, another set of problems with the standard model emerges. "Externalities," such as damage from pollution, long-term resource depletion, overuse of common property resources, and insufficient provision of environmental public goods, are not taken account of in free-trade models. The remedy for this, in a standard economic perspective, is appropriate government policies such as pollution or resource depletion taxes, public management of common property resources, and public funding or subsidies for environmental preservation. But all this assumes the jurisdiction of a national or state government over such policies. Once we enter an international free-trading arena, consistency in such policies across national borders becomes difficult to achieve. This implies that those nations with the lowest environmental standards and the least resource-conserving policies will acquire a comparative cost advantage over those with high standards and conservation-oriented policies. A lowest-common-denominator effect may therefore undermine environmental protection in all trading nations.

The most commonly proposed solution to this problem is the "harmonization" of environmental standards — the acceptance of common standards by nations within a free-trade area. But note that this solution is not "free trade" but something else — the creation of a supranational authority with the power to set environmental standards. This approach has been taken within the European Union, but in other free-trade areas such as the North American Free Trade Agreement (NAFTA) no such institutions exist. The World Trade Organization (WTO), the successor to the General Agreement on Tariffs and Trade (GATT), has no provision for any enforceable supranational environmental regulations. While the Standards Code adopted after the most recent Uruguay Round negotiations calls for international harmonization of environmental standards (Esty 1994, 172), there is no basis for this process to be other than voluntary. Indeed, critics feel that a harmonization undertaken in the closed, business-dominated atmosphere of the WTO standards committees would be likely to harmonize standards down rather than up in many cases.[4]

According to the logic of "free trade," environmental legislation that restricts or taxes the flow of traded commodities (as it must to be effective) can be challenged as a barrier to trade. Under this provision, GATT has found U.S. regulations on dolphin protection to be in violation of its free-trade rules.[5] Similarly, in regional trade agreements, Denmark's reusable bottle law has been overturned by the European Economic Court of Justice, and numerous U.S. and Canadian regulations for forest and fisheries protection, asbestos safety, pesticide management, acid rain reduction, and recycled paper content have come under challenge either based on U.S.-Canada free-trade agreements or GATT rules.

When we add these considerations to the already substantial list of problems with the standard trade model, the justification for a policy goal of free trade becomes murkier. In response to social and environmental critiques, neoclassical economists have risen to the defense of free trade, arguing that "promoting free trade and a protected environment simultaneously does pose problems, but none that are beyond resolution with goodwill and imaginative innovation" (Bhagwati 1993; see also Esty 1994, chap. 3). Nonetheless, the cumulative impact of social and environmental challenges to the free-trade doctrine should impel us to consider an alternative perspective. Is there a general, systematic problem with the standard analysis that gives rise to all these theoretical and practical problems? Can we do better in theory and in practice?

Trade and Sustainability — An Alternative Perspective

An ecological economics perspective acknowledges the specific theoretical and practical problems with the standard model of free trade, but also goes a step further by rejecting the fundamental framework of the standard model in favor of an alternative conceptualization.[6] One of the reasons that the many well-grounded criticisms of the standard model have made so little impression on theoretical perceptions and policy recommendations is that no systematic alternative has been presented. Rejection of free trade therefore appears to imply a descent into policy chaos and uncontrolled protectionism. Thus theorists like Paul Krugman, who have gone furthest within standard economics to develop criticisms of the basic model, tend to fall back on advocacy of free trade as a "useful target in the practical world of politics" (Krugman 1990), if not a theoretical *summum bonum.*

From an ecological economics perspective, the fundamental problem with formal trade theory is its grounding in a static Ricardian model of increasing short-term consumption benefits with fixed resource endowment. Even if environmental costs can be internalized, the model still gives no consideration to longer-term issues of sustainability, growth, and the social and institutional impacts of trading patterns. Lacking these, our analysis of trade will at best be one-dimensional and susceptible to multiple problems in real-world applications. At worst, its policy implications will be directly opposed to the requirements of a sustainable economic system.

What then would a model of trade and sustainability entail? Of primary importance is the concept of natural resources as capital. When we take "natural capital" into account, we find that nations may diminish their long-term wealth even as they boost current conventionally measured welfare through expanding exports of natural resources or increasing the output of resource-intensive industries. In theory, private property rights should induce natural resource owners to take account of natural capital depreciation and to conserve resources that are expected to be in short supply in the future. But this is vitiated in practice, especially in developing nations, due to the common-property nature of many resources, weak institutional structures and uncertain property rights, use of relatively high current interest rates for private and lender project evaluation, and high implicit interest rates to small operators. What results is essentially the plundering of a national heritage for short-term benefit. In the absence of major institutional changes, "free" trade accelerates this process by expanded export outlets for natural resource products.

Revised systems of national income accounting have been developed by Repetto, El Serafy, and others to adjust for environmental damage and natural resource depreciation (Repetto 1989, 1991, 1992; El Serafy 1993a). Efforts have been made to systematize environmental and natural resource accounting (United Nations 1993; World Bank 1993) and to evaluate its implications for economic theory and macroeconomic policy (El Serafy 1993b). If applied to trade theory, this revised accounting can provide a very different interpretation of the welfare effects of trade. According to one World Bank estimate, taking account of natural asset depletion reduces "genuine savings" (net of foreign borrowing, depreciation, and asset depletion) to close to zero, or below zero, for many developing nations.[7]

This kind of analysis can be applied to alter estimates of the economic benefits of trade expansion. In the case of the North American Free Trade Agreement (NAFTA), for example, one notable major result of U.S.-Canada free trade, and a projected result of U.S.-Mexico free trade, is an acceleration of oil, gas, and large-scale hydro development. Standard trade theory considers only the welfare effects of the current production of energy, assessing the lowering of energy prices through more abundant supply as a net gain to consumers.[8] Including the long-term costs imposed on the nations involved by resource depletion and irreversible environmental damage would give a different perspective. Also relevant are the effects of lower energy prices in undermining conservation and alternative energy development, as well as promoting investment in fossil-fuel-dependent capital stock and increasing carbon dioxide emissions.

The goal of maximizing short-term welfare through free trade is thus in conflict with the goal of long-term sustainability. Sustainability requires a process of national, regional, and local resource and environmental planning, which is in direct conflict with the principle of free trade. Free trade, as Daly and Cobb have argued (1989), inherently undermines community control of resources by eliminating export and import controls and replacing these with an impersonal control by international market allocation. This is not merely a side effect associated with free trade — it is its very essence. While GATT includes a provision known as Article XX for exceptions to general trade rules for measures "relating to the conservation of exhaustible natural resources," the competitive pressures of international trade make it very difficult for nations to adopt such measures.[9]

Acceptance of the free-trade paradigm thus necessarily involves the willingness to abandon national or local control over resources in favor of the proposition that in a free global market individual or corporate resource owners will make the best possible decisions concerning resource use ("optimize resource allocation," in the economists' terminology). Even setting aside the problem of common property and free-access resources, all private decisions on resource use will be made subject to market rates of interest. For example, if sustainable forestry yields a 4 percent annual return, while market interest rates are 6 percent, it makes more sense for the private owner to clear-cut his forest tract and invest the proceeds elsewhere. If erosion depletes soil productivity by 1 percent per annum, but intensive agricultural production for export can increase revenues 20 percent, it makes economic sense for farmers to continue erosive practices.[10] Unless there is specific social intervention, resource depletion or environmental damage effects extending more than twenty years into the future are unlikely to be considered in current decision making by private agents.

Long-term sustainability is thus necessarily a public responsibility. Whether the focus of social and environmental policy-making is local, regional, national, or global, planning for sustainability requires the power to override market allocation of resources when necessary to achieve environmental or social goals. It has not escaped the notice of international trade officials at GATT and the WTO that this principle fundamentally conflicts with the ground rules of free trade. The success of the GATT/WTO process in promoting free trade has largely been due to a sweeping simplicity of principle: multilateral elimination of trade barriers, with very limited exceptions. This in turn traces to neoclassical economic theory. Making an "exception" of environmental and resource issues opens a Pandora's box of problems for trade negotiations. As continued economic growth increases global ecological stresses, almost any goods production sector has important environmental impacts (energy resources, mining, metals, plastics, chemicals, agriculture, lumber, pulp and paper, fisheries, etc.). Putting sustainability first means putting free trade second. But free trade by its nature demands primacy over all other social or environmental considerations. The problem is that this primacy, a reasonable possibility in an earlier era, is no longer feasible without the sacrifice of fundamental social and environmental values.

The 1996 Report of the WTO Committee on Trade and Environment is clear evidence of the unresolved tension between the principles of free trade and environmental protection. The committee originated as a response to complaints by nongovernmental organizations that the negotiations that set up the WTO failed to consider environmental issues. Calls for a "Green Round" of negotiations led to the establishment of the Committee on Trade and Environment, which was charged with reviewing WTO rules and procedures as they related to environmental policies. Unfortunately, the committee's report is entirely equivocal. On issue after issue, it notes fundamental differences of opinion among participants, but fails to resolve these differences or present any specific proposals for modification of WTO rules (WTO 1996).

The committee's difficulties reflect the theoretical dichotomy that we have outlined above. Some theorists who argue for the compatibility of free trade and environmental protection have called for institutional reform of the WTO to take better account of environmental issues. Esty, for example, advocates broadening the resource and environmental "loophole" represented by GATT Article XX, specific recognition by the WTO of multinational environmental agreements, and legitimizing some "extraterritorial" measures that, like the U.S. Marine Mammal Act, invoke trade measures in support of environmental goals extending beyond national boundaries (Esty 1994). He also, together with C. Ford Runge (1994), favors the establishment of a Global Environmental Organization to counterbalance the WTO's one-sided emphasis on trade. The problem, evident in practice, is that such reforms are fiercely resisted both by policymakers deeply committed to traditional free-trade principles and by nations who fear any interference with their current resource-depleting and environmentally damaging policies.

The Global Dynamics of Trade, Growth, and Environment

A further difference between the "standard economics" and "ecological economics" view of trade concerns the relationship between trade and long-term economic growth. In standard macroeconomic models, economic growth is universally viewed as desirable, and in practice is usually seen as essential to prevent recession and unemployment. The real benefits of a relatively free world trading system in the post–World War II period have not been the static welfare gains from exchange of commodities, but the dynamic boost to growth given by an expanding global market. This is clearly reflected in the continual efforts of World Bank development advisers to promote export-led growth in developing nations. It is also the reason why the NAFTA agreement was seen by the Mexican government as so vital to Mexico's continued development. But from an environmental standpoint, the impact of continuous economic growth is not necessarily so positive.

In general, the throughput of energy and resource inputs to the economy, along with waste and pollution outputs, increases with growth. Increasing economic demands exacerbate the problems of resource limits and environmental stresses. Consider the dimensions of projected global economic growth over the next 40 years. According to the World Bank's 1992 World Development Report, *Development and the Environment,* "between 1990 and 2030, as the world's population grows by 3.7 billion, food production will need to double, and industrial output and energy use will probably triple worldwide and increase fivefold in developing countries" (World Bank 1992). The environmental implications of economic growth on this scale will clearly involve unprecedented strains on soil, water, fishery, forest, and other ecological systems, together with a steady accumulation of atmospheric carbon unless drastic changes in energy use patterns occur. Here the achievement of "free" trade — rapid growth in agricultural and industrial production — becomes its own environmental nemesis. In the real world, the success of free trade is based not on hypothetical welfare gains but on its contribution to promoting economic growth. But if environmental protection implies either growth limitation or a very different kind of growth (labor- and information-intensive rather than energy- and resource-intensive), then free trade cannot be the basis of sustainability in the way in which it has been the engine of growth.

The standard economic theory response to this problem is that "the primary cause of environmental problems is not liberalized trade but the failure of markets and governments to price the environment appropriately."[11] But an ecological analysis of environmental problems strongly implies that measurement of environmental costs as externalities is insufficient. The health or deterioration of whole ecosystems cannot be adequately reflected in individual prices for goods and services. Sound policies for maintaining a productive soil base and healthy water, forest, natural resource, and fisheries systems require constraints on development that are unrecognized in the free-trade model. Global ecosystem analysis must include consideration of the carbon cycle, ocean food systems, ozone depletion, nitrate fixation, the phosphate cycle, freshwater systems, and so forth. These problems are inherently transboundary and cannot be dealt with simply by modifying prices, even if individual nations were willing to impose trade disadvantages on themselves by internalizing environmental costs.

Defenders of the standard paradigm of trade and growth have often relied on what has come to be known as the Environmental Kuznets Curve (EKC) principle, which asserts that environmental damage increases in the early stages of growth, but diminishes once nations reach higher levels of income. The analogy is to a hypothesis regarding income inequality and economic growth, articulated by Simon Kuznets in his 1955 presidential address to the American Economic Association. Kuznets suggested that the relationship between national income and inequality in developing nations would have an inverted U shape, with inequality first increasing and then decreasing with economic growth.[12] The environmental variant of this principle implies that as nations reach higher income levels, they develop both greater capacity and greater demand for investment in environmental preservation. Thus after passing through a "dirty" stage of development, nations will put effort into "cleaning up" and may also shift to less polluting production methods. Some advocates of conventional growth and trade paradigms use the EKC hypothesis to argue that economic growth, rather than threatening the environment, is essential to protect the environment.[13]

The EKC principle is widely asserted to be supported by empirical data, with the work of Grossman and Krueger being most frequently cited (Grossman and Krueger 1995). However, its acceptance as a general principle may be extremely misleading. First, Grossman and Krueger tested only a limited number of air and water pollutants.[14] Other important environmental pollutants, such as nitrogen oxides, carbon monoxide, carbon dioxide, methane, and tropospheric ozone, were not included, nor were municipal wastes or measures of ecosystem degradation such as species loss, soil degradation, or groundwater depletion. Second, the "turning points" found by Grossman and Krueger vary considerably in income level, and other researchers have obtained different results depending on the data and statistical methods used. Third, even for those pollutants that seem to conform to an EKC, the "turning points" are high enough, ranging from $2,000 to $12,000 in income, to imply a considerable increase in pollution for most of the world's developing nations before any improvement would be noted.[15] According to an EKC study by Selden and Song, the estimated global "turning point" for sulfur dioxide would not come until 2085, by which time global emissions would be 354 percent above 1986 levels; suspended particulate matter would peak in 2089 at 421 percent higher emissions, and nitrogen oxides in 2079 with 226 percent higher emissions.[16] This projection seems to confirm rather than refute assertions that, absent major policy changes, global growth threatens increasing environmental degradation.

Social and Distributional Issues

Closely allied to the ecological critique is a social-institutional analysis of the impacts of trade. In the standard trade model, it is accepted that trade will create winners and losers, and that the losers may include whole industries, regions, or occupational classes.[17] Trade is nonetheless considered optimal in economic terms because overall output and consumption increases. Large-scale social disruption and increased inequality may very well result from expanded trade, but in the calculus of standard economics this is considered as a transitional problem, outweighed by the long-term gains from trade. As globalization of economies proceeds, however, the social costs become more evident and have begun to arouse concern even among economists.

To take one example, fully opening Mexico's agricultural sector to world trade will involve the collapse of the country's primarily small-producer (ejido) corn-farming sector. The resulting migration of displaced small producers from rural areas to overcrowded cities will intensify the already unmanageable problems of urban areas. In theory, this adjustment of a protected industry to the world price of corn represents an improvement in economic efficiency and welfare; in practice its effects could be socially disastrous. Furthermore, the world price itself reflects overproduction through heavily subsidized and unsustainable intensive agricultural techniques in the United States and Europe.[18] In situations like this, the breakdown of communities resulting from expanded trade can be damaging to social cohesion, to the environment, and to public health. Measured in terms of growth in agricultural and industrial output, gross domestic product (GDP) increases, while social problems multiply and income inequality may well increase. Eddy Lee of the International Labor Organization cites evidence that other Latin American economies also show increased wage inequality in the wake of trade liberalization (1996).

Rising inequality is also a problem for relatively wealthy industrialized nations engaging in trade with much lower wage countries. In the United States, there is little doubt that income inequality has increased over the last fifteen years. According to Richard Freeman, "an economic disaster has befallen low-skilled Americans, especially young men. Researchers using several data sources — including household survey data from the Current Population Survey, other household surveys, and establishment surveys — have documented that wage inequality and skill differentials in earnings and employment increased sharply in the United States from the mid-1970's through the 1980's and into the 1990's" (1995). However, there is an extensive debate among economists as to what portion of this increasing inequality can be attributed to trade.

In a review of the literature on trade and wage inequality, Belman and Lee find that "most of the research, using a range of empirical methods and theoretical assumptions, has found that increased trade (or import competition) is associated to some extent with reduced domestic employment or wages, with the employment effect usually estimated to be several times larger than the direct wage impact" (1992). They estimate that international trade accounts for about 10 to 20 percent of the increase in wage inequality in the United States, with trade with labor-abundant developing countries being especially significant. Nor is the effect confined to a limited number of workers: 70 to 80 percent of U.S. wage earners may be affected to some degree.

Some economists place greater importance on the impact of trade. Adrian Wood argues that "the main cause of the deteriorating situation of unskilled workers in developed countries has been expansion of trade with developing countries" (1995). Wood identifies his position as a "minority view" among economists, but even according to a more mainstream view, "trade is a moderate contributing source of income inequality trends; it may not overshadow other sources, but it cannot be shrugged away" (Richardson 1995). Perhaps this rising inequality might be considered an acceptable cost of economic progress if governments increased social measures aimed at supporting lower-income workers. This might be a rough application of the economic principle that, with unequal gains from trade, the winners could compensate the losers.[19] However, as Eddy Lee points out, the opposite is generally true of public policy. Globalization has reduced "the capacity, and perhaps even the will, of governments to take such compensatory or ameliorative action" (1996).

Perhaps even more significant than the issue of increasing wage inequality is the question of power relations. Exposure to the global economy systematically undermines the institutions through which the less well-off have traditionally defended their interests, such as labor unions and community organizations. From a technical point of view, economists would say that lower-income, lower-skilled workers face greater elasticity of demand in the market.[20] From a social point of view, the losers in the global economy are essentially at the mercy of the winners, dependent on the questionable goodwill of those who have benefited from economic growth and trade liberalization. Among the prime beneficiaries are the multinational and transnational corporations that can exploit the expanded profit opportunities in a global economy, while facing weakened labor unions and less effective government control. It is not surprising that those who enjoy most of the benefits of globalization should continually sing the praises of free trade, and it is equally not surprising that there is rising political opposition to trade expansion among those whose situation is clearly worsened by it — even if trade is only a contributing cause, rather than the main cause, of their problems.

A Practical Example — The NAFTA Agreement

The NAFTA agreement, concluded in August 1993, was hailed by its proponents as going "further than any trade agreement in addressing environmental concerns and actively promoting environmental protection."[21] In addition to a side agreement on the environment that set up the tripartite Commission for Environmental Cooperation (CEC), another side agreement, the North American Agreement on Labor Cooperation (NAALC), dealt with labor issues. This specific attention to social and environmental aspects of trade was remarkable and almost unprecedented in trade agreements. While this unusual aspect of NAFTA persuaded some environmental groups in the United States to support the agreement,[22] the record of implementation after three years is not encouraging.

The enforcement powers of the Commission for Environmental Cooperation are extremely limited. It has no power to upgrade or harmonize environmental regulations; the NAFTA agreement merely contains a statement of good intentions by the parties to pursue harmonization "to the greatest extent possible," which in fact is "largely unenforceable" (Johnson and Beaulieu 1996). The CEC may respond to a country's failure to enforce existing environmental regulations, but its role is generally limited to producing a fact-finding report and recommendations to the government involved. If the government fails to respond, it could in theory be subject to fines and trade sanctions, but only after a protracted process. This process has never been attempted to date — the CEC has rejected the two cases brought before it that might have involved fines or sanctions.[23]

The benign tone of the commission's annual reports, indicating inter-governmental cooperation on environmental protection, is belied by on-the-ground reports on environmental deterioration in Mexico. One of the prime concerns of environmentalists prior to NAFTA was the disastrous environmental condition in the "maquiladora" zone along the U.S.-Mexican border.[24] The NAFTA side agreement promised funds to improve maquiladora conditions. Three years later, virtually no funds have been forthcoming and conditions have deteriorated significantly. Rather than being dispersed, as NAFTA proponents had predicted, the concentration of industries in the border zone has grown. Controls on the extensive volume of hazardous wastes produced in the maquiladora industries are virtually nonexistent. There have been no improvements in water and sewage facilities, despite a 20 percent increase in the maquiladora work force. Border air pollution has increased. The incidence of disease linked to environmental contamination has increased. Further, the Mexican government has waived the requirement for environmental impact statements (EIS) for new investments in many industries.[25]

On labor issues, the record is no better. Complaints brought before the NAALC of significant labor and human rights violations in Mexico have not resulted in any reinstatement or compensation for workers fired for attempting to organize independent unions. The NAALC has essentially been ignored by multinational corporations taking advantage of repressive labor conditions in Mexico; corporations named in complaints have uniformly refused even to participate in hearings. A report to the NAALC on the labor impact of NAFTA in the United States found that "NAFTA has created a climate that has emboldened employers to more aggressively threaten to close, or actually close their plants to avoid unionization." The report called for a "significant expansion of both worker and union rights and employer penalties," but the NAALC is powerless to achieve such reforms.[26]

The clear failure of NAFTA to live up to its exaggerated promise of environmental and labor protection was a key factor in the defeat of the proposed "fast track" trade bill in 1997. Despite strong support from the U.S. administration, the Republican congressional leadership, and most leading press editorialists, the bill went down to defeat, as the swing votes that had narrowly approved NAFTA in 1993 swung the other way. A major reason that the administration had sought "fast track" was to move forward on negotiation of a "Free Trade Area of the Americas," expanding NAFTA to include other Latin American countries. This level of resistance to "free trade" was unprecedented in postwar U.S. history. While the opponents of "fast track" were widely criticized as inward-looking protectionists, the coalition opposing "free" trade had clearly expanded well beyond the specific import-competing industries and unions who have historically supported protective tariffs. This shift in the public policy arena parallels the shift in thinking on economic trade theory that we have discussed. Supporters of the free-trade paradigm view this as a temporary development, a bump in the road of progress toward global free trade. But perhaps it represents a more fundamental shift, implying the need for new concepts of trade theory and policy that could replace the dominant free-trade model.

A Strategy for Trade and Sustainability

The "free"-trade model has never been as "free" as its theoretical proponents imply. Nominally "free"-trade agreements have always contained strong strategic elements. The exclusion of textiles and agriculture from GATT regulations was clearly a deliberate global protection strategy on the part of developed nations.[27] The U.S.-Canada "free"-trade agreement specifically exempts oil and gas development from antisubsidy rules — these rules can, however, be invoked against subsidies for energy efficiency and conservation[28] (Shrybman 1991). Recent trade controversies over intellectual property rights and bioengineering clearly have strong strategic interest aspects, pitting developed nations and multinationals against developing nations in disputes over appropriate ground rules.[29] Japan's trading policy has always been a classic example of strategic trade planning. The European Economic Community was conceived partly as a strategic move to counter U.S. economic predominance. U.S. advocates of expanding NAFTA to encompass a "Free Trade Area of the Americas" typically argue that a U.S.-centered free-trade area is necessary to preclude agreements between Latin American countries and the European Union, to the strategic disadvantage of the United States.[30] The inclusion of environmental sustainability in trade strategies and agreements is therefore entirely feasible, and its legitimacy is at least as great vis-à-vis "free" trade as the frequent national-interest considerations that have shaped global trade.[31]

A balanced view of the relationship between growth and the environment should acknowledge both the greater pressures placed on the environment by rising economic output and the possibility of policy changes leading to "greener" economies. But a number of factors — the scale of current environmental problems, the rising importance of issues of wage inequity, the much greater social and ecological problems potentially associated with a projected tripling of global GNP — make it foolhardy to rely on a regime of liberalized trade and faster growth. Strategies for sustainability will need to be specifically included in trade policies and trade agreements at all levels, from global to local.

In the global arena the sweeping multilateral principles of GATT must give way to a more balanced treatment of trade, environment, and social issues. This could well involve the creation of a Global Environmental Organization, as Esty (1994) and Runge (1994) have suggested, to balance the World Trade Organization. It will also involve significant modification in the one-sided rules of the GATT/WTO regime. These institutional changes, however, are not as easily compatible with the goals of liberalized trade as Esty and Runge suggest. The multilateral application of "free"-trade principles will have to give way to a greater emphasis on specific sectoral agreements consistent with global sustainable-development strategies. For example, agreements on agricultural subsidies should permit the redirection of farm subsidies to soil conservation and development of low-input agricultural techniques, preserving farms while reducing overproduction. As global CO_2 emissions continue to rise, trade in the energy sector will have to be adapted to accommodate a substantial carbon tax or tradable permit scheme to be implemented both nationally and internationally.[32] Global agreements on forest and biodiversity preservation will likely also involve specific trade restrictions, labeling systems, and tariff structures. The troika of international institutions dating to the 1940s — IMF, World Bank, and GATT/WTO — must be reoriented to substitute goals of global sustainability for their present ideological commitment to a model of free trade and unlimited economic growth.

At the regional level, there can be no single dominating principle for future trade agreements, but some guidelines might be suggested for regional trade negotiations. First, in regional agreements such as NAFTA where no supranational rule-making body is involved, trade agreements should be specific, sectoral, and based on consideration of national strategies for environmental sustainability and social justice. A revised U.S.-Mexico agreement that genuinely implemented a major border cleanup and provided for significant expansion of worker and union rights on both sides of the border could be consistent with sustainable trade, but is a far cry from the present realities of NAFTA. A "green" trade agreement would also have to place the goal of sustainable agriculture above simple tariff reduction. NAFTA rules currently do give precedence to international environmental treaties (Basel on hazardous wastes, Montreal on ozone-depleting substances, and CITES on endangered species). This principle should be expanded to all national environmental protection policies, and the imposition of sanctions for environmental violations needs to be much more effective.

Second, in regional trade groupings such as the European Union where elected supranational policy-making bodies exist, these bodies must take responsibility for environmental and social issues to the extent that their legitimate democratic mandate allows — otherwise, these responsibilities must be ceded to national governments. Transboundary issues are a logical area for supranational bodies to be responsible for environmental rule-making. Where they are empowered to intervene in national policy-making, the process must be oriented toward "leveling up" rather than "leveling down" standards. This means that countries within the common market must retain the power to impose higher social and environmental standards where they see fit.

At the national and local levels, it is important to reassert the power of democratic decision making vis-à-vis multinational corporations. Hines and Lang (1996) propose a radical increase in local powers to control trade and capital flows and activities of multinational corporations. Their approach, oriented toward promoting local sustainability, probably goes well beyond what is politically practicable; but they make the essential point that where community sustainability is threatened by global market forces, there must be some recourse even if it involves measures usually viewed as "protectionist." At a minimum, national governments have a responsibility to consider community impacts before entering trade agreements, and to reassert their powers of control over corporate entities rather than passively accepting a free-trade logic that tilts the playing field in favor of the multinationals.

The general presumption derived from Ricardian free-trade theory, that freer trade will always bring *overall* greater benefits, despite losses to specific sectors, will no longer hold in the emerging twenty-first century global economy, which will be characterized both by resource and environmental limits and by a much more important role for the presently developing nations (where almost all of the net population growth will occur). There will still be clear benefits from trade in terms of increased efficiency, technology transfer, and the import/export of sustainably produced products. But in the future, the effects of trade must be evaluated in terms of social and ecological impacts, and the structure of regional or global trade agreements must reflect these assessments.

NOTES

An earlier version of this article (Harris 1993) set out the basic ecological critique of free trade. Since then there has been both extensive theoretical discussion and significant practical experience with trade and environment policy. I attempt here to provide an update and overview of sustainable trade issues that will be accessible both to economists and noneconomists.

1. For an overview of the ecological economics critique of free trade, see Ekins et al. 1994 and Costanza et al. 1995. Theorists who have attempted to reconcile the goals of liberalized trade and environmental protection include Esty (1994) and Runge (1994).

2. Colin Hines and Tim Lang are among the few critics of free trade who have actually welcomed the label of "protectionist," attempting to alter the perception of protectionism as a defense of narrow, inefficient special interests. Instead, they propose that we should support "protection" of workers, communities, and the environment from the destructive effects of globalization (Hines and Lang 1994, 1996).

3. There is an extensive literature dealing with the impact of trade on employment and distribution of income, with widely differing estimates of its significance; this issue is discussed further below.

4. See Goldsmith (1997) on GATT/WTO harmonization and Johnson and Beaulieu 1996, chap. 4: "NAFTA's Downward Pressure on Environmental Norms and Upward Harmonization."

5. The 1991 "Tuna/Dolphin" panel decision in favor of Mexico, which found portions of the U.S. Marine Mammal Protection Act to be GATT-illegal, was reaffirmed by another GATT panel in 1994, in response to a European challenge to the "secondary embargo" provision of the Marine Mammal Protection Act (see Esty 1994, 268–69).

6. For a brief summary of the ecological economics critique, see also Daly 1993.

7. Hamilton 1994. See also Serageldin and Steer 1995, chap. 7.

8. Advocates of NAFTA often cited expanded access to Mexico's estimated 65 billion barrel oil reserves as a major advantage of the agreement (see, e.g., Orme 1993).

9. Also, as Esty points out, "the scope of Article XX fails to cover important natural resources such as the atmosphere, the oceans, the ozone layer, and other elements of the global commons. Indeed, the tuna/dolphin decision implies that Article XX cannot be used to justify environmental trade measures aimed at harms outside the jurisdiction of the nation imposing the measures" (Esty 1994, 49).

10. Defenders of free trade point out that in some cases agricultural production for export, such as tree crops, may be environmentally preferable to the more erosive local production of cereals or legumes. However, there is no reason to expect that trade-induced reallocations of resources will generally be environmentally beneficial. And in this particular case, the negative social effects of a shift away from basic food needs production should also be considered.

11. World Bank 1992, 67. See also Panayotou 1993.

12. The Kuznets hypothesis for income inequality appears to be borne out by cross-section data, but the paucity of time-series data, and the persistence of high levels of inequality in nations such as Brazil, leave it in some doubt as a general principle (see, e.g., Gillis et al. 1996).

13. See, e.g., Beckerman 1992. Bhagwati (1993) also emphasizes this argument in his defense of free trade.

14. Sulfur dioxide, smoke, and particulate matter in air; oxygen regime, fecal contamination, and heavy metal contamination in water.

15. According to the 1996 *World Development Report,* 91 of the world's nations have GNP per capita below $3,000, and 106 have GNP below $8,000.

16. Selden and Song 1992, quoted in World Wildlife Fund 1996.

17. This is codified in what is known as the Heckscher-Ohlin theory, which states that scarce factors lose from trade. For example, workers in a relatively labor-scarce economy will lose when trade is opened up with a labor-abundant economy. A stronger form of this theory is the factor price equalization theorem, according to which the price of labor and other factors of production will be equalized across trading nations.

18. The Uruguay Round agreement on gradual reduction of agricultural subsidies is a case in which freer agricultural trade probably represents an environmental gain. However, many environmentally destructive subsidies to agriculture, such as energy or irrigation subsidies, are indirect and are therefore not covered by the recent agreement.

19. The principle of Pareto optimality, fundamental to economic welfare analysis, states that if "winners" in a new economic arrangement (such as liberalized trade) can compensate "losers" for their losses, and still be better off, the new situation is unambiguously preferable. However, such compensation rarely takes place. Economists get around this difficulty by accepting the idea of "potential compensation" rather than requiring actual compensation as a condition for "optimality." This allows a situation to be judged an economic improvement, even if some people — perhaps a substantial number — are clearly worse off.

20. For an explanation of this point and a review of evidence, see Rodrik 1997, chap. 2: "Consequences of Trade for Labor Markets and the Employment Relationship."

21. Carla Hills, U.S. Trade Representative, in a presentation to U.S. Senate Finance Committee, September 8, 1992. Quoted in Johnson and Beaulieu 1996, 66.

22. NAFTA was endorsed by the National Wildlife Federation, the World Wildlife Fund, the Environmental Defense Fund, the Natural Resources Defense Council, and the National Audubon Society. It was opposed by the Sierra Club, Friends of the Earth, Greenpeace, the Humane Society of the United States, and the American Society for the Prevention of Cruelty to Animals, as well as numerous other environmental groups.

23. See Commission for Environmental Cooperation, *1995 Annual Report.*

24. Maquiladoras are production facilities engaged in processing or assembly of imported components for re-export, on a duty-free basis.

25. Public Citizen and RMALC 1996; Economic Policy Institute et al. 1996; Varady and Mack 1995; Wheat 1996.

26. Bronfenbrenner 1996, 1997, quoted in Economic Policy Institute et al. 1997.

27. Under the Uruguay Round agreement, agricultural and textile quotas will be gradually abolished over the period 1994–2004.

28. See Shrybman 1991 on this and other strategic biases damaging to the environment and social policy in U.S.-Canada trade agreements.

29. See, for example, Shiva and Holla-Bhar 1996 for a critique of the Trade Related Intellectual Property (TRIPS) regime as it applies to biodiversity and the patenting of life forms.

30. See, for example, the U.S. Trade Representative's 1977 *Report to the Congress on Recommendations on Future Free Trade Area Negotiations* (U.S. Department of Commerce 1997).

31. As Charnovitz 1996 documents, there is an extensive history of trade measures being used to protect the environment and public health, dating back to the *Phylloxera* agreement of 1878 (to prevent trade in infected grapevines), the migratory bird protection treaty of 1902, and the Phosphorous Match Convention of 1906 (prohibiting trade in phosphorous matches to protect worker health).

32. The 1996 Kyoto agreements to reduce developed-nation emissions of CO_2 by 7 percent below 1990 levels will clearly require carbon taxes or some equivalent system to accomplish, although the agreement merely sets goals and does not specify implementation.

REFERENCES

Beckerman, Wilfred. 1992. Economic Growth and the Environment: Whose Growth? Whose Environment? *World Development* 20, no. 4: 481–96.

Belman, Dale, and Thea M. Lee. 1992. International Trade and the Performance of U.S. Labor Markets. In Robert A. Blecker, ed., *U.S. Trade Policy and Global Growth.* Armonk, NY: M. E. Sharpe.

Bhagwati, Jagdish. 1993. The Case for Free Trade. *Scientific American* 269 (November): 42–49. Summarized in Krishnan et al. 1995.

Bronfenbrenner, Kate. 1996. Final Report: The Effects of Plant Closing or Threat of Plant Closing on the Right of Workers to Organize. Cornell University. Report Commissioned by the Labor Secretariat of the North American Commission for Labor Cooperation.

———. 1997. We'll Close! Plant Closings, Plant Closing Threats, Union Organizing, and NAFTA. *Multinational Monitor* 18, no. 3: 8–13.

Charnovitz, Steve. 1996. Trade Measures and the Design of International Regimes. *Journal of Environment and Development* 5, no. 2: 168–96.

Commission for Environmental Cooperation. 1995. *Annual Report.* Washington, DC.

Costanza, Robert, John Audley, Richard Borden, Paul Ekins, Carl Folke, and Jonathan Harris. 1995. Sustainable Trade: A New Paradigm for World Welfare. *Environment* 37, no. 5 (June).

Daly, Herman E. 1991. *Steady-State Economics.* 2d ed. Washington, DC: Island Press.

———. 1993. The Perils of Free Trade. *Scientific American* 269 (November 1993): 50–57. Summarized in Krishnan et al. 1995.

———. 1996. *Beyond Growth: The Economics of Sustainable Development.* Boston: Beacon Press

Daly, Herman E., and John B. Cobb Jr. 1989. *For the Common Good: Redirecting the Economy toward Community, the Environment and a Sustainable Future.* Boston: Beacon Press.

Economic Policy Institute et al. 1997. *The Failed Experiment: NAFTA at Three Years.* Washington, DC: Economic Policy Institute <http://www.epinet.org>.

Ekins, Paul, Carl Folke, and Robert Costanza. 1994. Trade, Environment, and Development: The Issues in Perspective. *Ecological Economics* 9, no. 1: 1–12.

El-Serafy, Salah. 1993a. The Environment as Capital. In Ernst Lutz, ed., *Toward Improved Accounting for the Environment.* Washington, DC: World Bank.

———. 1993b. *Country Macroeconomic Work and Natural Resources.* World Bank Environment Department Working Paper no. 58.

Esty, Daniel C. 1994. *Greening the GATT: Trade, Environment and the Future.* Washington, DC: Institute for International Economics.

Freeman, Richard B. 1995. Are Your Wages Set in Beijing? *Journal of Economic Perspectives* 9, no. 3: 15–32.

Gillis, Malcolm, et al. 1996. *Economics of Development.* New York: W. W. Norton.

Goldsmith, Edward. 1997. Can the Environment Survive the Global Economy? *Ecologist* 27, no. 6: 242–48.

Goodland, Robert, and Herman E. Daly. 1992. Ten Reasons Why Northern Income Growth is Not the Solution to Southern Poverty. In Robert Goodland, Herman E. Daly, and Salah El Serafy, eds., *Population, Technology, and Lifestyle.* Washington, DC: Island Press.

Grossman, Gene, and Alan Krueger. 1995. Economic Growth and the Environment. *Quarterly Journal of Economics* 110, no. 2: 353–77.

Hamilton, Kirk. 1994. Green Adjustments to GDP. *Resources Policy* 20:155–68.

Harris, Jonathan M. 1993. 'Free' Trade and Environmental Sustainability. *Praxis: The Fletcher School Journal of Development Studies* 10, no. 2: 77–84. Medford, Massachusetts: Fletcher School of Law and Diplomacy, Tufts University.

Hines, Colin, and Tim Lang. 1994. *The New Protectionism.* London: Earthscan Publications.

———. 1996. In Favor of a New Protectionism. In Mander and Goldsmith, eds. 1996.

Johnson, Pierre Marc, and André Beaulieu. 1996. *The Environment and NAFTA.* Washington, DC: Island Press.

Krishnan, Rajaram, et al. 1995. *A Survey of Ecological Economics.* Washington, DC: Island Press.

Krugman, Paul. 1990. Is Free Trade Passé? In Philip King, ed., *International Economics and International Economic Policy: A Reader,* New York: Mc-Graw Hill.

Krugman, Paul, ed. 1994. *Rethinking International Trade.* Cambridge: MIT Press.

Lee, Eddy. 1996. Globalization and Employment: Is Anxiety Justified? *International Labour Review* 485–97.

Mander, Jerry, and Edward Goldsmith, eds. 1996. *The Case Against the Global Economy.* San Francisco: Sierra Club Books.

Orme, William A. 1993. *Continental Shift: Free Trade and the New North America.* Washington, DC: Washington Post Company.

Panayotou, Theodore. 1993. *Green Markets: The Economics of Sustainable Development.* San Francisco: Institute for Contemporary Studies Press.

Public Citizen and Red Mexicana de Acción frente al Libre Comercio (RMALC). 1996. *NAFTA's Broken Promise: The Border Betrayed.* Washington, DC: Public Citizen Publications.

Repetto, Robert, and Wilfredo Cruz. 1992. *The Environmental Effects of Stabilization and Structural Adjustment Programs: The Philippines Case.* Washington, DC: World Resources Institute.

Repetto, Robert, et al. 1989. *Wasting Assets: Natural Resources in the National Income Accounts.* Washington, DC: World Resources Institute.

———. 1991. *Accounts Overdue: Natural Resource Depreciation in Costa Rica.* Washington, DC: World Resources Institute.

Richardson, J. David. 1995. Income Inequality and Trade: How to Think, What to Conclude. *Journal of Economic Perspectives* 9, no. 3: 33–55.

Rodrik, Daniel. 1997. *Has Globalization Gone Too Far?* Washington, DC: Institute for International Economics.

Runge, C. Ford. 1994. *Freer Trade, Protected Environment: Balancing Trade Liberalization and Environmental Issues.* New York: Council on Foreign Relations.

Selden, Thomas M., and Daqing Song. 1994. Environmental Quality and Development: Is There a Kuznets Curve for Air Pollution? *Journal of Environmental Economics and Management* 27, no. 2: 147–62.

Serageldin, Ismail, and Andrew Steer, eds. 1993. *Valuing the Environment.* Washington, DC: World Bank Environmentally Sustainable Development Proceedings Series no. 2.

Shiva, Vandana, and Radha Holla-Bhar. 1996. Piracy by Patent: The Case of the Neem Tree. In Mander and Goldsmith, eds. 1996.

Shrybman, Steven. 1991–92. Trading Away the Environment. In *World Policy Journal* 9, no. 1 (winter): 93–110.

United Nations Department for Economic and Social Information and Policy Analysis. 1993. *Integrated Environmental and Economic Accounting.* New York: United Nations.

United Nations Development Programme (UNDP). 1992. *Human Development Report, 1992.* New York: Oxford University Press.

United States Trade Representative. 1997. *Report to the Congress on Recommendations on Future Free Trade Area Negotiations.* U.S. Commerce Department.

Varady, Robert, and Maura Mack. 1995. Transboundary Water Resources and Public Health in the U.S./Mexico Border Region. *Journal of Environmental Health* 57, no. 8: 11.

Wheat, Andrew. 1996. Troubled NAFTA Waters. *Multinational Monitor* 17, no. 4: 23–25.

Wood, Adrian. 1995. How Trade Hurt Unskilled Workers. *Journal of Economic Perspectives* 9, no. 3: 57–80.

World Bank. 1992. *World Development Report, 1992: Development and the Environment.* New York: Oxford University Press.

———. 1995. *Monitoring Environmental Progress.* Environmentally Sustainable Development Series. Washington, DC: World Bank.

World Trade Organization. 1996. *Trade and the Environment: Report of the WTO Committee on Trade and Environment.* Geneva, World Trade Organization Information and Media Division <http://www.unicc.org/wto>.

Worldwide Fund for Nature. 1996. *Dangerous Curves: Does the Environment Improve with Economic Growth?* Switzerland: Worldwide Fund for Nature.

Part 2
Sustainability and Institutions in Practice

Introduction to Part 2: Power, Knowledge, and Institutions in Development Practice

Jonathan M. Harris

Economic theories of development tend to underplay political and institutional considerations. The focus of economic development theory is on such issues as markets, trade, investment, agricultural productivity, and industrialization. The unspoken assumption underlying much development economics is that there is a well-defined path and a known goal of development. The path is that already followed by the presently developed economies, and the goal is to become similar to those economies in terms of gross domestic product (GDP) per capita. This view has been criticized by advocates of sustainable development, who argue that the planet cannot support the levels of material consumption implied in this model without environmental disaster.[1] But there are also other grounds to dissent from a standard economic model of development, as some writers within the economics profession have realized.

Joseph Stiglitz, for example, suggests that the problems facing the developing economies are significantly different from those of European and North American development:

> Many economists took the position that there were certain stages of economic growth through which an economy had to go in the process of becoming a mature economy; just as a child has to go through certain stages in becoming an adult. Thus, urbanization and industrialization were taken to be virtually synonymous with development.
>
> This view is, I think, fundamentally incorrect. The central problem facing England, France and the United States was one of innovation, of developing new techniques and technologies. . . . The LDC's are in the position of imitators. For them, the questions of concern are much closer to those addressed in the classical theory of comparative advantage, modified by certain important dynamic

considerations. The rapid improvements in agricultural technology during the past two decades mean that significant improvements in standards of living can occur without urbanization and industrialization. The LDC's thus face a choice about the appropriate path of development.[2]

Stiglitz uses an information-theoretic approach, as distinct from a standard neoclassical model, to explain such phenomena as sharecropping, relatively high urban wages, and low savings in developing nations. He suggests that the course of development is strongly influenced by institutional factors and technological choices (noting the possibility that "advanced" technologies may be "inappropriate" for developing countries). He also emphasizes the potential for an agriculturally oriented development strategy as an alternative to market-oriented industrialization.

Another development in modern economics, endogenous growth theory, has focused on issues such as technological diffusion from leader to follower countries, learning by doing, and the importance of human capital — information embodied in trained or educated people.[3] While these variants on standard economic theory are not especially oriented toward sustainability issues, they do suggest that much more consideration should be given to what Neva Goodwin calls "contextual" economics — economics in the context of specific institutions, cultures, and natural environments. The standard economic model of development, in which GDP growth is a function of capital, labor, and exogenous technological progress, is well suited to mathematical modeling, but too narrowly conceived to capture many of the issues involved in development, sustainable or otherwise. The interplay between existing cultures and institutions on the one hand, and technologically driven economic "progress" on the other, is central to the shaping of development.

Let us try to view things from the perspective of a local community within a developing nation. What forces drive the economic development of this community? At the local level, the needs, aspirations, and skills of its people, together with the available natural resources, will provide a basis for development. But other powerful forces will also be brought to bear on this community. If the community is part of a country that is integrated into the world market, globally set prices will strongly affect the resource use and labor choices of the community. Often the policies of multilateral development agencies will also have a significant impact on these choices, directly or through policies urged on national governments. Powerful national elites will also have their own agendas, and considerable institutional power to implement them. Finally, local elites will seek to turn economic development to their own advantage, and the process of development may itself create or strengthen local elites (such as wealthy farmers taking advantage of Green Revolution technologies).

Viewed this way, it is evident that much will have to be done to transform rhetoric about "community participation" and "locally oriented sustainable development" to reality. Local communities are confronted by — one is tempted to say are at the mercy of — strong economic and political forces that are beyond their control. Will the influence of these forces be benign? Will they be consistent with social or ecological sustainability? If not, what can be done to alter the picture? While leading economic and political actors at all levels have been quick to adopt the rhetoric of sustainability, it is far from clear that either the impersonal forces of the global marketplace or the self-interested actions of the politically powerful will in fact promote sustainable development at the local level.

Cultural Paradigms and Political Power

The essays in this section of the volume focus on examples of development practice that demonstrate the relationship between political institutions and development. Allan Hoben links issues of culture and sustainability in his examination of the success or failure of environmental policies in Africa. His focus is not, as one might expect from the title, on indigenous cultures, but rather on the culture of the First World as manifest through development agencies. Northern practitioners of development economics like to think of their approach as rational. Hoben sees it rather as driven by cultural paradigms that dominate the thinking of development professionals, often to the exclusion of practical evidence to the contrary. In the environmental policy area, Hoben argues that the uncritical acceptance of a simplistic neo-Malthusian theory, linked to a disdain for the knowledge and adaptability of indigenous peoples, has led to poorly conceived, wasteful, and counterproductive policies. Far from being scientific or rational, this approach is based on a "faith in unproven assumptions" and a refusal to consider inconvenient empirical evidence. Hoben sees this unfortunate syndrome as having great durability due to the political needs of bureaucratic organizations.

In criticizing neo-Malthusian paradigms, Hoben is not denying the importance of environmental issues. Rather, he is pointing out the degree to which "asymmetric power relations" between Northern development professionals and local communities in Africa can lead to a complete mis-specification of the nature of environmental problems. He acknowledges some movement in development organizations toward recognition of the importance of a participatory approach, and of relying on local knowledge. Hoben remains skeptical, however, of whether these organizations are institutionally capable of translating this focus from rhetoric to successful practice.

Robert Paarlberg also traces many environmental problems in developing countries to imbalances of political power. He focuses on the widespread environmental abuses associated with agriculture. Resource access and control, rural land ownership patterns, and political power, in Paarlberg's view, are the key factors in determining patterns of environmental use and abuse. This is true both on marginal lands stressed by overuse, and on high-quality agricultural lands farmed with "modern" techniques. Poverty in itself is not the problem, since poor people often have developed quite sophisticated techniques of conservation and agroforestry; rather, it is the breakdown of stable traditional institutions under the impact of outside political and economic forces.

Expansion of markets and privatization of land, generally viewed favorably in economic theory, can be destructive to local systems of resource protection. Paarlberg sees the introduction of intensive, Green Revolution technologies as essential to prevent extensive conversion of wildlife habitat and marginal lands to cropland. At the same time, he argues that modernization can contribute not only to social inequity and dislocation, but to environmental damage. It can create a dualistic system of rural land ownership, in which the wealthier farmers abuse the land by overuse of chemical inputs and irrigation, while the poorer farmers are forced onto marginal lands and excluded from lucrative market connections.

Paarlberg dissents from the commonly advocated economic paradigm of private property rights and market-based incentives for environmental protection. It is not that these policies are ill-advised in themselves, but that they ignore political power relations. Property rights are intertwined with political power, and the interests of the politically powerful are often hostile to conservation. Huge fortunes have been made in poor countries through resource exploitation; Paarlberg rightly points out that it is "naive" to expect the politically powerful to subordinate their own interests to the recommendations of well-intentioned economists.[4]

Paarlberg specifically criticizes the impact of market-oriented reforms in Mexico under the North American Free Trade Agreement. Greater economic efficiency is the goal of these reforms, but they will also result in expansion of pesticide-dependent agriculture, the disruption of rural livelihoods, greater landlessness, and damage to marginal soils and forest ecosystems. A combination of market forces and feudalistic power relations makes for ruthless exploitation both of people and of natural resources; yet this combination is more the rule than the exception in many developing nations. Paarlberg sees "fundamental political and social change" as essential for sustainable development in rural areas. This, he suggests, is the missing link between organizational proclamations of a new environment/development focus and actual progress at the ground level.

New Institutions for Agricultural Development

The development of a sustainable agriculture paradigm with a strong grassroots base requires, in Hoben's terms, that the organizational cultures of the First World adapt to those of the Third World rather than the other way around. Jules Pretty and Robert Chambers discuss the specific changes needed for this to occur, and they see some hopeful signs. The more general acceptance of the concept of sustainable agriculture by development organizations is not, in their view, mere lip service. But the major international research and policy bureaucracies have yet to make the necessary transition.[5] Pretty and Chambers applaud the movement of agricultural research and development focus into an "ecological stage," replacing the simplified concept of "modernization" in which farmers were seen as passive recipients of intensive production technologies. Now — at least in theory — there is much broader recognition of the need for the indigenous knowledge of farmers to be fully incorporated into the process of research and development. However, they feel that we are just at the start of an "institutional stage" in which development organizations must develop new, more democratic structures that involve farmers as full partners with researchers, theorists, and managers.

In the new organizational structures envisioned by Pretty and Chambers, experiential learning and problem solving replace a unidirectional teaching and extension structure. "Modernized" agriculture has relied on relatively simple, easily replicable formulas for combining high-yield crop varieties, fertilizer, pesticides, and irrigation. The role of the researcher is to develop ever more productive systems, and the role of the extension agent to transfer these new systems to farmers. This approach is being challenged by approaches such as participatory rural appraisal. Rather than relying on a general formula, the new methods are context-specific, providing for the dissemination of successful techniques while always respecting the unique character of local production. Institutional support for such approaches has been slow to develop, but Pretty and

Chambers cite a number of success stories, widely distributed through-out the developing world.[6]

One notable feature of the new agricultural development systems is the much larger role for nongovernmental organizations (NGOs) in their implementation. While NGOs generally lack the breadth of cover-age that national or multinational organizations can achieve, they offer vital flexibility and responsiveness to local conditions. Developing part-nerships between NGOs and government organizations therefore be-comes an important element of the new development paradigm.[7]

Pretty and Chambers are less optimistic about progress in the inter-national agricultural research agencies, which remain wedded to the professional-centered, top-down approach to development of farming techniques. A handful of staff within these research organizations are open to new approaches, but often lack sufficient institutional support. Nonetheless, Pretty and Chambers present a number of examples of successful participatory research in the Philippines, Latin America, In-dia, and Africa. Interestingly, they note that a high proportion of the pioneering scientists in this area are women (just as women often play a leading role in local agricultural systems).

Dianne Rocheleau, Laurie Ross, and Julio Morobel have docu-mented in detail the importance of gender roles in the planning and management of agricultural ecosystems. Using case studies from the Dominican Republic, they demonstrate the interconnections between social and gender relationships and responsibilities for production and resource conservation at the village level. They show how ecological stability, household subsistence, and commercial activity are linked to-gether, with women playing a central role in managing integrated land use systems. These systems are vulnerable both to new technologies introduced by the market and to the ministrations of planners who are generally unaware of the complexity of the relationships involved in local production and conservation.

Rocheleau, Ross, and Morobel suggest that "sustainable" develop-ment planning may be just as vulnerable to failure as more mainstream efforts if its advocates are not sufficiently sensitive to these complex systems of social and ecological functions. In particular, the tendency of government functionaries, development professionals, or commercial interests to deal primarily with men in shaping labor and land use deci-sions can undermine sustainable systems. Men and women both serve as reservoirs of local ecological knowledge, and it is important to preserve a balance that supports the role of women in managing local ecosystems.

Molly Anderson and John Cook discuss issues of community food security, picking up on many of the themes developed by Pretty and

Chambers and by Rocheleau, Ross, and Morobel. They criticize the narrow concept of "food security" based simply on food as a commodity, suggesting instead a more inclusive concept of community food security. Community food security is based, in their view, on local knowledge and stable local institutions; these may be threatened by the social, political, and institutional effects of globalization. Dependence on food imports, often seen by economists as a desirable strategy for releasing productive factors for industrial development,[8] puts local people at the mercy of varying external food prices. It also destroys the reservoirs of local knowledge that, as detailed by Rocheleau, Ross, and Morobel, are essential both for food security and for ecological management. Anderson and Cook suggest, however, that communities both in industrial and in developing nations can successfully "deglobalize" and thus defend their own food security, social stability, and environment.

Anderson and Cook are not opposed to food trade or to large-scale agricultural production per se; but they distinguish between sustainable trade that supports local food systems and a global market system of food trade that can often be environmentally and socially destructive. The focus of their analysis of hunger is primarily on the United States, showing that even in one of the world's richest economies, a major agricultural exporter, significant numbers of people suffer food insecurity. They cite numerous practical examples of progress toward community food security in the United States and in developing nations. Although limited in scope, these initiatives are successfully fighting the tide of globalization, homogenization, and loss of community cohesion.

Rethinking Assumptions and Reforming Institutions

The authors of the articles in part 2 thus bring varied perspectives to the issue of sustainability in development practice. But some general themes are common to their differing perspectives and are supported by the many specific cases discussed. It is clear that sustainability, in agriculture and in development in general, cannot be seen simply as an issue of conserving natural resources and protecting the environment. It must involve a rethinking of the assumptions of standard economics, and a reworking of the power relationships that are associated with economic development. The powerful actors in national and global economic development are not in general oriented toward sustainability. The spread of global markets is not necessarily friendly to, and may be actively destructive of, sustainable economies. The ideology that still pervades most transnational development organizations is that of standard rather than sustainable economics. Thus efforts to promote sustainability at the grass roots face many strong forces that can impede their progress.

The underlying reasons for this incompatibility between grassroots sustainability and dominant political and economic institutions can be traced to the nature and control of knowledge. Richard Norgaard, in his book *Development Betrayed,* makes this link between development practice and the sociology of knowledge:

> Western and westernized societies — whether capitalist or socialist, democratic or authoritarian — increasingly sanctioned technocrats during the nineteenth and first half of the twentieth century to combine shared values, beliefs, and knowledge and act on behalf of the public. This authorization of agricultural scientists, engineers, foresters, planners, and eventually economists was rooted in a common vision of progress, and a common faith in how science and technology could accelerate development. The international discourse on sustainable development, however, challenges that common faith and vision of progress and challenges the shared assumptions, understandings, and rationalizations that evolved while experts reigned through progressive institutions.[9]

As Hoben suggests, and as Pretty and Chambers document in detail, new and more democratized approaches to the formulation of values, beliefs, and knowledge are essential to truly sustainable development. The situation is by no means hopeless, since despite the power of major "old model" institutions, there is extensive evidence of more creative and successful work within national and transnational organizations, in nongovernmental organizations, and at the community level. However, it is unlikely that these efforts will prevail without certain changes in the larger forces affecting local community development.

The development of a single global market system, apparently an inescapable reality at the threshold of the twenty-first century, must be moderated and balanced to take account of social and environmental factors. Multinational development agencies must restructure away from top-down, large-scale money-moving bureaucracies toward more decentralized, transparent, and democratized forms. National and local political forces, often oligarchical and corrupt, must be challenged by more democratic forces. Without progress in all these areas, sustainability will remain merely a catchphrase to be bandied about by institutions that continue to undermine social and ecological systems in the name of progress. The contributions to this volume suggest that real sustainability is a definable and achievable goal, but that much of the work is still before us.

NOTES

1. See, for example, Alan Durning's *How Much Is Enough? The Consumer Society and the Future of the Earth* (1992).

2. Joseph E. Stiglitz, "Economic Organization, Information, and Development," in Chenery and Srinivasan 1988.

3. Theories of endogenous growth are reviewed in Barro and Sala-i-Martin 1995.

4. A parallel that comes to mind here is the massive expropriation of the resources of the former Soviet Union, often by criminal organizations, under the rubric of "privatization."

5. The proceedings of a recent workshop held under the auspices of the Food and Agriculture Organization of the United Nations (FAO) and the Winrock International Institute for Agricultural Development (Breth 1996) document efforts by development professionals to grapple with sustainability issues, while remaining primarily within a standard development framework.

6. Many detailed case studies in sustainable development, with specific attention to the issues of democratic participation, are presented in Samad, Watanabe, and Kim 1995.

7. Detailed discussion of numerous specific examples of NGO/governmental cooperation on two continents are available in Wellard and Copestake 1993 and Farrington and Lewis 1993.

8. Jeffrey Sachs, Director of the Harvard Institute for International Development, suggests, for example, that "the frustrating record of tropical agriculture may mean that we should begin to accept as normal a situation in which Africa and other tropical regions are fed by temperate-zone exports, and in which the tropics earn their way in the world through manufacturing and service exports rather than primary commodity exports" (Sachs 1997).

9. Norgaard 1994.

REFERENCES

Barro, Robert J., and Xavier Sala-i-Martin, eds. 1995. *Economic Growth*. New York: McGraw-Hill.

Breth, Steven A., ed. 1996. *Integration of Sustainable Agriculture and Rural Development Issues in Agricultural Policy*. Morrilton, AR: Winrock International.

Chenery, Hollis, and T. N. Srinivasan. 1988. *Handbook of Development Economics*. Amsterdam: Elsevier Science Publishers.

Durning, Alan. 1992. *How Much Is Enough? The Consumer Society and the Future of the Earth*. New York: W. W. Norton.

Farrington, John, and David J. Lewis. 1993. *Non-Governmental Organizations and the State in Asia*. New York and London: Routledge.

James, Valentine Udoh. 1995. *Women and Sustainable Development in Africa*. Westport, CT: Praeger Publishers.

Norgaard, Richard B. 1994. *Development Betrayed: The End of Progress and a Coevolutionary Revisioning of the Future.* New York and London: Routledge.

Sachs, Jeffrey. 1997. The Limits of Convergence: Nature, Nurture, and Growth. *The Economist,* June 14–20, 1997.

Samad, Syed Abdus, Tatsuya Watanabe, and Seung-Jin Kim, eds. 1995. *People's Initiatives for Sustainable Development: Lessons of Experience.* Kuala Lumpur, Malaysia: Asian and Pacific Development Center.

Wellard, Kate, and James G. Copestake. 1993. *Non-Governmental Organizations and the State in Africa.* New York and London: Routledge.

CHAPTER 6

Stories People Tell: The Cultural Construction of Environmental Policy in Africa

Allan Hoben

Much has been written about culture and development. For the most part this rather inconclusive literature focuses on the culture or cultures of groups in the Third World. This essay, instead, is concerned with the culture of the First World. It is concerned with the ways Western images of nature and concepts of conservation have shaped the environmental policies of development agencies, African governments, and nongovernment organizations working in Africa. It argues that these policies often rest on historically grounded, culturally constructed paradigms that at once describe a problem and prescribe its solution. Whatever their origins, variants, and elaborations, these paradigms are rooted in a narrative, a story with a beginning, a middle, and an end, that tells us how things were in an earlier time when man lived in harmony with nature, how human agency has altered that harmony, and of the calamities that will plague man and nature if dramatic action is not taken soon. It is not surprising that the narratives remind us more or less explicitly of humanity's fall from Eden and are neo-Malthusian.

It is striking and discouraging that environmental policy narratives used in sub-Saharan Africa have often been wrong, misrepresenting environmental conditions and trends, the role of human agency in causing the trends, or both. This has been costly in many ways. It has contributed to a great waste of scarce development resources. It has failed to protect or conserve natural resources. It has fostered inappropriate investments and regulations and encouraged rent seeking by officials. It has exacerbated conflict between stakeholders over access to natural resources. In some cases, such as the imposition of state licensing systems and the creation of rangeland reserves, national parks, and state forests, it has enabled governments and elites to appropriate natural resources at the expense of the rural peoples whose livelihoods depend on them. Laws and regulations established in support of misconceived

151

environmental policies have, at times, reduced rural incomes, increased rural work loads, and criminalized rural producers by banning their indigenous farming practices. All of these problems are illustrated in the cases discussed in this essay.

Policy narratives have a number of distinctive characteristics. Whatever their origins in religion, myth, or Western scientific findings, they *emerge from and represent the views of articulate first world experts or first world domestic constituencies.* They are enhanced through the *incorporation of the donor nation's dominant symbols and ideologies,* as, for example, those associated with Christianity and expulsion from the Garden of Eden, or the deep-set notion that Africans are innately less creative and rational than white men. Frequently the narratives are grounded in the *real or imagined historical experience of Western donor nations.* This is illustrated in several cases discussed later. The American dust bowl experience informed the way experts viewed soil erosion in Kenya and the wider process of "desertification" in the Sahel, while successful American efforts to stop degradation in the western states through range management at the turn of the century became the explicit model for a series of range management schemes intended to stop what was conceptualized as the tragedy of the commons in Africa. Environmental policy narratives deployed in Africa are thus culturally constructed and reflect the hegemony of Western development ideas.

To the extent that a particular development narrative, with its associated assumptions, becomes influential in expert and donor communities' development discourse, it becomes actualized in specific development programs, projects, packages, and methodologies of data collection and analysis. Over time, development discourse thus comes to be exemplified by past programs and projects. Through the agency of these exemplars, known to professionals in the field, development discourse becomes not merely a set of beliefs or a theory, but a blueprint for action as well.[1] Elsewhere I have referred to these well-established cultural models of and for action as cultural paradigms (Hoben 1995). The cases presented next exemplify many aspects of this process. They concern land degradation in Kenya, desertification in the Sahel, and environmental reclamation in Ethiopia.

Cases

The following cases have been drawn from recent academic research and the author's experience.[2] They are not meant to be comprehensive, exhaustive, or necessarily representative. Instead, they have been purposely selected to illustrate the rich diversity of case material, much of which has yet to be explored, and the many facets of the problem that have yet to be satisfactorily understood.

Each case is unique in the way it played itself out. Yet the narratives associated with them have much in common. Following the seminal work of Blaikie (1985) it is useful for heuristic purposes to piece together the key elements underlying all of them.

> Before the coming of the white man, Africans practiced a subsistence economy in harmony with nature, based on shifting agriculture and herding. They did, however, suffer the effects of drought, pestilence and warfare, which limited their numbers. Under beneficent colonial rule Africans and their livestock multiplied. Soon human and animal populations began to exceed the carrying capacity of the land. This resulted in environmental degradation, including soil erosion, the deterioration of the range and deforestation. These changes, in turn, reduced the retention of water and rainfall, and increased the frequency of drought and famine. This downward spiral is accelerating, ending in human and environmental disaster unless appropriate actions are taken. These actions are primarily technical measures, such as terracing, bunding, closures and tree planting, and regulatory, such as enforced reduction in stocking levels. Both types of action require strong state intervention, as local people do not have the knowledge, organizational skill or will to take them on their own.

Case 1: Land Degradation in Machakos District, Kenya

One of the best-documented cases revealing how an environmental policy paradigm shaped the way planners perceived and dealt with an environmental problem comes from Machakos District in Kenya.[3]

Two things are striking about the case. One is that policymakers and experts persisted in their belief that the area was being degraded by poor farming techniques, overstocking, and increasing population pressure, in the face of clear evidence to the contrary. The second is that the successful conservation measures eventually adopted by local farmers were not those recommended by experts and were not financed by official credit programs.

Machakos District, inhabited by the Akamba people, lies in a semi-arid area of east central Kenya. Its highest hills, in the northwest, are 1,800 meters above sea level and have a mean rainfall of about 1,000 millimeters. In the southeastern lowlands, mean rainfall is only

500 millimeters. Throughout the district, rainfall is characterized by great interyear and interseasonal variation. Though some early travelers on caravan routes through the district gave "glowing reports" of its "wonderful grass" (Peberdy 1958, 2), colonial observers described it as degraded by the late 1920s. In 1927 the district commissioner wrote: "Since 1917 the reserve has become desiccated beyond knowledge" (English 1992). In 1929 another report claims: "A journey through the area east and south of Machakos reveals that over large stretches of hillsides vegetation has been almost wholly removed" (Cobb et al. 1929, cited in English 1992).

By 1931 the authorities thought a massive program was needed to recondition pastureland. Eighty hectares of steep, eroded land was treated with a variety of measures and closed to cattle as a demonstration to the Akamba of what could be achieved. In 1934 grazing was restricted and reclamation work undertaken with volunteer and prisoner labor. The Akamba, then as later, showed little enthusiasm for this effort, which earned them the reputation of being uninterested in farming.

In 1937 two studies were carried out to document the extent of soil erosion in Machakos. One reported:

> The Machakos Reserve is an appalling example of a large area of land which has been subject to uncoordinated and practically uncontrolled development by natives whose multiplication and the increase of whose stock has been permitted, free from the checks of war and largely from those of disease, under benevolent British rule.
>
> Every phase of misuse of land is vividly and poignantly displayed in this Reserve, the inhabitants of which are rapidly drifting to a state of hopeless and miserable poverty and their land to a parching desert of rocks, stones and sand. (Maher 1937)

The report added that "the greater part of the Reserve" had lost its topsoil and much of its subsoil as well. The causes of degradation in descending order of importance were found to be deforestation, overstocking, cultivation of slopes, overcultivation, ploughing (the plough was newly introduced), increases in the cultivated area, road drainage, and livestock damage. The other report by Barnes (1937, cited in English 1992), though more moderately written, came to similar conclusions. What neither report brings out is that the Akamba had been deprived of much of their former rangeland that surrounded their arbitrarily gazetted reserve. They had been prevented from grazing their livestock on land set aside for European farms in 1913 and banned from grazing on Crown lands in 1924.

In short, the environmental problems of Machakos in the late 1930s were seen as a classic example of the effects of population growth in a subsistence economy based on haphazard cultivation and overstocking, exacerbated by several unusually dry years. To combat these effects the colonial administration pressured the Akamba to build terraces and bunds to control runoff on cultivated land and to reduce stocking levels. There was great resistance to the latter, and it was not pursued with force. The construction of terracing gained momentum after World War II. The failure of these efforts to improve the environmental situation was attributed to unusual drought, the need for more funding and a greater effort, and a lack of Akamba interest. It also was seen to validate the underlying premise, that Akamba subsistence agriculture and over-population were the root cause of the problem.

By the 1950s it was clear, at least to the Akamba, that the narrow-based terraces designed to control runoff were useless. By then, however, a new type of wider "bench" terrace had been introduced by a Kamba who had traveled in Asia. The bench terrace improved the perco-lation of rain and raised production. It was adopted spontaneously, without significant government help or credit. By the late 1960s and 1970s it was almost universally adopted. In all, more than 200,000 hect-ares were terraced, representing a very large Akamba investment of labor and cash in improving their land resources.

From the 1950s onward, a process of agricultural innovation and growth accelerated. Improved maize was introduced, the use of the plough increased. Coffee and, later, new high-value vegetables were planted on the terraced land. Migrant labor, which had been exten-sive earlier in the century, slowed, and locally owned small enterprises were started by prosperous Akamba. Throughout this period Machakos's population grew at approximately 3 percent per annum, and the livestock population grew as well.

In spite of these signs of growing agricultural and economic prosper-ity, expert prophecies of environment degradation and collapse contin-ued. Projections in the 1950s, 1960s, and 1970s all foresaw a severe wood-fuel shortage. Yet this has not occurred. Indeed, there is more tree cover in the district today than there was in the 1930s or at any time since. In the mid-1970s the Consortium for International Development undertook a major study as part of the effort to understand and arrest arid-land problems in Kenya. After examining the evidence on eleven indicators, the study found that population pressure was causing a long-term process of deterioration in the physical and human condition of Machakos (Ber-nard 1978).

It is somewhat astonishing, in light of all earlier assessments, that a thorough interdisciplinary review and field study, carried out in 1990 and 1991 by Mary Tiffen, Michael Mortimore, and a team of seven faculty members of the University of Nairobi, found no evidence that Machakos has been undergoing a vicious circle of degradation (Tiffen and Mortimore 1994). The picture that emerges from this study contrasts with that of the environmental degradation paradigm in almost every respect. In the four decades between 1930 and 1990 population increased fivefold. The number of cattle and small ruminants each nearly doubled, though they declined in per capita terms. Agricultural output per capita (in terms of livestock, fruits and vegetables, cash crops, and food) is estimated to have risen more than two and one-half times, while agricultural output per kilometer was up more than sevenfold. Many households had off-farm income from remittances or nonfarm sources as well. The area cultivated has increased four or five times. Bush, scrub, and grazing land has been correspondingly reduced.

Over the same period, degradation, in the paradigm's colloquial sense, has been reduced. The rate of soil erosion on cropped land has been sharply reduced. The nutrient content of the soils of cropped fields is lower than that of land under natural vegetation, but their productive capacity has been raised, and there is no evidence that their composition is declining under current practices. Rangeland appears to have more woody species than previously, but it is not clear whether this is due to grazing practices or other factors, including the prohibition of annual burning, a reduction in the elephant population, and Akamba efforts to encourage tree growth. It cannot be shown that, even today, livestock densities have reached carrying capacity. There are far more trees than before, though there has been a change in the species composition, favoring species planted and used by Akamba. Photographs of the same sites taken in 1937 and 1991 reveal dramatic changes. Heavily grazed slopes with a few scattered areas of cultivation have been replaced by terraces supporting continuous cropping, widespread settlement and, in many cases, substantially more trees than before. What has happened illustrates Shepherd's observation that, as in many cases from other countries, "what has gone on is a process of improvement upon what nature gave in the first place. A tract of bush is turned into a farm with trees on it, through careful processes of selection and enrichment" (1989, 27).

Many factors, some of them unique to Machakos, contributed to its success story. The relative importance of these factors and likely future scenarios for the district and its people are subject to debate. Such issues are, however, beyond the scope of present analysis. The significance of the Machakos case for this discussion is that it shows how an environmental development paradigm, once set, can dominate experts' and policy-makers' views for decades, in the face of mounting evidence that it does not describe or account for what is happening on the ground. Today the paradigm is giving way, at least in leading development organizations like the World Bank and AID, to new paradigms in which sustainable agriculture is to be achieved by adopting a more participatory approach and building on local people's knowledge and self-interest. Whether this new paradigm will prove more productive and more flexible than the old one remains to be seen.

It may seem puzzling that the findings of so many competent experts appeared to support the degradation narrative. The literature suggests this intellectual sleight of hand was achieved in at least three ways. First, researchers, like more casual observers in the district, focused their attention only on those indicators that were significant in terms of the degradation paradigm and their scientific discipline. Thus, for example, they looked for natural species of trees but took little note of trees planted by the Akamba. Second, using the assumptions of the degradation paradigm uncritically, they interpreted the occurrence of an indicator to be evidence that it had been caused by the events described in the narrative. For example, an increase of woody species in the rangeland was taken as proof of overgrazing. Third, experts were commissioned to carry out their studies after an unusual series of dry years had alarmed government officials. The Consortium study was based on observations after six consecutive years of below-normal rainfall. More recent analysis of long-term rainfall patterns has revealed that there are several independent rain cycles in Machakos that together produce expectable, if not entirely predictable, runs of dry years. Projections based on observations made after a number of low rainfall years were inevitably pessimistic. Rainfall, not surprisingly, tended to improve in the years following the investigations, but this was written off by relieved officials as good luck.[4]

Case 2: The Rise and Decline of Desertification

The story of desertification exemplifies the power and endurance of an environmental narrative that caught the imagination of donors' domestic constituencies and suited the needs of donor agencies. It also shows how a narrative and its assumptions, once embedded in policy and organizational interests, can resist mounting scientific counterevidence and, ultimately, transform most of its content while retaining the utility of its evocative name. Finally, it illustrates the way the same narrative can be used by different stakeholders, in this instance donors and national governments, to pursue very different objectives. The schematic account that follows is based on the work of Jeremy Swift (1996) and my own experience while serving as the Senior Anthropologist for Policy in AID.

The desertification narrative, without the label, took shape in West Africa in the 1920s and 1930s in response to officials' concern with the apparent drying out of extensive areas in the French and, later, British West African colonies. The narrative was first clearly articulated in the writings of E. P. Stebbing, a forester from the Indian Forest Service who traveled from the coast forest zone across the savanna and onto the Sahara desert in 1934.

By 1938 he had systematized his ideas in writings that contained all of the key assertions and assumptions that still are found in writings on desertification today:

> In West Africa the process [of the advancing Sahara] owes its commencement to the system of farming the bush or degraded type of forest which covers much of the countryside, this system being a form of shifting cultivation. With an increasing population the same areas are refarmed at shorter intervals, with a consequent more rapid deterioration of the soil constituents, until a stage is reached when the soil is no longer sufficiently productive for agriculture.
>
> It may then be made over for stock raising. The grazing and browsing, accompanied by the universal practice of annually firing the countryside, reduces the quality, height and density and therefore the resisting power to sand penetration of the now much-degraded forest or bush, and the soil becomes covered with a sandy top, gradually increasing in depth. Once this stage has developed the rapidity in the degradation of the bush increases until it no longer affords sustenance to cattle; then the sheep disappear; and under the final exploitation by goat herds to feed their flocks the savannah succumbs and the desert has encroached and extended its boundaries. (Stebbing 1938, 12–13, cited in Swift 1996, 74–75)

To counter the encroachment of the desert, which he estimated to have been moving at the rate of one kilometer per year for the previous three centuries (Stebbing 1937, 24, cited in Swift 1996, 5), Stebbing recommended international cooperation in the creation of a continuous forest belt and the strengthening of central and local government power to regulate farming and ban unregulated burning.

Even before Stebbing had published the article quoted above, an Anglo-French commission of scientists, established at Stebbing's insistence, conducted research after an unusually wet season and set out a counternarrative. They refuted most of Stebbing's assertions and concluded that there was no evidence of climate change, but rather of periodic variation in rainfall, with vegetation suffering in dry years and regenerating most rapidly in wet years. Summing up the report, Dudley Stamp, an eminent Africanist geographer, concluded that what was being observed was the worldwide problem of local soil erosion, rather than a desert on the march.

Over the following decade, however, Stebbing's version of the narrative seems to have gained adherents in the French colonial forest service, perhaps because it legitimized their claims to greater authority over natural resources and people. In 1949 A. Aubreville, a French forester, first introduced the term *desertification* (cf. English 1992). Despite his participation with the commission, he now insisted that African farming and herding practices were almost entirely responsible for the destruction of the forest and savannah zones. Nevertheless, the two narratives, along with their entailed assumptions, assertions and recommendations, coexisted uneasily during the 1950s and 1960s, which saw above-average rainfall.

The Sahelian drought, which began in the late 1960s and reached its climax in 1973, precipitated a revival of interest in desertification. As is the case with other natural disasters, the crisis presented both a challenge and an opportunity for donors and African governments: a challenge because they needed to mobilize resources to alleviate human suffering and an opportunity because it enabled them to obtain the funding to initiate new programs and projects. To seize the opportunity, however, donors had to choose a narrative, preferably the same one adopted by the donor community as a whole. The more dramatic Stebbing version was selected by all major institutional actors.

Without being cynical, one can say that the drought could not have come at a better time for AID. The agency was still recovering from a threat to its funding, if not its existence, caused by the backlash against the Vietnam War and was trying to cope with a new congressional mandate that directed it to work with low-income rural people without an increase in its budget. The drought, which was vividly reported on television and in the press, created an opening for the agency to lobby Congress for additional funds. And this it did. I have described the agency's success in lobbying Congress, creating new bureaucratic structures, and, eventually, funding research and communication networks in the Sahelian region and elsewhere (Hoben 1998).

AID officials concerned with the Sahel were well aware of the debate over the nature and causes of changes in the Sahara-Sahel boundary.

Indeed, they commissioned a yearlong review of the evidence by prestigious MIT. Nevertheless, they aggressively adopted the desertification narrative and made it the centerpiece of their drive for congressional funding for a major new program for the Sahelian region. In 1972, well before the results of the MIT program were available, AID's Office of Science and Technology stated unequivocally, without citing sources, that

> measurable encroachment in the northern areas of [the Sahelian] countries has occurred and is continuing. While specific areal data are lacking, a rough estimate of magnitude of encroachment south of the Sahara is that about 150,000 square miles of arable land (*i.e.*, suitable for agriculture or intensive grazing) has been forfeited to the desert in the past 50 years. . . . Several studies of the Sahara have concluded that there has been a net advance in some places, along a 2,200 miles southern front, of as much as 30 miles a year. (AID 1972, 2–4, cited in Swift 1996, 77–78)

If the desertification narrative was useful for a time in AID's Africa Bureau, it become the centerpiece for the United Nations Environmental Program (UNEP), a new UN agency trying to define its distinctive role and a rationale for funding new programs. As it gained prominence in donors' development discourse, the narrative also justified the efforts of African governments to legitimate their claims to control over natural resources and the farmers and herders who used them.

Two studies carried out in the mid-1970s provided key elements in UNEP's desertification discourse. The first, commissioned by the Sudanese government, UNESCO, and UNEP, was a three-week survey combining aerial reconnaissance with a ground survey carried out by Hugh Lamprey. Using a number of indicators and comparative data from a 1958 survey, the study concluded that the southern edge of the Sahara had moved south 90 to 100 kilometers in seventeen years. This tentative finding was transformed into fact and fixed in desertification discourse as proof that the Sahara was moving south 6 kilometers a year along its entire southern edge. With the advantage of hindsight, it is interesting to note that far more intensive multiyear research carried out subsequently in the same region failed to verify any of Lamprey's observations (Helldén 1991, 379).

The other influential study was a book by Fouad N. Ibrahim based on his research in northern Darfur, Sudan. His work supported the conviction that the Sahara was advancing — 650,000 square kilometers in the past fifty years — and that "man is the real cause of this desertification" (Ibrahim 1984, 17, cited in Swift 1996, 79). The desertification narrative had been grounded in scientific data, located along the southern edge of the Sahara, and fixed, along with its images and rhetoric, in the discourse that was to dominate other views and evidence in UNEP for more than a decade.

International concern with desertification culminated in the United Nations Conference on Desertification (UNCOD) held in Nairobi in 1977. At the conference, for which four extensive state-of-the-art reviews of scientific knowledge had been commissioned, many scientists involved expressed uncertainty about the causes and the extent of desertification.[5] The final UNCOD report ignored these doubts and concluded that the problem of desertification was "more widely shared, and require[s] greater and longer term action than expected" (UNCOD 1977, 1). More than one-third of the earth's surface was natural desert and semidesert, another 10 percent was man-made desert, and another 19 percent was threatened by the increased intensity of inappropriate land use.

To combat the advance of desertification, UNCOD produced a Plan of Action to Combat Desertification, which was to be implemented by the year 2000. In addition to twenty-eight detailed recommendations, the plan proposed large-scale transnational projects that, among other things, would construct a Sahelian greenbelt 50 to 100 kilometers wide from the Atlantic to the Red Sea and a somewhat narrower northern greenbelt of similar length. UNEP was given the mandate to monitor progress on implementing the plan (Swift 1996, 80–81). UNSO was to be the key implementing agency, but aside from interagency squabbling over jurisdiction little came of the effort, and the major projects were never funded.

On the basis of a twenty-nine-page questionnaire sent to ninety-one countries, a new set of figures supporting the desertification narrative was issued by UNEP in 1984 (UNEP 1984). The report made no mention of the doubts and strong reservations of a panel of outside advisers asked to provide an overview of the data. The new figures, which further concretized the narrative and the urgency of the threat it described, passed into the Brundtland Commission report and from there into many other reports, with or without attribution. Though many dryland scientists never accepted it, the official UNEP position became part of the orthodox donor discourse on desertification.

UNEP was never able to obtain funding for the major projects envisaged by UNCOD. Nevertheless, the crisis scenario the agency promulgated and the narrative that supported it were used by some African governments to justify and intensify the *dirigiste* approach to rural development that was already being challenged. In the name of combating desertification they sought to legitimize their attempts to strengthen central governments' bureaucratic control over natural resources and over those who lived in the drylands. Pastoral nomads, in particular, were singled out, as their uncontrolled movements and actions were viewed as threats to state sovereignty and security.

Adherence to the dominant desertification narrative, with its confusion of *drought* (two or more years of well-below-average rainfall), *desiccation* (a more general process of drying out over a period of a decade or more, leading to changes that may be reversed over the long run), and *dryland degradation* (persistent decrease in the productivity of vegetation and soils, caused largely by inappropriate land use), has masked very real natural resource management problems and distracted donor and government attention from addressing them. During the following decade, the weight of evidence and scientific opinion eroded support for the desertification narrative and began to shift donors to the alternative, less drastic discourse that focused on specific, localized cases of man-made soil degradation.

By the time of the Earth Summit in Rio de Janeiro in 1992, much of the content of the desertification narrative had changed. Some of the old figures were still used, but human action was no longer seen as the sole cause. Climate variation was viewed as equally important, and solutions to land degradation were formulated in the more current discourse of poverty alleviation, environmental education, better incentives for farmers and herders, and community-based natural resource management.[6] Today the best available evidence suggests strongly that human activities have no impact at all on climate variation in the Sahel, all of the variation being accounted for by phenomena similar to El Niño in the North Atlantic. Yet it would be difficult to say that desertification had been entirely demythologized or depoliticized. Its emotive images and crisis scenario remained. And it was reinserted in the great North-South development debate as the industrial nations insisted on the primacy of global warming and the developing nations held out for the salience of desertification, which seemed more relevant to their situation and their prospects of obtaining development assistance. The international Convention to Combat Desertification signed in 1994 must be seen in this light. Summing up his analysis of what has changed and what has not, Jeremy Swift, himself a participant in the debates surrounding the rise and decline of the desertification narrative, remarks:

> There are few scientists or international administrators now who would defend the received narrative of desertification, although it lingers on in many government departments in dryland areas and

some development agencies, and is often raised as a critical issue in project formulation in dry areas. A simple idea, adorned with powerful slogans, proves remarkably hard to change, even when shown to be patently inaccurate. (Swift 1996, 85)

Case 3: Crash Environmental Reclamation Programs in Ethiopia

This case, which I have analyzed elsewhere in detail (Hoben 1995), illustrates the way the adoption of a common narrative can enable powerful organizations with divergent interests and values to overcome their differences, craft a common policy, and coordinate their activities when they are under pressure to act quickly. It also shows the damage that can be done in such situation if the dominance of the narrative overrides the need for adequate scientific research and the wishes and interests of local people.

In the aftermath of the drought and famine of 1985, Western donors and NGOs needed a narrative that would give them a rationale for justifying the continuation of food aid to Ethiopia, a blueprint for what to do with it, and a way of coordinating their program with the Ethiopian regime, for which they had little sympathy. Under these circumstances, an Ethiopianized version of the neo-Malthusian African narrative, the idea that the underlying cause of Ethiopia's periodic famines was environmental degradation due to population increase, poverty, and poor farming practices, had great appeal. It depoliticized the granting of assistance. It focused on environmental causes rather than many other factors that contributed to the famine. It suggested that food-for-work could be used to alleviate short-term food shortages while at the same time addressing the long-term root causes of food deficits. It suggested that it was plausible to address the food problem at the local level through the agency of nongovernmental organizations while largely bypassing Ethiopia's authoritarian and *dirigiste* regime.

Thus, in the wake of the 1985 famine, the donors and the Ethiopian government launched an ambitious program of environmental reclamation supported by donors and nongovernment organizations and backed by the largest food-for-work program in sub-Saharan Africa. Over the following five years, peasants constructed more than one million kilometers of soil and stone bunds on agricultural land and built almost one-half million kilometers of hillside terrace. They also closed off more than 80,000 hectares of hillside to most forms of use to foster the regeneration of naturally occurring plant species and planted 300,000 hectares of trees, much of it in community woodlots.

In retrospect, it is clear that much of this effort was wasted or counterproductive. The long- and short-term soil conservation benefits of the structures and trees are uncertain. The most rigorous research conducted to date shows that under most conditions terracing has lowered agricultural production, instead of raising it as had been anticipated (Herweg 1992). Farmers have been unwilling to construct or maintain structures without food for work or coercion, and many of the structures have fallen into disrepair. Most community woodlots have been harvested or destroyed. Hillside closures had mixed results. Where they were built best, they tended to reduce household income from livestock, to cause environmental damage by concentrating livestock on the remaining pasture, and to harbor wild animals and pests.

Many factors contributed to the reclamation program's poor performance. It was based on inadequate scientific and technical knowledge. It was implemented with a standardized approach and with little regard to regional or local agroecological conditions. The views and interests of the rural men and women it was intended to benefit were not solicited or heeded. Instead, implementation was top-down, authoritarian, and politicized. Peasant interest in investing in long-term environmental management, to the extent that it had existed, had been undermined by the government's program of agrarian reform. Above all, however, it was the ideational role of the environmental degradation narrative, its corollaries, and associated activities that made it possible for such a massive and misguided program to be carried out.

And what of the truth value of the narrative itself? How well does it explain the root causes of Ethiopian food deficits? There is little doubt that the population of Ethiopia is increasing at over 2.5 percent per year, that many Ethiopians are poor, hungry, and vulnerable to famine, and that soil erosion is a serious problem in many highland areas. What is in question is whether the neo-Malthusian environmental degradation paradigm provides an adequate framework for understanding the genesis of these phenomena, their causal interrelations, or what should be done to alleviate them. Elsewhere I have tried to show that there are major difficulties with the narrative and its supporting "data stories" (Hoben 1995). They misrepresent what has happened, often exaggerating the rate of degradation and the ways in which human activity is causing it. They preclude the examination of alternative hypotheses based on a careful investigation of Ethiopian data and the experience of other countries, and they inhibit scientific inquiry.

A new regime came to power in Ethiopia in 1991. Since then, a number of policy changes have been made at the national level. "Respect for indigenous knowledge" and "broadly based participation in development planning" have been incorporated into the national discourse on environmental management. Nevertheless, old attitudes die hard. At the regional and lower levels of administration, where environmental programs are controlled as a result of decentralization, the top-down community mobilization approach and its attendant narrative still prevail.

The Ethiopian famine of 1985 was in many ways unique. What lessons, then, can be drawn from this case study? The Ethiopian case suggests that the power of a development narrative varies with the context in which it is used. Generally, it is enhanced when: (1) donor experts and their domestic constituencies are strongly attached to such a narrative; (2) there is political, strategic, or moral pressure on donors to act quickly; (3) there has been little technical and socioeconomic research, and there is a weak data base on the problem in the recipient nation; (4) the recipient country must rely heavily on expatriate experts for advice; (5) the recipient government is dependent on foreign assistance; and (6) the recipient government, being weak or authoritarian or both, does not have the institutional capacity to hear and learn from its rural people.

Analysis

The cases presented above illustrate the way systems of ideas and images, narratives and paradigms come to play a central role in all aspects of policy and project-level decision making. They do this by structuring options, defining what are to be considered relevant data, and ruling out the consideration of alternative paradigms from the outset. These systems are robust, exercising great influence at the pre-attentive stage of choice, thus discouraging scientific research that can discredit them. They do this by defining the parameters of legitimate research methods and what is to be considered credible data in both first and third world research communities.[7] They are hard to challenge and slow to change, even in the face of mounting evidence that does not support them. In sum, they influence what is considered "reasonable" to think and say and do.

Policy narratives and their embedded assumptions are transferred to project implementation, training, institution-building, and investments. These activities also create interest groups, in donor and recipient nations alike, which become constituencies supporting the paradigm and making it politically and institutionally difficult to discard or replace.

Environmental policy discourse is also infused into African urban and rural national culture through formal education and media campaigns, which seek to associate it with national symbols and political figures. It permeates to local-level development discourse as community leaders learn what to say to get assistance, even if it is in stark contradiction to their experience and knowledge of local conditions (Leach and Mearns 1996, 25–28). Narratives thus become culturally, institutionally, and politically embedded in developing countries.

For all of these reasons, the influence and durability of a dominant development policy narrative is not necessarily related to its economic, social, or environmental consequences. The narrative and the resource flows associated with it become hard to challenge and may remain current in the aid-recipient nation, even if it loses its currency in the donor community.

All the problems associated with these processes are evident in a broad spectrum of cases. Each in its own way illustrates the force and tenacity of environmental narratives in African environmental policy. Among the best documented are range management, tropical deforestation, and the "wood-fuel shortage." A generation of pastoral livestock projects costing over $600,000,000 was predicated on the "tragedy of the commons" narrative, which combined the out-of-Eden emotive theme with Garrett Hardin's model of rational herders destroying common property (Hardin 1968). The narrative was powerful but incorrect. The projects failed to meet their ecological, economic, or social goals (cf. Bromley and Cernea 1989; Behnke and Scoones 1993; Hoben 1979; Roe 1991; Scoones 1996). Throughout the present century foresters and planners in the West African nation of Guinea have incorrectly attributed deforestation on the edge of the savanna to human activity when, in fact, local people have been causal agents of afforestation (Fairhead and Leach 1996). In eastern and southern Africa, numerous community woodlot projects were launched by donors and NGOs based on an incorrect narrative that portrayed deforestation as a direct result of villagers' inflexible need for a domestic fuel supply (Dewees 1989; Leach and Mearns 1988).

Summary and Conclusions

In this essay I have outlined the key elements of a framework for analyzing the way narratives and associated discourse influence environmental policy and practice in sub-Saharan Africa. It is a framework that attempts at once to examine the role of unconscious and semiconscious structures of thought in shaping the discourse; to analyze the many ways that development discourse is used by individuals and institutions to address perceived environmental problems, and to justify their actions in the pursuit of wealth, power, and prestige; and to understand the way reliance on narratives mediates the impact of environmental programs.

The framework raises a number of questions: Where do narratives and discourse come from? How are they grounded in the general culture and imagined history of their adherents? How do they incorporate and draw power from dominant symbols, myths, and images? Under what circumstances and through what processes do they become institutionalized in development organizations and discourse? How are they elaborated into recommendations for specific policies and projects? How are they transmitted? How do they attract constituencies in both the developed and the developing world? Why do they appeal to certain groups? How do they enable their adherents to explain their apparent failures? Why do some persist longer than others do? What kinds of strategies do competing interest groups use to establish the legitimacy and primacy of their discourse? How are they challenged, changed, and replaced, and what is the role of science and politics in these processes?

I have not addressed all of these questions. Rather, I have tried to make a beginning. Drawing upon the work of a group of Africanist historians, I first suggested that an earlier European image of "Africa as Eden" was transformed during the colonial period into one of Africa in crisis or "Paradise Lost." Then I tried to illustrate the ways that particular variants of this generalized narrative took shape, became institutionalized in specific contexts, and influenced the formulation and implementation of environmental policies in Kenya, the Sahel, and Ethiopia. In each case I suggested that the environmental policies discussed are not only based on incorrect assumptions but are counterproductive as well. They created negative incentives for sustainable natural resource management, caused hardships for rural people, or both.

The use of narratives and cultural paradigms in decision making is not peculiar to development planning. Indeed, it plays a fundamental role in all social action. In the most general terms, these narratives represent uniquely human symbolic condensations of past experience that enable people to respond appropriately to complex situations with which they have not had previous personal experience, since they at once classify and describe a situation and also prescribe or suggest what should be done about it. In addition to their puzzle-solving role, they have important social, communicative, politicoeconomic, and expressive-integrative functions, which are often not fully recognized by the actors. They are, to a greater or lesser extent, grounded in the general cultural beliefs — the values, logic, and symbolic forms — of their adherents and therefore provide intellectual, normative, and aesthetic coherence to decision-making processes. Because they are institutionally and culturally situated or embedded, those cultural paradigms that are central to the interests and activities of their adherents are not easily challenged, discarded, or replaced.

Simplifying narratives, discourse, and paradigms play an especially prominent role in development work. In part this is because they enable development agency, government, or NGO personnel working under severe information and time constraints to produce a steady supply of projects and programs that are consistent with current policy trends and funding availability (Hoben 1989; Tendler 1975). Development discourse simplifies and speeds up the process of program and project design. In part it is because development activities must make sense to donor personnel and constituencies, rather than to third world officials (let alone low-income intended recipients). This creates serious problems since, for many types of development assistance, there is virtually no "unfiltered" feedback from intended beneficiaries to first world constituencies or their elected representatives. For both of these reasons, development narratives and paradigms tend to dominate country- and site-specific information, transforming local landscapes and problems to fit general donor policy (Hoben 1980). For the same reasons, they follow periodic fads sweeping across development organizations. Environmental concerns, for example, penetrated AID, the World Bank, and other international donors only after they became widespread in the West.

The domination of imported narratives in development work is especially problematic in sub-Saharan Africa in relation to agroecological and environmental issues. There are several reasons for this. First, African governments tend to be "policy takers" because of their economic dependence on foreign assistance and the weakness of their research institutions. This is particularly true of environmental policy, which has seemed less pressing than many other issues to most regimes. Second, Western experts, and their African counterparts, have been trained to think in terms of models based on research in the temperate zones. Because of this, Africa's ecological and farming systems have been poorly understood by Western experts, leading them to make policies and recommendations that are technically, economically, and socially inappropriate. Third, negative stereotypes of rural people's skills and knowledge inherited from the colonial period still predominate among many African officials, as does a top-down approach to extension. For all of these reasons, policymakers have been reluctant to take seriously the views of rural people or to adopt a learning, error-embracing approach to policy implementation.

In the last analysis, what is the value of trying to understand the role of narratives in African environmental policy? I believe there are two answers to this question. The first is that only by understanding the powerful and problematic role of narratives, their embedded assumptions, and entailed development practice can environmental policy in Africa be improved. Understanding is, of course, only the beginning of change. Much remains to be done, but this is beyond the scope of this essay.

The second and more general answer is that this tentative and incomplete analysis demonstrates the usefulness of re-examining other development policies and processes in the same way. Including the "culture of the developers" in the analysis of what they do helps us understand what otherwise appears to be puzzling and irrational behavior that, in some instances, harms people and wastes development resources. It helps us to understand the extraordinary shifts and fads that have characterized donors' development policies in sub-Saharan Africa since independence.

NOTES

The research upon which this article is based was supported by a grant from the MacArthur Foundation to the Global Development and Environment Institute at Tufts University.

Portions of this article are reprinted from Allen Hoben, "The Role of Development Discourse in the Construction of Environmental Policy in Africa," in Marcussen and Arnfred, eds., *Concepts and Metaphors: Ideologies, Narratives, and Myths in Development Discourse* (Roskilde, Denmark: Roskilde University, 1998); and from Allan Hoben, "Paradigms and Politics: The Cultural Construction of Environmental Policy in Ethiopia," *World Development* 23 (6): 1007–22 (1995), with permission from Elsevier Science.

1. This point is illustrated in relation to the Agency for International Development's work in Africa in Hoben 1989.

2. Key works dealing with environmental narratives include Anderson and Grove 1987, Leach and Mearns 1996, and McCann 1999.

3. The most comprehensive treatment of the case is found in Tiffen et al. 1994.

4. In a similar vein, Katherine Homewood has shown how experts were misled in their careful studies of rangeland carrying capacity in Baringo District, Kenya (Homewood 1987, in Anderson and Grove 1987).

5. The report reflected a new consensus that desertification, to the extent it was occurring, preceded from gradually expanding patches rather than along a broad front. This view was accepted by UNEP and other agencies, but the image of the advancing Sahara continued to be evoked in development discourse.

6. See UN 1992, Agenda 21, chap. 12.

7. For examples of the way science can be influenced by received wisdom, see Fairhead and Leach 1996 and Stocking 1996.

REFERENCES

AID. 1972. *Desert Encroachment on Arable Lands: Significance, Causes, and Control*, 2–4. Washington, DC: USAID, Office of Science and Technology.

Anderson, David, and Richard Grove, eds. 1987. *Conservation in Africa: People, Policies and Practice.* Cambridge: Cambridge University Press.

Barnes, R. C. 1937. Report on the Ukamba Reserve, July 1937 — Memorandum on Soil Erosion, Ukamba Reserve KNA DC/MKS/10A/29/1, unpublished.

Behnke, R. H., and I. Scoones. 1993. Rethinking Range Ecology: Implications for Rangeland Management in East Africa. In R. H. Behnke, I. Scoones, and C. Kerven, eds., *Range Ecology at Disequilibrium,* 1–30. London: Overseas Development Institute.

Bernard, F. E. 1978. Population Pressure in Machakos and Kitui Districts. In *Consortium for International Development: Kenya Marginal/Semi-arid Lands Pre-investment Inventory: Human Resources and Social Characteristics.* Final Report: Machakos/Kitui/Embu-Baring/Kerio Valley, Report no. 6. Mimeo prepared for the Government of Kenya.

Blaikie, Piers. 1985. *The Political Economy of Soil Erosion in Developing Countries.* London: Longman.

Bromley, D. W., and M. M. Cernea. 1989. The Management of Common Property Resources: Some Conceptual and Operational Fallacies. World Bank Discussion Papers 57. Washington, DC: World Bank.

Dewees, Peter. 1989. The Woodfuel Crisis Reconsidered: Observations on the Dynamics of Abundance and Scarcity. *World Development* 17, no. 8: 1159–72.

English, John C. 1992. Land Resource Management in Machakos District, Kenya, 1930–1990. Draft. Washington, DC: World Bank, Policy and Research Division.

Fairhead, James, and Melissa Leach. 1996. *Misreading the African Landscape: Society and Ecology in a Forest-Savanna Mosaic.* Cambridge and New York: Cambridge University Press.

Hardin, G. 1968. The Tragedy of the Commons. *Science* 162:1243–48.

Helldén, U. 1991. Desertification: Time for an Assessment? *Ambio* 20, no. 8: 372–83.

Herweg, Karl. 1992. Major Constraints to Effective Soil Conservation. Experiences in Ethiopia. Paper presented to the Seventh International Soil Conservation Conference: People Protecting their Soil. ISCO, Sept. 27–30: Sidney, Australia.

Hoben, Allan. 1979. Lessons from a Critical Examination of Livestock Projects in Africa. Washington, DC: USAID, Working paper of the Studies Division, Office of Evaluation.

———. 1980. Agricultural Decision Making in Foreign Assistance: An Anthropological Analysis. In Peggy Barlett, ed., *Agricultural Decision Making: Anthropological Contributions to Rural Development*, 337–69. Orlando, FL: Academic Press.

———. 1989. USAID: Organizational and Institutional Issues and Effectiveness. In R. J. Berg and D. F. Gordon, eds., *Cooperation for International Development: The United States and the Third World in the 1990s*, 253–78. Boulder: Lynne Rienner.

———. 1995. Paradigms and Politics: The Cultural Construction of Environmental Policy in Africa. *World Development* 23, no. 6: 1007–22.

———. 1998. The Role of Development Discourse in the Construction of Environmental Policy in Africa. In Henrik Marcussen and Signe Arnfred, eds., *Concepts and Metaphors*. Occasional Paper no. 19. International Development Studies. Roskilde University, Roskilde, Denmark.

Homewood, Katherine, and W. A. Rodgers. 1987. Pastoralism, Conservation and the Overgrazing Controversy. In Anderson and Grove 1987.

Ibrahim, Fouad N. 1984. Ecological Imbalance in the Republic of the Sudan with Reference to Desertification in Darfur. Bayreuther Geowissenschaftliche Arbeiten 6. Bayreuth: Druckhaus Bayreuth Verlagsgesellschaft.

Leach, G., and Robin Mearns. 1988. *Beyond the Woodfuel Crisis: People, Land and Trees in Africa*. London: Earthscan Publications.

Leach, M., and R. Mearns, eds. 1996. *The Lie of the Land: Challenging Received Wisdom on the African Environment*. Oxford: The International African Institute, in association with James Currey, and Portsmouth, NH: Heinemann.

Maher, C. 1937. Soil Erosion and Land Utilisation in the Ukamba Reserve (Machakos). Report to the Department of Agriculture.

McCann, James C. 1999. *Green Land, Brown Land, Black Land*. Portsmouth, NH: Heinemann.

Peberdy, J. R. 1958. Machakos District Gazetteer. Kenya: Machakos District Office, Ministry of Agriculture.

Roe, Emory. 1991. "Development Narratives" or Making the Best of Blueprint Development. *World Development* 19, no. 4: 287–300.

Scoones, Ian. 1996. Politics, Polemics and Pasture in Southern Africa. In M. Leach and R. Mearns, eds., *The Lie of the Land: Challenging Received Wisdom on the African Environment*. Oxford: The International African Institute, in association with James Currey, and Portsmouth, NH: Heinemann.

Shepherd, G. 1989. Assessing Farmers' Tree Use and Tree-Planting Priorities. A

Report to Guide the ODA/Government of Kenya Embu-Meru-Isiolo Forestry Project. London: Overseas Development Institute.

Stebbing, E. P. 1937. *The Forests of West Africa and the Sahara: A Study of Modern Conditions*. London: Chambers.

———. 1938. The Man-Made Desert in Africa: Erosion and Drought. *Journal of the Royal African Society,* Supplement (January): 3–35.

Stocking, Michael. 1996. Soil Erosion: Breaking New Ground. In M. Leach and R. Mearns, eds., *The Lie of the Land: Challenging Received Wisdom on the African Environment*. Oxford: The International African Institute, in association with James Currey, and Portsmouth, NH: Heinemann.

Swift, Jeremy. 1996. Desertification: Narratives, Winners and Losers. In M. Leach and R. Mearns, eds., *The Lie of the Land: Challenging Received Wisdom on the African Environment*. Oxford: The International African Institute, in association with James Currey, and Portsmouth, NH: Heinemann.

Tendler, Judith. 1975. *Inside Foreign AID*. Baltimore: Johns Hopkins University Press.

Tiffen, M., M. Mortimore, and F. Gichuki. 1994. *More People, Less Erosion: Environmental Recovery in Kenya*. Chichester: Wiley.

UN. 1992. *Agenda 21: The United Nations Plan of Action from Rio*. New York: United Nations.

UNCOD. 1977. Round-Up, Plan of Action and Resolutions. UN Conference on Desertification, Nairobi, August 29–September 9. New York: United Nations.

UNEP. 1984. *General Assessment of Progress in the Implementation of the Plan of Action to Combat Desertification 1978–1984: Report of the Executive Director*. Governing Council, Twelfth Session, UNEP/GC.12/9. Nairobi: UN Environment Programme.

CHAPTER 7

Political Power and Environmental Sustainability in Agriculture

Robert L. Paarlberg

Environmental damage from agriculture is widespread, but the specific types of damage vary widely from country to country and between developing and industrialized nations. In developing nations, lands unsuited to sedentary farming are being cleared and plowed, and soil nutrients exhausted. Farmers and ranchers cut and burn trees, degrade watersheds, and allow rivers and dams to silt up. Irrigated land is becoming waterlogged or saline, and farmworkers are threatened with exposure to toxic pesticides while pest populations become more resistant. In the agriculture of industrialized nations, environmental problems include wetlands loss, farm chemical ground and surface water pollution, and overpumping of groundwater, as well as problems of pesticide residues and pest resistance. What explains the patterns of environmental damage in world agricultural systems?

The most frequently offered explanations for environmental damage in farming typically make no reference to political power. The source of the problem, we often hear, is either poverty, or population growth, or too much (or too little) use of science-based farm inputs, or a "market failure" caused by technical error in the construction of the institutions that govern the ownership or the pricing of resources. From the point of view of a scholar of political science, these various *nonpolitical* explanations for environmental damage in farming appear unsatisfactory. Uneven or unbalanced power relationships — between farmers and nonfarmers, between farmers and governments, and between big farmers and small farmers — are a more powerful explanation for the environmental problems that so often arise in agriculture. A review of some of the most prominent nonpolitical theories of resource degradation shows why they fall short of providing a convincing picture, and it focuses attention on the role of political power and institutions.

Poverty and Resource Degradation

When we consider actual agricultural cases, we find that most conventional explanations for environmental damage in farming are unsatisfactory. Poverty is not a convincing explanation, since so often the perpetrators of environmental damage in farming are rich rather than poor. In the Brazilian Amazon, some of the most environmentally damaging cattle ranching schemes of the past several decades were perpetrated not by poor subsistence farmers in search of land, but by wealthy corporate conglomerates speculating in land, or in search of tax breaks, government subsidies, and a shelter for their wealth against inflation (Branford and Glock 1985). In Saudi Arabia, deep-water aquifers are being mined and depleted to produce wheat, not by poor Bedouin nomads, but by wealthy and heavily subsidized oil sheikhs. In Mexico, large-scale commercial fruit and vegetable growers are overirrigating and jeopardizing the safety of farm workers by spraying too many dangerous chemicals.[1]

Furthermore, many poor farming communities do conserve resources under the right circumstances (see Jazairy et al. 1992). Hill farmers in some of the poorest countries in Africa have constructed elaborate terracing systems and have maintained those systems for hundreds of years. Poor farmers in Africa today are willing to plant slow-maturing perennial crops when given access to market-based price incentives along with the necessary credit structures. Poor pastoral communities, in traditional circumstances, have found ways to prevent overgrazing (Mink 1993).

The resource-protecting systems used by poor farmers can easily be destroyed or disrupted, however, because they usually depend on the health of traditional social institutions or distinctive and traditional patterns of local labor use. Powerful outside actors — such as colonial administrators, international companies, forestry department bureaucrats, megaproject engineers, centralized irrigation authorities, and government land-titling agencies — can undermine a farmer's secure sense of local control and hence the operation of many resource-conserving systems. Poverty alone is seldom the problem; in fact, sometimes it is poverty reduction that actually does the damage. When roads and commerce are first brought into remote rural areas, for example, or when male labor is drawn away from farms by lucrative new employment in urban areas, traditional systems of resource protection can quickly break down.[2]

Population Density and Population Growth Rates

Population density is also suspect as an all-purpose explanation for environmental damage from farming. Neither the Amazon nor the Saudi desert is densely populated. Nor is Africa densely populated, even though Africa is currently where the most devastating environmental damage from farming can be found — including deforestation, rangeland destruction, and soil nutrient depletion. Economists know that it is sometimes only when population density *increases* that land-protecting investments finally become profitable (Boserup 1981). Indeed, it is in some of the most densely populated parts of Africa that African farming is today most sustainable, in environmental terms.

In the close-settled zone of Kano in northern Nigeria, a semiarid region with poor soils and variable precipitation, a dense and rapidly growing local population — more than 500 people per square kilometer — supports itself with systems of farming based on high labor inputs. The area produces a diversified mix of high-value crops, partly for sale in nearby urban centers, with no evidence of declining outputs, decreased soil fertility, or recent erosion (Turner and Benjamin 1984; Mortimer 1989). In Kenya, farmers in the densely settled, semiarid Machakos district have avoided serious damage to their marginal soil endowments by making heavier land-protecting investments in terrace systems, by using improved seeds in combination with purchased fertilizer inputs, and by shifting more of their production from low-value to higher-value commodities, including horticultural crops (see the article by Hoben in this volume). A 1991 Overseas Development Institute study argued that this kind of intensification had helped reverse land degradation problems in Machakos.[3]

Furthermore, a sparse human population is no guarantee of resource protection. The sparsely populated Amazon basin is undergoing widespread deforestation followed by rapid degradation of pasture and cropland. In much of Africa, rural labor shortages frequently cause many traditional resource-conserving tasks — such as proper soil preparation, mulching, terrace maintenance, and weeding — to be left undone.

High population growth rates can be more damaging than high population densities. Slowly growing populations have time to innovate, and resource control systems will have time to evolve from open-access regimes toward more secure, common property systems and perhaps eventually toward individual private property systems. Such an evolution can protect resources in densely settled areas. When population grows rapidly, however, this desired evolution of institutions can be disrupted or even reversed. Well-functioning common property systems can break down under the sudden pressure of higher numbers — of people, animals, or both — and revert to damaging open-access systems.

Rapid population growth is not, however, the only source of such disruption. In South Asia since the 1950s, local common property systems have been broken not just by population growth but also by inequitable, state-sponsored land privatization schemes (Jodha 1991). In Africa, effective local control over land and trees has often been lost due to nationalization of property—a practice African governments originally learned from colonial administration—or due to government land-titling programs that function as patronage schemes to please urban elites by granting them cheap access to exploitable resources (Land Tenure Center 1990). In Latin America, indigenous resource management institutions never had a chance to evolve after the land seizures and the massive depopulation of indigenous peoples that followed European conquest; the indigenous population fell by roughly 75 percent between 1492 and 1650.

Input Use in Agriculture

Green Revolution farming—which increases crop yields by replacing bio-diverse fields of local crop varieties with laboratory-developed versions designed to rely more heavily on irrigation, inorganic fertilizer, and pesticides—is often blamed for environmental problems by advocates of sustainable agriculture.

In many industrial-country settings, as well as in some parts of the developing world, agricultural water and chemical use is damaging enough to validate this charge. Input use tends to be greatest where farmers receive the heaviest subsidies. Yet, in most of the developing world, agriculture is still taxed rather than subsidized, and consequently levels of input use—especially in Africa—are still too low rather than too high. Fertilizer use in Africa averages 12 kilograms per hectare—only one-fourth the average level in India and one-eighth that in the United States. Irrigation covers only 4 percent of cultivated area in sub-Saharan Africa compared to 26 percent in India and 44 percent in China. Africa's meager production gains in recent years have resulted not so much from boosting yields as from environmentally destructive practices, such as cutting more trees, grazing drier lands, and shortening fallow times to mine more nutrients out of the soil (Cleaver 1993).

Is it possible, then, to blame resource degradation on too *little* use of purchased inputs? Advocates of farm modernization often cite the success of the Green Revolution in India and in Machakos and propose similar intensification elsewhere to slow the environmentally damaging cultivation of still more fragile lands.

This approach can encounter serious social and institutional constraints. In Latin America, for example, land ownership is so badly distributed that farm modernization can malfunction and become an impediment to environmental protection. Particularly in Central America and Mexico, farm modernization has tended to benefit the few, harm the many, and damage the rural environment.[4]

When Central American countries built better roads and infrastructure after World War II, they were able to make a technical shift to higher-profit, input-dependent farming (Williams 1986). Maize and beans gave way to cotton, tomatoes, strawberries, and bananas. The value of farmland naturally increased, which benefited privileged landowning elites but led many poor farmers—who had previously been allowed to live and plant subsistence crops on land they did not own—to be promptly evicted.[5]

These farmers had no choice but to move on to drier lands, forests, hillsides, or lands with shallow and less fertile soils. Here, with insecure tenure, they had little means or incentive to conserve the soil or trees. The constant threat of being evicted a second time made them more inclined to farm in a destructive hit-and-run fashion. Political and social exclusion from the elite-dominated growers' associations that controlled marketing channels, as well as distance from the best roads, made it hard for poor farmers to participate in the lucrative export-oriented agricultural intensification that was under way in the region (Tucker 1992).

Dualistic land ownership structures can also cause Green Revolution farming to malfunction at the other end, among the more powerful and privileged commercial growers who adopt modern practices. These farmers use their influence to demand environmentally damaging input subsidies, which in turn lead them to overmechanize, overirrigate, and overspray.

This environmentally damaging exercise of power by larger commercial farmers is also visible in the industrializing countries of East Asia, where land ownership is typically not as imbalanced. Here, politically sophisticated and well-organized farmers use their influence to demand commodity price supports, trade protection, and generous input subsidies. Asia's Green Revolution, which helped relieve a first generation of environmental problems, such as soil erosion, tree cutting, and habitat destruction, has thus become associated with a second generation of environmental problems such as excess water and fertilizer use, inadequate nutrient and waste containment, and excessive reliance on pesticides. Technically, these are resource management problems that should not be inevitable with a switch to high-yield farming. Nevertheless, they are a predictable development because they are induced by the subsidies that commercial farmers usually gain the power to demand when societies undergo an industrial transformation.

Market Failures

When most Western-trained economists come to explain environmental damage from farming, they turn to a concept called *market failure*. Economists like to say that environmental damage comes from resources that are either unowned, unpriced, or underpriced, or from contracts that are unenforceable, or from excessive transaction costs, or from externalities that have not been internalized—problems that are often compounded by unwise government regulations and subsidies (Panayotou 1993). The remedies these experts recommend are familiar and technically valuable: creation of secure and transferable property rights; enforceable contracts; subsidy removal; use of market-based incentive policies rather than bureaucratic command-and-control regulations; and the adoption of "green" accounting methods that valuate natural resources, such as forests and soil, alongside man-made capital.

The drawback to this economistic approach is that it pulls attention away from power relations and real conflicts of interest. It implies that suboptimal economic and environmental outcomes are largely unintended and result from little more than technical oversight. This is naive. It is hardly due to a technical oversight that many small peasant farmers in Latin America lack secure property rights while commercial farmers are receiving fertilizer and pesticide subsidies. Nor is it for lack of accounting skills that a wasteful exploitation of public timber resources by politically favored concessionaires in Southeast Asia will be represented by governments as a gain to gross domestic product rather than as a loss. When wealthy industrialists gain access to generous subsidies and tax breaks as a reward for cutting trees and grazing cattle in the Amazon, this represents more than a technocratic market failure. It is a deliberate use of political power to seek and provide rents at the expense of the rest of society (Mahar 1989). It is not for lack of sound advice from international financial institutions that so many governments in Africa, dominated by urban elites, continue to underinvest in agricultural research, rural infrastructure, and farm extension services. Economists may construe this as a technical failure to provide public goods, but it is more easily understood as a conscious choice by self-interested urban elites who govern without adequate accountability to the countryside.

Governments do not mismanage resources by accident. In the Philippines, for instance, only 16.5 percent of potential logging rents were collected by the government between 1979 and 1982. This environmentally damaging public giveaway was not so much a public resource pricing failure as it was an example of the corrupt "crony capitalism" of the regime of President Ferdinand Marcos. In China, political authorities are pursuing the environmentally destructive Three Gorges Dam project, but not because they have failed to figure environmental costs into their calculations. Even using a more narrow commercial calculus, the $34.4 billion that the project is expected to cost is unlikely ever to be recovered through power generation or flood control. The failure is not one of cost accounting techniques, but of bureaucratic momentum and unchecked leadership pride (Qing 1994; Kahn 1994). Public resource mismanagement on this scale can be described as a market or policy failure, but it is better understood as a consequence of unaccountable government power.

Seeking to correct deeper political problems of power abuse with superficial technical remedies can be dangerous. In Africa, legitimate demands by the World Bank and the International Monetary Fund for public sector spending cuts have induced many African governments to cut capital spending for farm-to-market roads, while continuing to pay swollen wages to bureaucrats working in the capital city.[6] In Southeast Asia, good-faith efforts to use the courts to clarify the rights of local resource-users have at times resulted in a further dispossession of the rural poor because the courts themselves are biased against them (Arnold 1992). In India, when government authorities began to privatize well-functioning common property resource systems in the 1950s in the name of clarifying ownership and helping the poor, the traditional protection of pastures, forests, rivers, and village ponds collapsed and the poorest households received only one-third to one-half the amount of land given to more prosperous households (Jodha 1991). Mexico's technocratic decision to amend Article 27 of its constitution to permit private sale or rental of communal *ejido* lands may boost incentives to invest in resource protection; however, it could also trigger a mass exodus of labor from subsistence farming at a time when the rest of the economy may not be creating enough jobs (Martin 1993).

Although Mexico deserves credit for having embraced a bold series of market-oriented reforms since 1988 — including significant improvements in budget and monetary policy, subsidy removal, market deregulation, and free trade under the North American Free Trade Agreement (NAFTA) — the rural environmental effects are likely to be mixed. Subsidy removal reduces the incentive for Mexico's commercial farmers to overirrigate, overmechanize, overfertilize, and overspray in some areas, but pesticide-dependent agriculture in irrigated districts such as Sonora will nonetheless expand as sales of Mexico's winter vegetables to the United States will increase. Meanwhile, Mexico's financial privatization programs could disrupt rural credit relationships, forcing peasants into property foreclosures for lack of a means to repay debts.[7] If landlessness in rural Mexico increases as a result, soil and forest conservation will suffer.

Political Explanations for Agricultural Degradation

The plethora of examples previously cited should create a persuasive case that a good explanation for environmental damage in farming must be political from the start, grounded in the sometimes unbalanced power relationships that exist between farmers and governments, farmers and nonfarmers, and big and small farmers.

We know that such power relationships are of prime importance in the establishment of agricultural policies around the world. Economists and political scientists have been able to demonstrate that in highly industrialized countries where farmers are wealthy, educated, and *well organized politically* — for example, in western Europe — farming tends to be heavily subsidized, while in nonindustrial societies where farmers tend to be numerous but poor, poorly educated, and *poorly organized politically* — for example, in most of Africa — farming tends to be heavily taxed rather than heavily subsidized. Governments around the world, in order to stay in power themselves, must cater to those in their society who are powerful, rather than those who are weak, and in rich industrial countries farmers tend to be powerful, while in poor nonindustrial countries farmers tend to be weak. In Africa, for example, even though farming provides 80 percent of all employment, the farm sector gets less than 10 percent of public spending, and farm commodity prices tend to be kept artificially below world market prices, to the disadvantage of farmers and the advantage of government and industrial workers. Accordingly, it is a reasonable hypothesis that the political strength or weakness of farmers also tends to determine where and when environmental abuse from farming will take place, and perhaps even the kind of abuse that will tend to take place.

To explore this possibility, consider an inventory (table 7.1) of some of the most prominent forms of environmental abuse in agriculture, sorted out by who suffers the most from this abuse (farmers themselves, farmers and nonfarmers alike, or nonfarmers primarily) and also sorted by where these forms of damage are most visible (comparing western Europe where farmers are politically strong to sub-Saharan Africa where farmers are politically weak).

If the factual judgments made in table 7.1 are accurate, then an important pattern has been identified. Where farmers are politically weak (as in Africa) most environmental damage from farming is done on the farm, and to the primary disadvantage of farmers themselves. Where farmers are politically strong (as in western Europe), damage is being done by farmers, but it mostly shows up off-farm, and nonfarmers tend to suffer most from that damage. This is just what those who study power relations would expect to find. The weak (farmers in Africa) are forced into damaging farm practices from which they will suffer the most, while the strong (farmers in Europe) are permitted to engage in damaging practices that place burdens primarily on others.

Political Power Mechanisms in Agriculture

What are the mechanisms that drive these outcomes forward? The actual political power mechanisms that generate these outcomes are sometimes direct and obvious. In Africa, weak farmers who fear that they might lose access to land (which can easily be taken away in most African countries, by government land-management bureaucracies, irrigation ministries, or state-owned agribusiness firms) will have no incentive to make resource-protecting investments in the land (such as building terraces, mulching or carrying in nutrients, or planting trees). But these mechanisms are indirect as well. The levels of taxation or subsidy imposed by governments on their agricultural sectors (both in absolute terms and relative to other sectors) are powerful determinants of the kind of environmental damage

TABLE 7.1.   Environmental Damage from Agriculture

Damage Type	West Europe	Africa
1. Damage to interests of farmers primarily		
Soil erosion and nutrient depletion	no	yes
Overgrazing and desertification	no	yes
Waterlogging and salinization	no	yes (Egypt)
Watershed destruction, flooding, siltation	no	yes
Pesticide poisoning of farm workers	no	yes
2. Damage to both farmers and nonfarmers		
Forest loss	no	yes
Biodiversity loss	some	yes
3. Damage to interests of nonfarmers primarily		
Wetlands loss	yes	no
Farm chemical group and surface water pollution	yes	no
Air pollution	yes	no
Pesticide residues on food	yes	yes
Water shortages for urban and industrial use	yes	not yet

likely to be done. In regions such as western Europe, where farm production is heavily subsidized, farmers will have an artificial incentive to apply too many chemical inputs (such as fertilizers and pesticides), and so the risk of downstream surface and groundwater pollution from farming will increase. In regions such as Africa, where farm production is heavily taxed, farmers will have too little incentive to apply inputs, so soil nutrients will be depleted, and an excessively "extensive" model of farming will be employed, with damaging implications for protection of forests and fragile lands.

The political power of farmers even helps to explain the kinds of environmental protection schemes that governments will embrace once damage from farming starts to be noticed. In the United States, where (much as in western Europe) farmers tend to be well organized and politically powerful, environmental protection policies in the farm sector tend to rely, not surprisingly, more on subsidies than on penalties. Instead of following the usual "polluter pays" approach, U.S. policy in the agricultural sector has tended toward an opposing "pay the polluter" approach. Since 1985, under the Conservation Reserve Program (CRP), the U.S. government has been paying farmers to keep a portion of their more fragile crop lands (about 36 million acres in all) out of production. Farm lobbies in Congress designed the CRP as a voluntary program, knowing this would force the Department of Agriculture to offer generous inducements for participation. Without generous inducements, farmers would elect to continue collecting normal farm subsidies (deficiency payments) by keeping their land in production. In effect, the U.S. government then had to bid against itself, first offering farmers deficiency payment subsidies that encouraged production, then having to offer farmers even more lavish subsidies under the CRP so they would voluntarily take fragile land out of production. Rental payments consequently tend to be very generous, sometimes two or three times the local cash rental rate for land.

More recently, the U.S. government has tried to discourage groundwater pollution in U.S. agriculture by enacting, in 1990, a "water quality incentive program," which again uses cash inducements rather than penalties or regulations to pursue environmental objectives. The 1990 farm bill also contained an "environmental easement program" based on annual cash payments to farmers plus up to 100 percent cost sharing and an "integrated farm management program," which provided financial assistance to farmers to help them introduce state-of-the-art conservation practices. These programs have had positive effects on the environment, but they have been a costly approach to the problem. Yet where farm interests are so well organized and so powerful, this seems the only way to proceed.

Latin American Agriculture and the Case of Argentina

The distribution of political power in Latin American agriculture differs both from that in Africa and from that in western Europe and the United States. In Latin America as a whole, the structure of agriculture tends toward a pronounced dualism. Some farmers — especially the largest commercial farmers who typically own a disproportionate share of the best farming lands — may enjoy a strong measure of political access and influence. But a majority of farmers — especially small peasant farmers who seek to earn a living on dry and sloping lands, or by cutting down trees on the forest margins — tend to be politically weak. This dualistic coexistence of powerful and weak farmers side by side in Latin America can result in the coexistence of two completely different kinds of environmental damage from farming side by side. The small dryland or upland peasant farmers may behave much like politically weak African farmers: they will cut trees, allow soils to erode, and not add enough fertilizer. Meanwhile, larger commercial farmers in Latin America are sometimes politically powerful enough to get subsidies — especially subsidized credits to over-irrigate, overfertilize, and overspray — and they can end up doing environmental damage similar to the kind done by highly subsidized farmers in western Europe or the United States. In Mexico such a dualistic pattern of environmental damage has derived from an underlying dualistic pattern of farm structure and rural political organization.

Within Latin America, Argentina is quite a different case. Argentina does have a highly dualistic farm structure, with more than half of the land in the hands of a small minority of farmers who have holdings larger than 1,000 hectares each. Yet this minority of large-scale farmers in Argentina can be considered politically weak rather than politically powerful. In recent decades these large-scale Argentine farmers have been much less successful than large-scale commercial farmers elsewhere in Latin America (in Brazil, for example), in securing governmental production inducements, or income and credit subsidies. Between 1979 and 1989, the overall producer subsidy equivalent (PSE) in Brazil was roughly 20 percent (meaning that roughly 20 percent of the income of Brazil's farmers derived from government policy). This represented a modest level of subsidization relative to the 40 percent PSE noted in western Europe over this period, or the 60 percent PSE noted in Japan, but at least Brazilian farmers were being subsidized.

In Argentina, over this same 1979 through 1989 time period, the PSE was a *negative 40 percent* (Anderson 1992, table 2). In other words, Argentine farmers were not being subsidized by the government; they were being heavily taxed. Even large-scale Argentine farmers were being heavily taxed. This perhaps helps to account for the curious fact that in most recent years the dominant form of farming in the pampas — farming organized around large-scale capitalist firms with an exclusively rural income base — has been unprofitable (Solbrig 1997, 10).

What kinds of environmental damage should we expect to see from Argentine farmers that have been overtaxed rather than oversubsidized? We would expect, most of all, to see damage resulting from inadequate on-farm investments in soil nutrient replacement (fertilizers) or soil protection technologies (conservation tillage technologies, windbreaks).

Adequate investments in resource protection may have been unprofitable in the pampas for many reasons, not only because of a history of excessive Argentine taxes on farm production. Excessive subsidies on farm production in the United States and in the EU are also in part to blame. Consider the protectionist meat trade policies of the EU, which between 1962 and 1983 transformed the EU from a market that imported 13 percent of its beef and veal consumption into a market that actually became a net exporter of these meats. This meant a significant closing off of meat export opportunities for Argentina. This discouraged the beef production for which Argentina has always been so well suited and made it that much more difficult for Argentine farmers in the pampas to practice environmentally sound crop-livestock rotations. Or consider the grain export subsidy policies employed so lavishly by both the EU and the United States. When international commodity prices collapsed in the mid-1980s, these EU and U.S. export subsidies knocked prices even lower for exporters in Argentina. So if farmers in Argentina have in the past been denied the incentives they need to make resource-protecting investments, it is a problem for which authorities in the United States and the EU, not just authorities in Argentina, must be held accountable.

Power Imbalances and the Potential for Change

As these examples make clear, agricultural resource abuse reflects imbalances in political power, at both the national and international levels. It grows out of unbalanced power relationships among farmers, between farmers and nonfarmers, between farmers and their own governments, and between governments of different nations. Placing many of the earlier partial or more superficial explanations into this political framework provides a deeper level at which to understand them.

Farming communities with sufficient power to control their own resources are seldom prone to destructive practices. Dangers arise when privileged rural elites or nonaccountable governments either take away or threaten to take away local control. Incentives to conserve resources then disappear. As Alan Durning has argued, "access to a resource without control over it is calamitous. Nothing incites people to deplete forests, soils, or water supplies faster than the fear that they will soon lose access to them" (1989, 41). Nonaccountable government agencies — such as forestry departments, centralized irrigation bureaucracies, and parastatal marketing boards — often constitute the greatest single threat to secure local control by ordinary farmers.

Power imbalance also explains the environmental damage being done by wealthy commercial farmers and agribusinesses, both in the developing world and in industrialized nations. These producers, situated at the other end of the political spectrum, are powerful enough to demand trade protection and subsidies that encourage excessive or distorted input use. In developing nations, the resulting downstream chemical pollution and groundwater depletion will mostly harm the rural poor, who will not have enough political or social influence to hold the large growers accountable. Only when politically influential urban communities or consumers in rich nations start to become harmed by these effects will commercial farmers be placed under environmental discipline.

Democratization might seem the answer to problems of maldistribution and nonaccountable power, but the superficial procedures of democracy are sometimes no solution at all to environmental and social justice problems in rural areas. In the developing world, democratization has often been a political movement initiated and dominated by the urban middle class. When democracy does spread to rural areas under these circumstances, traditional elites find vote counts easy to control or manipulate, and so their own position of dominance can go unchallenged (Fox 1994). Traditional rural elites in such countries as Brazil, the Philippines, and Mexico have at times used superficially democratic procedures to consolidate and extend their power. Technocratic political reforms can therefore be just as unsatisfying as the technocratic economic reforms discussed above.

Fundamental political and social change in rural areas should be the goal. New and less abusive power relationships must evolve between the landed and the landless, between indigenous and nonindigenous peoples, and between citizens and governments. Ordinary peasant farmers need to gain control over the resource base on which they and their children depend.

Linking environmental protection to power relations is nothing new. In the agricultural sector, this linkage has been acknowledged by a full range of conventionally technocratic institutions, including the World

Bank (1922), the Food and Agriculture Organization of the United Nations (1991), the World Resources Institute (1992), and the United Nations Conference on Environment and Development (1992). It is nonetheless a daunting conclusion to reach because it implies a need for real political change — not just policy change or technical change — to win the looming battle of producing sufficient food at an acceptable cost to the natural environment.

NOTES

This article incorporates portions of an earlier article, "The Politics of Agricultural Resource Abuse," which appeared in *Environment* 36, no. 8 (1994).

1. In the Culiacan Valley, tomato growers have sprayed insecticides on their crops as often as twenty-five to fifty times per growing season. See Wright 1990.

2. A recent case is the rapid degeneration of Yemen's terracing systems (the "hanging gardens of Arabia") following the emigration of the labor necessary for terrace maintenance to the oil-rich Persian Gulf states. See Srivasta and Alderman 1993.

3. Overseas Development Institute 1991; see also English et al. 1994.

4. Even in Mexico, which prides itself on having accomplished land reform, the top quintile of landholders still controls 77 percent of all land. In the Dominican Republic, the top quintile controls 89 percent; in Guatemala, the figure is 90 percent. See Jazairy et al. 1992, table 10.

5. As many as 3 million people in Central America today — roughly one-fifth of all rural inhabitants — have recently been displaced by such commercial evictions, political intimidation, or war. See Annis et al. 1992.

6. The gains promised to agriculture from structural adjustment in Africa have been elusive in part because of how little adjustment has actually taken place. After a decade of trying to coax policy reforms out of urban-biased governments in Africa, the World Bank reported in 1994 that only 17 of 29 countries surveyed had reduced tax burdens on farming, while some had actually increased those burdens, and only 4 of these 29 countries had eliminated parastatal marketing boards for major export crops (World Bank 1994).

7. According to an analysis prepared by the U.S. embassy in Mexico City in 1994, the shift to private lending had already had "abrupt and socially catastrophic" consequences in rural Mexico and had triggered protests in fourteen of Mexico's thirty-one states ("Excerpt from U.S. Cable on Mexican Agriculture," *Inside NAFTA,* 1994).

REFERENCES

Annis, S., et al. 1992. *Poverty, Natural Resources, and Public Policy in Latin America.* New Brunswick, NJ: Transaction Publishers.

Arnold, J. E. M. 1992. Policy Issues Related to the Role of Trees in Rural Income and Welfare Security. In H. Gregersen, P. Oram, and J. Spears, eds., *Priorities for Forestry and Agroforestry Policy Research: Report of an International Workshop*. Washington, DC: IFPRI.

Boserup, E. 1965. *Conditions of Agricultural Growth*. London: Allen and Unwin.

————. 1981. *Population and Technology*. Chicago: University of Chicago Press.

Branford, S., and O. Glock. 1985. *The Last Frontier: Fighting over Land in the Amazon*. London: Zed Books.

Cleaver, K. M. 1993. A Strategy to Develop Agriculture in Sub-Saharan Africa and a Focus for the World Bank. Africa Technical Department Paper no. 203, 27. Washington, DC: World Bank.

Durning, A. B. 1989. Poverty and the Environment: Reversing the Downward Spiral. Worldwatch Paper no. 92 (November): 41. Washington, DC: Worldwatch Institute.

English, J., M. Tiffen, and M. Mortimore. 1994. *Land Resource Management in Machakos District, Kenya, 1930–1990*. Environment Paper no. 5. Washington, DC: World Bank.

Excerpt from U.S. Cable on Mexican Agriculture. 1994. *Inside NAFTA* 1, no. 8 (April 20): 17–18.

Food and Agriculture Organization of the United Nations. 1991. *Elements for Strategies and Agenda for Action*, 11. Draft Proposal. Rome.

Fox, J. 1994. The Difficult Transition from Clientelism to Citizenship: Lessons from Mexico. *World Politics* 46 (January): 151–84.

Jazairy, I., M. Alamgir, and T. Panuccio. 1992. *The State of World Rural Poverty: An Inquiry into Its Causes and Consequences*, 24. New York: New York University Press.

Jodha, N. S. 1991. Rural Common Property Resources: A Growing Crisis. Gatekeeper Series no. 24. London: International Institute for Environment and Development.

Kahn, J. 1994. Despite Vast Obstacles, Chinese Move to Tap Power of Historic River. *Wall Street Journal*, April 18, 1.

Land Tenure Center. 1990. *Security of Tenure in Africa: A Presentation to the Agency for International Development*. Madison, WI.

Mahar, D. J. 1989. *Government Policies and Deforestation in Brazil's Amazon Region*. Washington, DC: World Bank, World Wildlife Fund, and Conservation Foundation.

Martin, P. L. 1993. *Trade and Migration: NAFTA and Agriculture* (October), 108. Washington, DC: Institute for International Economics.

Mink, S. D. 1993. *Poverty, Population, and the Environment*. Discussion Paper no. 189. Washington, DC: World Bank.

Mortimore, M. 1989. *Adapting to Drought: Farmers, Famines and Desertification in West Africa*. Cambridge: Cambridge University Press.

Overseas Development Institute. 1991. *Environmental Change and Dryland Management in Machakos District, Kenya: 1930–90*. Working Paper no. 56, 38. London.

Panayotou, T. 1993. *Green Markets: The Economics of Sustainable Develop-*

ment. San Francisco: ICS Press for Harvard Institute for International Development and the International Center for Economic Growth.

Qing, D. 1994. *Yangtze! Yangtze!,* trans. N. Liu, W. Mei, S. Youngeng, and Z. Xiaogang, ed. P. Adams and J. Thibodeau, 155–62. London: Earthscan.

Repetto, R. 1992. Earth in the Balance Sheet: Incorporating Natural Resources in National Income Accounts. *Environment* (September): 12.

Srivastava, J. P., and H. Alderman, eds. 1993. *Agriculture and Environmental Challenges: Proceedings of the Thirteenth Agricultural Sector Symposium,* 25. Washington, DC: World Bank.

Tucker, S. K. 1992. Equity and the Environment in the Production of Nontraditional Agricultural Exports. In Annis et al. 1992.

Turner II, B. L., and P. A. Benjamin. 1994. Fragile Lands: Identification and Use for Agriculture. In V. W. Ruttan, ed., *Agriculture, Environment, and Health: Sustainable Development in the Twenty-first Century,* 104–45. Minneapolis: University of Minnesota Press.

United Nations Conference on Environment and Development. 1992. *The Global Partnership for Environment and Development: A Guide to Agenda 21* (April), 99. Geneva.

Williams, R. G. 1986. *Export Agriculture and the Crisis in Central America.* Chapel Hill: University of North Carolina Press.

World Bank. 1992. *World Development Report 1992: Development and the Environment,* 143. New York: Oxford University Press.

———. 1994. *Adjustment in Africa: Reforms, Results, and the Road Ahead,* 1–2, 47, 76–88. New York: Oxford University Press.

World Resources Institute. 1991. *Accounts Overdue: Natural Resources Depreciation in Costa Rica* (December). Washington, DC.

———. 1992. *World Resources 1992–93: Toward Sustainable Development,* 33–34. New York: Oxford University Press.

Wright, A. 1990. *The Death of Ramon Gonzales: The Modern Agricultural Dilemma.* Austin: University of Texas Press.

CHAPTER 8

Toward a Learning Paradigm: New Professionalism and Institutions for Agriculture

Jules N. Pretty and Robert Chambers

The Context of Change

The 1987 Farmer First workshop marked the growing strength of a new worldview in agriculture: put farmers' needs and views first, and the potential for growth and regeneration in complex, diverse, and risk-prone areas is far greater than previously supposed. To do this on a large scale, though, was to require great changes in professionals and the institutions in which they work.

The transfer-of-technology approach for agricultural research and extension that has served for industrial and Green Revolution agriculture has been recognized to fit poorly many of the conditions and needs of complex, diverse, and risk-prone agriculture. In the transfer-of-technology paradigm, research decisions are made by scientists, and technology is developed on research stations and in laboratories, then handed over to extension to pass on to farmers. In the alternative paradigm, farmers' needs and priorities are put first, and farmers participate in research and extension. When this is done, the potential of the "resource-poor" becomes greater than previously supposed. But achieving real participation, putting farmers' priorities first, facilitating their analysis, and supporting their experimentation, requires changes that are personal, professional, and institutional.

A new and complementary paradigm for agricultural research, development, and extension has emerged both from a recognition of the failures of current approaches and from advances in other domains. The dominant positivist and modernist frameworks have singularly failed to help poor people and reduce inequity. Reductionist science and transfer of technology remain strong in controlled, predictable, and simplified conditions, and at the microscopic level; but their limitations are now clearer. They have missed local complexity; determinist causality has failed to account for uncertainties, variability, and the adaptive performances of farmers; technologies successful in one context have been applied irrespective of context, with widespread failure; and professionals and institutions have engaged in self-deception as a defense against having to learn the lessons of failure (Kuhn 1962; Lincoln and GABA 1985; Chambers 1997; Chambers et al. 1989; Harvey 1989; Russell and Ison 1991; Pretty 1995a, 1998).

In parallel, advances in a wide range of disciplines and fields of investigation are providing insights for an emerging learning paradigm.[1] Together, these insights challenge assumptions underlying modernization and rationalist thought. They have several themes at their core, namely:

- the affirmation of individuals and their differences, and the necessary coexistence with these multiple perspectives;
- a pluralist stance giving voice to individuals and groups so as to participate in decision making;
- knowledge and associated technology are seen as contextual in time and space, and so limited in their transferability, while ways of learning have wider validity;
- the future is recognized as uncertain and indeterminate, with a sensitive dependence on current and contextual conditions.

These paradigmatic themes underpin and resonate with farmer-first and participatory approaches. Expressed in practical terms, the components of this new paradigm imply a new professionalism and new institutional settings. The core challenge is how best to proceed in a context of uncertainty, indeterminacy, diversity, mutual causality, increasing complexity, and often accelerating change.

Changing Phases in Agricultural Research, Extension, and Development

Robert Rhoades's (1989) historical review of forty years of agricultural research and development helps to clarify the nature of the challenge. He characterizes four overlapping periods of steadily shifting emphases: the *production stage* (roughly 1950–75); the *economic stage* (roughly 1975–85); the *ecological stage* (roughly 1985–95); and the *institutional stage* (roughly from 1995 onwards). Even though each wave of enthusiasm for a new approach has grown out of antecedents, there has been a tendency for those who pioneer and embrace each new direction to play down the accomplishments of earlier approaches, and so the "old" always argues that the "new" is not so new ("we were doing it all along") while the "new" fiercely defends what it perceives to be the wave of the future (Rhoades 1989). This distracts from the new potential, as these four stages are, of course, not mutually exclusive and should be seen as overlapping dimensions of a single interdisciplinary whole.

Any vision for a future institutional phase will best be grounded in experience. Two domains of recent innovation are relevant: new learning environments and participatory approaches and methods. These in turn imply new institutional settings for much agricultural research and development in order to support a new professionalism.

New Learning Approaches and Environments

The central concept of the new paradigm is that it enshrines new ways of learning about the world. Teaching and learning, though, are not the same thing. Learning does not necessarily result from teaching. Teaching implies the transfer of knowledge from someone who knows to someone who does not know. Teaching is the normal mode in curricula; it underpins the transfer-of-technology model of research; and it is central to many organizational structures (Ison 1990). Universities and agricultural institutes reinforce the teaching paradigm by giving the impression that they are custodians of knowledge that can be dispensed or given (usually by lecture) to a recipient (a student).

Teaching can impede learning. Gibbs (1981) commented that the "preoccupation with teaching . . . actually constrained the effectiveness of higher education and limited its abilities to meet society's demands. . . . We might say that we are now beginning to perceive that the purpose of education is learning. And we are beginning to realise that frequently teaching interferes with learning." Professionals who are to work with local complexity, diversity, and uncertainty need to engage in sensitive learning about the particular conditions of rapid change. Where teaching does not include a focus on self-development and enhancing the ability to learn, "teaching threatens sustainable agriculture" (Ison 1990).

A move from a teaching to a learning style has profound implications. Everyone involved in agriculture, including farmers, trainers, educators, researchers, extensionists, and administrators becomes important, as do their interactions. The focus is then less on what we learn, and more on how we learn. Institutions will need to provide creative learning environments, conditions in which learning can take place through experience, through open and equal interactions, and through personal exploration and experimentation. The pedagogic goals become self-strengthening for people and groups through self-learning and self-teaching. Russell and Ison (1991) have distinguished between first-order R&D and second-order R&D, in which "the role and action of the researcher is very much a part of the interactions being studied." Responsibility then replaces objectivity as an ethic, and perception and action are based on the individual's experiential world.

Types of Participation

The many ways that development organizations interpret and use the term *participation* can be resolved into seven clear types. These range from passive participation, where people act out predetermined roles, to self-mobilization, where people take initiatives largely independent of external institutions (table 8.1). This typology suggests that the term participation should not be accepted without appropriate clarification.

TABLE 8.1.   A Typology of Participation

Typology	Characteristics of Each Type
1. Passive Participation	People participate by being told what has been decided or has already happened. Information being shared belongs only to external professionals.
2. Participation by Consultation	People participate by being consulted or by answering questions. Process does not concede any share in decision-making and professionals are under no obligation to take on board people's views.
3. Bought Participation	People participate in return for food, cash, or other material incentives. Local people have no stake in prolonging technologies or practices when the incentives end.
4. Functional Participation	Participation is seen by external agencies as a means to achieve their goals, especially reduced costs. People participate by forming groups to meet predetermined objectives.
5. Interactive Participation	People participate in joint analysis, development of action plans and formation or strengthening of local groups or institutions. Learning methodologies are used to seek multiple perspectives, and groups determine how available resources are used.
6. Self-Mobilization and Connectedness	People participate by taking initiatives independently to change systems. They develop contacts with external institutions for resources and technical advice they need, but retain control over how resources are used.

Source: adapted from Pretty 1995b.

The problem with participation as used in types 1 to 3 is that any achievements are likely to have no positive lasting effect on people's lives. The term participation can be used, knowing it will not lead to action. Types 4 through 6, by contrast, involve building of social and human capital. Great care must, therefore, be taken in both using and interpreting the term participation. The term should always be qualified by reference to the type of participation, as some types will threaten rather than support the goals of community regeneration. It is important for institutions and individuals to define better ways of shifting from the more passive, consultative, and incentive-driven participation towards the interactive end of the spectrum. This can partly be done by adopting one or more of the more than fifty different systems of social learning and deliberative democracy that have emerged in recent years.[2]

These new approaches and methods imply shifts of initiatives, responsibility, and action downward in hierarchies, especially to farmers and rural people themselves. Earlier investigations which were extractive, with researchers collecting data and taking it away for processing, are increasingly superseded by investigation and analysis by farmers themselves, who share their knowledge and insights with outsiders.

Methods such as participatory mapping, analysis of aerial photographs, matrix scoring and ranking, flow and linkage diagramming, seasonal analysis, and trend diagramming are not just the information of outsiders, but for farmers' own analysis. They are, in effect, conducting their own farming systems research (Chambers 1992a). Farmers' groups have come into prominence, as more and more design and conduct their own trials and evaluations (Ashby et al. 1989; Heinrich et al. 1991). Farmers using these methods have shown a greater capacity to observe, diagram, and analyze than most outsiders have expected and are also proving good facilitators for other farmers (Shah 1999). Participatory approaches and methods have proved increasingly popular and powerful and are taking different forms in different places.

New Institutional Settings

Many current agricultural institutions, whether universities, research organizations, or extension agencies, are characterized by restrictive bureaucracy. They have centralized hierarchical authority, specialized disciplinary departments, standardized procedures, and uniform packaged outputs provided in a mode of supply-push to farmers. Personal promotion and institutional survival depend less on external achievement, such as farmers adopting the products of research, and more on internal criteria, such as performance according to professional norms and bureaucratic public relations with funding sources. Such institutions are stable partly through self-deception: they are sustained by modes of learning that present misleading feedback from the peripheries, giving falsely favorable impressions of the impact of their packages and programs.

Institutions that respond better to open learning environments and participatory methods must be decentralized and heterarchical, with an open multidisciplinarity, flexible teams, and heterogeneous outputs responding to demand-pull from farmers. In these conditions, personal promotion and institutional survival should depend more on external achievement, such as responding to farmers' diverse expressed needs. The new institutions will be learning organizations (Senge 1990), with realistic and rapid feedback flows for adaptive responses to change. Multiple realities will be understood through multiple linkages and alliances, with continuous dialogue and participation (table 8.2).

Old and New Professionalism

The new roles of farmers, the new participatory approaches and methods, and the new learning environments all imply new roles for agricul-

TABLE 8.2. Comparison between Old and New Institutional Settings

	From the Old Institutional Setting	To the New Institutional Setting
Mode of decision making	Centralized and standardized	Decentralized and adapted to context
Mode of planning and delivery of technologies or services	Static design, fixed packages, supply-push	Evolving design, wide choice, demand-pull
Response to external change	Collect more data before acting	Act immediately and monitor consequences
Mode of field learning	Field learning by rural development tourism and questionnaire surveys; error concealed or ignored	Learning by dialogue and participatory inquiry and methods; error embraced
How those in institutions learn (especially at the top)	Self-deceiving; misleading feedback from peripheries give falsely favorable impressions of impact	Learning through feedback and feedforward; for adaptive and iterative processes
Linkages and alliances	Institutions work in isolation	Institutions linked formally and informally to each other

tural scientists and extensionists. Scientists must and will continue their normal science, in laboratories and on research stations, in support. But in addition, through these participatory means they are now better able to learn from and with farmers, and so to serve diverse and complex conditions and farming systems, as well as to enable farmers to learn for themselves. The new roles for outsider professionals include convenor for groups; catalyst and consultant to stimulate, support, and advise; facilitator of farmers' own analysis; searcher and supplier for materials, principles, and practices for farmers to try; and travel agent and tour operator to enable farmers to learn laterally from each other (Chambers 1992a, 1993; Pretty 1995b). These new roles require a new professionalism with new concepts, values, methods, and behavior.

To characterize an old and a new professionalism is to risk polarized caricature between the bad and the good. A distinction is needed here between the strengths of traditional science as bodies of knowledge, principles, and methods, and the weaknesses of the beliefs, behavior, and attitudes that often go with it. It is mainly the beliefs, behavior, and attitudes that present problems and opportunities, and that the new professionalism seeks to change.

The contrasts stand out. Typically, old professionals are single-disciplinary, work largely or only on research stations, are insensitive to diversity of context, and are concerned with themselves generating and transferring technologies. Their beliefs about farmers' conditions and priorities often differ from farmers' own views. The new professionals, in contrast, are either multidisciplinary or work closely with other disciplines, are not intimidated by the complexities of close dialogue with farmers and rural people, and are continually aware of the context of inquiry and development (see table 8.3).

A Vision for the Future

This vision for the future, in which the new professionalism becomes the norm in new institutional structures and partnerships, has already been achieved in certain places. There are, for example, an increasing number of well understood environmental and economic successes in complex, diverse, and risk-prone areas, where agricultural regeneration has been achieved. Local groups supported by new professionals (in state organizations and NGOs) working in enabling institutions have increased yields, reduced environmental impacts, built capacities and resilience, and reduced dependencies. The major challenge for institutionalizing the Farmer First vision is to point to the ways of scaling up these successes.

TABLE 8.3. Changing Professionalism from the Old to the New

	From the Old Professionalism	To the New Professionalism
Assumptions about reality	Assumption of singular, tangible reality	Assumption of multiple realities that are socially constructed
Scientific method	Scientific method is reductionist and positivist; complex world split into independent variables and cause-effect relationships; researchers' categories and perceptions are central	Scientific method holistic and postpositivist; local categories and perceptions are central; subject-object and method-data distinctions are blurred
Strategy and context of inquiry	Investigators know what they want; prespecified research plan or design. Information is extracted from respondents or derived from controlled experiments; context is independent and controlled	Investigators do not know where research will lead; it is an open-ended learning process. Understanding and focus emerge through interaction; context of inquiry is fundamental
Who sets priorities?	Professionals set priorities	Local people and professionals set priorities together
Relationship between all actors in the process	Professionals control and motivate clients from a distance; they tend not to trust people (farmers, rural people, etc.) who are simply the object of inquiry	Professionals enable and empower in close dialogue; they attempt to build trust through joint analyses and negotiation; understanding arises through this engagement, resulting in inevitable interactions between the investigator and the object of research
Mode of working	Single disciplinary — working alone	Multidisciplinary — working in groups
Technology or services	Rejected technology or service assumed to be fault of local people or local conditions. Careers are inward and upward — as practitioners get better, they become promoted and take on more administration	Rejected technology or service is a failed technology or service. Careers include outward and downward movement — professionals stay in touch with action at all levels

For this vision, recent empirical evidence suggests there are three essential areas to tackle. These are:

1. New methodologies for partnerships, dialogue, participatory analysis, and sharing;
2. New learning environments for professionals and rural people to develop capacities;
3. New institutional environments, including improved linkages within and between institutions.

These three areas for action are shown in figure 8.1 as intersecting circles. From our empirical experience of the successes and failures, the most sustainable solutions lie in the overlapping central sector. The following assumptions underlie this conceptual framework.

- Participatory approaches and methods support local innovation and adaptation, accommodate and augment diversity and complexity, and enhance local capabilities, and so they are more likely to generate sustainable processes and practices. These are represented by the ECAB circle and include participatory approaches and methods such as participatory rural appraisal (PRA), participatory technology development, farmer participatory research, and others represented in farmer-first and people-first approaches.
- An interactive learning environment encourages participatory attitudes, excites interest and commitment, and so contributes to jointly negotiated courses of action. This is represented by the GBAD circle and includes adult education and new learning (Rogers 1985), training for transformation (Hope et al. 1984), and other training for development (Lynton and Pareek 1990).
- Institutional support encourages the spread between and within institutions of participatory methods and so gives innovators the freedom to act and share. This is represented by the FDAC circle, which includes where a whole organization shifts toward participatory methods and management, and where there are informal and formal linkages between different organizations.

The hypothesis is that participatory practices are least strong and least sustainable at the peripheries of the circles, with gradients to the central overlap where the best, most sustainable, and most spreading participatory practices are to be found. In this perspective, sectors G, F, and E represent starting points and preconditions, but none is likely to

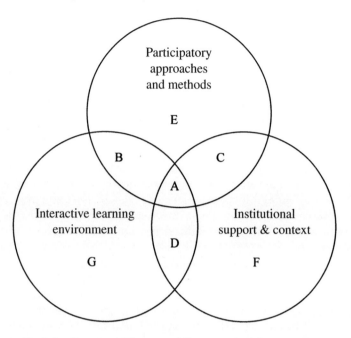

Fig. 8.1. Conceptual framework for a new learning paradigm

take root, be sustained, or spread well unless it receives support by moving into D, C, or B, and then into A.

In sector A support within institutions exists at the top. Authority is decentralized, and local diversity supported. There are incentives and encouragement to conduct participatory work. Linkages and sharing are encouraged with other institutions, whether NGO, government, or local organization. Spread is lateral, through sharing between and within organizations and through participants becoming trainers. The learning environment focuses on problem solving and is interactive and field-based. Error is embraced in the learning process. Responsibility is personal more than procedural, relying more on discretion and judgment and less on rules and manuals. Behavior and attitudes are democratic, stressing listening and facilitation, not didactic teaching. Methods and approaches are participatory and enabling, and seek to enhance capabilities. Local groups and organizations are supported and encouraged to conduct their own experiments and extension to manage themselves and to make demands on the system. Rapid adaptation to change occurs through devolved responsibility, local learning, and the responsive generation of a range of options.

Examples of these conditions, or conditions moving close to them, can now be found in many countries and contexts: Kenya for soil and water conservation (see case 8.1); Sri Lanka for irrigation (see case 8.2) (Uphoff 1992); India for watershed development (Shah 1999; Devavaram 1999; Mascarenhas et al. 1991; Pretty and Shah 1997); India for tank rehabilitation (Mosse 1992); Philippines for irrigation (de los Reyes and Jopillo 1986; Bagadion and Korten 1991); Nepal and India for credit groups (Rahman 1984; Uphoff 1990; Fernandez 1992); Botswana and Zambia for farmers' research (Heinrich et al. 1991; Drinkwater 1992; FARM Africa/IIED 1991); Burkina Faso for soil and water conservation (Critchley 1991). There are many others that are not in this list.

Case 8.1. A Success from Kenya: The Soil and Water Conservation Branch, Ministry of Agriculture
In 1974, the National Soil Conservation Programme was established in the Ministry of Agriculture. During the first ten years, emphasis was placed on the construction of mechanical protection works, mainly various forms of terracing. The extension services targeted those individual farmers who were willing and able to accept technical assistance. During the 1980s, it became increasingly apparent that this individual approach to extension was not supporting sufficient soil and water conservation measures. Erosion was outstripping conservation, despite the financial incentives and subsidies.

As a result, in 1987 the ministry adopted the catchment approach. This concentrates resources and efforts within a specified area for a limited period of time. A team with extension officers from different ministries works together for a week in a catchment are using Participatory Rural Appraisal methods for the catchment planning. They work with local people to analyze local ecological and social conditions, produce inventories of local knowledge and practices, and develop an action plan. This is discussed at an open meeting, or *baraza*, where farmers are able to comment and express their needs. A catchment committee of local people is elected, and this local organization coordinates soil and water conservation within the catchment area.

This group approach to extension planning has increased the credibility of extension staff as they are seen to be listening to and learning from local people. It does not make use of subsidies. Instead, it has mobilized communities around a productive interest. It has changed attitudes in both local and outside people. The approach has resulted in significant environmental and economic regeneration, with sustained increases in agricultural yields, resource conservation, and strength of local groups (MOALDM, Kenya, passim; Pretty et al. 1995).

Case 8.2. A Success from Sri Lanka: Irrigation and
Groups in Gal Oya
After involvement of the farmers in groups for the rehabilitation of
25,000 hectares of agricultural land:

> water use efficiency increased, and farmers increased the cropping
> intensity and crop production;
> the number of complaints about water distribution dropped nearly
> to zero as adjustments were worked out amicably with field-level
> staff; and
> the problem of broken gates disappeared (formerly they were bro-
> ken 80 percent of the time).

Cooperation among farmers and with officials was catalyzed within a
few months despite a thirty-year legacy of conflict and noncooperation.
As officials were involved in measuring the impacts of these groups and
saw the positive results, their support grew and became more active.
The conditions for success included continuity of personnel, strong government support at high levels, and the right kind of leadership in communities. One impact was that "government personnel started working
more conscientiously and effectively once they came to know the real
conditions at village level through the systematic monitoring and evaluation system" (Uphoff 1992).

Role of Governments and State Institutions

Constraints on the Capacity of National Research and
Extension Systems

There is growing acceptance that participatory approaches can contribute to the development of technologies by and for resource-poor farmers, and to community management of natural resources. But this potential is unlikely to be realized until participatory approaches are adopted
by National Agricultural Research and Extension Systems (NARSs and
NAESs) and by government field organizations, and then applied on a
sustained basis and on a broad scale. Such participation requires that
farmers and communities be regarded as partners in the research, extension, and institutional development process, rather than as clients.

Government organizations are limited in their ability to conduct
and facilitate systems-based participatory agricultural research and development. This is accounted for by well-known factors at the macro-,

institutional, and individual levels. At the macroeconomic level, in many countries, tight limits are set by debt burdens, structural adjustment, low revenue, and budget deficits. At the institutional level, centralization, inflexible management, and standardized programs misfit diverse local conditions and generate often misleadingly favorable feedback based on centrally determined criteria. Lack of funds and inflexible budgets preclude responses to new opportunities. Government field agencies with the deadlines of financial years often concentrate on physical construction to meet targets to the neglect of community and farmer participation. In consequence, attempts to scale up NGO successes frequently founder (case 8.3). At the individual level, agricultural researchers are deterred from working in the field and with farmers by their conditioned attitudes and behavior, by reward systems based on scientific papers derived from on-station research, and by sheer lack of physical and financial means such as transport and travel allowances.

Case 8.3. The Hill Resource Management Program of Haryana, India
External institutions find social change much less easy to promote than technical and economic change. In this program, groups for natural resource management have been established to fill the gap left by the decline and near disappearance of indigenous management systems. The project began in Sukhomajri and Nada where prolonged and patient interaction between professionals of both government and nongovernment agencies and villagers led to the equitable distribution of irrigation and water from small antierosion dams and to "social fencing" through which degraded forest land was protected by villagers from grazing and grew fibre and fodder grasses as well as trees. The impact was remarkable: rope-making from the fibre grass yield which rose 400 to 800 percent, stall-fed livestock with a ninefold increase in milk sales, and crop yields which rose 100 to 400 percent.

The Haryana Forest Department became the lead agency for extension of the approach. But physical development preceded and outpaced social organization. At the time when fifty-seven dams had been built, in only 30 percent of the thirty-nine communities involved had the department established management societies. The program was vulnerable to local people becoming less and less involved in planning and management (Mishra and Madhu 1988; Poffenberger 1990).

Many problems, as well as strengths, were brought to light by the International Service for National Agricultural Research (ISNAR) in its study of nine NARSs[3] that had been conducting on-farm client-oriented research for at least five years. The study found that the hardest role of on-farm research to institutionalize was feedback from clients to affect research priorities (Merrill-Sands et al. 1991). As Merrill-Sands and Collion (1992) have put it: "This finding is particularly disturbing given that we were looking at relatively mature FSR efforts that had had time to train researchers in FSR methods."

Extension also thoroughly embodies the teaching, positivist paradigm. Extension means extending knowledge from a center of learning to those presumed to be in need of that knowledge. Researchers have the prestigious role of being the source of new technologies, while farmers are passive recipients. The erroneous assumptions underpinning much extension and transfer of technology follow.

Erroneous Assumptions Underpinning Much
Agricultural Research and Extension

- Real knowledge is the sole domain of the researcher.
- The farmer is a passive and malleable recipient of information.
- The initiative for disseminating information rests exclusively with the communicator.
- Increased production is the main criterion for farming improvement.
- Farmers' information needs are technical research results rather than in the area of management of their livelihood systems (Chambers et al. 1989; Ison 1990; Moris 1990).

This approach to formal extension is exemplified by the Training and Visit system (Benor et al. 1984). In this system, extension agents receive regular training to enhance their technical skills, which they then pass on to farmers through regular contact with the selected contact farmers. This technical advice and knowledge then diffuses from the contact farmers to other noncontact farmers. The secondary transfer of the messages, though, has been less successful than predicted, and adoption rates have commonly been low among noncontact farmers. In Somalia, for example, only one noncontact farmer adopted a high input package for each contact farmer (Mullen 1989). This was despite the fact that over several years maize and sorghum yields were 40 to 45 percent greater on contact farmers' fields (Chapman 1988). Farmers who choose not to adopt are then liable to be labeled as "laggards with attitudinal barriers" (Russell et al. 1989).

An alternative to this kind of extension would be group-based approaches that, when analyzed carefully, look nothing like extension as conceptualized and defined above. Extension becomes facilitation, through using and developing farmers' knowledge, teaching observational skills, and using adult education methods to develop joint decision-making skills (Röling 1992). Russell and Ison (1991) have suggested that "it is time to abandon the term extension altogether because of what it has come to mean in practice and the network of faulty assumptions which are at its core."

Government Successes

Despite these constraints, there are a growing number of successful innovations in national agricultural research and extension systems. Some were in existence at the time of the 1987 Farmer First conference (Chambers et al. 1989). Others have arisen and developed more recently. A selection includes:

- working groups, research teams, and joint interdisciplinary treks based in Lumle and Pakhribas Agricultural Centres, Nepal (Chand and Gurung 1991);
- catchment approach to participatory planning and implementation of soil and water conservation, Ministry of Agriculture, Kenya (MOALDM passim; Pretty et al. 1995);
- Adaptive Research Planning Teams and village research groups, Ministry of Agriculture, Zambia (Drinkwater 1992);
- farmer groups for technology research and extension in the Ministry of Agriculture, Botswana (see case 8.4) (Heinrich et al. 1991);
- innovator workshops in Bangladesh (Abedin and Haque 1989);
- farmer groups for National Landcare Programme, Australia (Campbell 1992);
- policy analysis network of universities in Nepal, coordinated by Winrock International (Gill 1993);
- participatory research teams, Tamil Nadu Agricultural University, India (Pretty 1995);
- farmer groups for technology adaptation and extension, Narendra Deva University of Agriculture and Technology, Faisabad, Uttan Pradesh (Maurya 1989).

Case 8.4. Agricultural Technical Improvement Project
(ATIP), Ministry of Agriculture, Botswana
In the ATIP, technologies are tested under farmer-managed, farmer-implemented conditions. The key component of the approach is local groups, referred to as Research-Oriented and Extension-Oriented Farmer Groups (ROFGs and EOFGs), which have become powerful

tools for examining the potential of a range of technologies under farmer management. Some 90 percent of the farmers attending meetings are women. The process involves researchers presenting a wide range of options gathered from many sources to farmers in villages. Selection is according to personal interest and specific resource constraints. Subgroups of farmers selecting the same options conduct trials and meet monthly to discuss progress and observations. As harvest approaches, field days are held to share interesting results with farmers outside the groups.

The strong and sustained dialogue between farmers and researchers has:

- given greater flexibility to the research process, as technology options can easily be moved into the testing phase, and researchers respond rapidly to needs and interests of farmers;
- increased the range of topics under joint examination, and so increased the diversity of options open to farmers;
- led to attitude change in scientists, as they appreciated the benefits to all that could be achieved and enjoyed personal success;
- developed improved linkages between on-station commodity researchers and FSR teams, as demand for their technologies and feedback from farmers grew;
- increased the total research capacity beyond the available research resources;
- increased linkages with NGOs, as they became involved in the ROFGs and EOFGs; and
- led to significant increases in grain (sorghum and millet) yields with low external input technologies — increase over three years of 71 percent for double ploughing, 23 percent for row planting, and 56 percent for small applications of phosphorus (20 kg/ha) (Heinrich et al. 1991; Norman et al. 1989).

These cases were successes because progress was made in several areas. There were incentives for change and a recognition that past approaches had failed. These incentives came in certain cases from external sources, including donors. There were enabling management structures, with support from senior staff giving the space to innovators who, in turn, were often charismatic individuals able to promote and achieve change. Smaller, autonomous groups within the larger bureaucracies innovated, and then became a model for the rest. Participatory methods were used not just for information gathering, but to establish new dialogues, change behavior, and empower local people. In Uphoff's (1992) words: "The precision of data is not as important as people's participation in its acquisition and assessment, since the real goal is changing behaviour (towards more productive processes)."

Replicability and New Problems

The last question is to what extent these successes are replicable. Three types of issues stand out: second-order problems arising from the approaches themselves; national policies; and international factors.

First, the most pressing new problems arising from the approaches themselves include:

- sustaining feedback from farmers: Feedback and learning from farmers' experiences are essential for further improvement of technologies and for sustained dialogue between scientists and farmers, but these have proved difficult to sustain on a large scale. In Botswana feedback has been effective, but on a small scale, from farmer groups in one region. In Nepal field staff could not devote sufficient time to supervision or collection of feedback because of the large number of on-farm activities;
- creating new reward systems: these are needed for agricultural scientists, to reduce emphasis on controlled on-station experimentation and the publication of conventional scientific papers, to give incentives to encourage and support researchers' working in the field and to develop new publication outlets for accounts of participatory research;
- successful groups become a threat: empowered local groups could be seen as a threat to state institutions, or themselves want to threaten them;
- overexpansion: the desire to scale up programs too fast to too large a scale can result in the sacrifice of quality;
- political takeovers: political patronage and hijacking can occur when successes are seen as vehicles for achieving other aims.

Second, the national policy environment has a major bearing, but is not directly addressed by these positive examples. For wider impact, attention has also to be paid to factors that impede the spread of locally led successes, such as macroeconomic policies (subsidies for inputs; food pricing policies; food for work schemes); regulatory policies (lack of land title for tenurial arrangements; lack of legal title for local groups); financial constraints; and the desire by politicians to maintain political control and direction of actions at all levels.

Third, international influences largely outside the control of states and of government organizations also present constraints. These include structural adjustment policies that reduce the capacity of the state; uncertainties over future development assistance policies and flows; imponderables concerning trade imbalances and agreements; and the difficulties of working in war-torn regions.

Given these problems, and the scale of the challenges and opportunity, it is evident that governments cannot and should not try to go it alone. There is then a compelling case for partnerships and alliances with NGOs, local groups, and international organizations.

Nongovernmental Organizations

The scale, scope, and influence of NGOs concerned with development has grown enormously in recent years (Korten 1990; Edwards and Hulme 1992; Farrington et al. 1993; Fowler 1992; Pretty 1995a). In the South, there are perhaps some 10,000–20,000 development NGOs, and in the OECD countries a further 4,000. Their activities are now very diverse. In some of the poorest areas and countries, they perform many of the service roles elsewhere carried out by government. Activities include not only relief, welfare, community development, and agricultural research and extension, but also advocacy and lobbying, development education, legal reform, training, alliance building, and national and international networking. These varied functions and roles mean they are both critical actors in their own right, as well as potential partners for government and international institutions.

Like state organizations and NARSs, NGOs have undertaken a range of activities relating to agricultural research, extension, and development. In some countries or parts of countries, the coverage by farmers' groups and NGOs in extension, training, and input supply is more extensive than that provided by the public sector, as in Ecuador, in eastern Bolivia, and in northern Ghana, where there are three times as many extension agents operating from church-based agricultural stations as from the public sector (Bebbington 1991; Farrington and Biggs 1990).

Elsewhere NGOs have trained government staff, particularly in India. There, NGOs such as the Aga Khan Rural Support Programme (India), Activists for Social Alternatives, MYRADA, OUTREACH, Seva Bharati, and SPEECH have been at the forefront of training agricultural researchers, extensionists, and officials in participatory approaches and methods (Hinchcliffe 1999). When federated into higher level organizations, they can be more effective in influencing policies and presenting the local case (Constantino-David 1992). Federations and networks also create the opportunity for more efficient and more effective disbursement of funds by donors, with lower administrative costs (Pretty and Scoones 1991).

A number of strengths of NGOs, often but not always found, contribute to their relative success:

- flexibility to choose the subject area and sources of information;
- freedom to develop their own incentives for professionals;
- capacity to struggle to get things right, and so more ability at the local level to question, puzzle, change, and learn;
- strength in supporting community-level initiatives, and helping to organize federations and caucuses; and
- ability to work on longer time horizons, as they are less affected by the time- and target-bound project culture.

Scaling up the Impact of NGOs

The scale of operation and range of activities of NGOs have raised new challenges and problems. NGOs are not elected and are not accountable to citizens and the public. Like any other organization, they can lose touch with local views. And where the public sector is weak or non-existent, there can be a growing statism of NGOs as they create structures that perform what are normally functions of the state but without feedback or responsibility to government.

NGOs that operate on a very large scale, like the Bangladesh Rural Advancement Committee, are the exception. Most NGOs are quite small, though quite often conspicuous. They can then appear to be doing a lot, but the observer is easily misled. Coverage by NGOs as a whole is usually patchy and small compared with that of government field organizations. If governments adopt a good approach and methods, even if quality is diluted, the total wider impact can be enormous. Once again, the challenge is to find the means to scale up, or widen, the impact of the successful actions of NGOs. Three strategies have been identified by Edwards and Hulme (1992):

- *additive:* NGOs increase their size and expand operations
- *multiplicative:* NGOs achieve impact through deliberate influence, networking, policy and legal reform, or training
- *diffusive:* NGOs achieve impact through informal and spontaneous spread of ideas, approaches, and methods

The additive strategy is widespread as donors' interest and support have fostered an operational and organizational expansion. But it has dangers. Some of the comparative advantage of NGOs is liable to be lost when they expand. Close relationships with farmers, the capacity to experiment, and the ability to be flexible in local contexts may all be weakened. Another problem is that internal organizational objectives may come to dominate and displace development objectives (Fowler 1992). Success in the provision of services by NGOs may be also cited to support an ideological case for reducing the scale of service delivery by the public sector.

The multiplicative strategy can take many forms. Intermediary NGOs, for example, in Latin America and West Africa, have provided stimulus, resources, and technical assistance for the formation and functioning of community-based organizations. NGOs in these cases can act as intermediaries, channeling financial and technical resources from other agencies to community-based organizations instead of using those resources themselves (Mitlin and Satterthwaite 1992).

The diffusive strategy entails developing and spreading ideas, approaches, and methods that others pick up, and that have a capacity to spread on their own. Examples include various forms of self-help savings and credit, such as that of the Grameen Bank, the very ideas of which may encourage others to try similar approaches, and the approaches and methods of participatory rural appraisal (PRA) (Mascarenhas et al. 1991; Chambers 1992d).

NGO-Government Partnerships

Much of the multiplicative strategy involves working with governments. The amount of human capital and resources locked up in government institutions usually represents a huge underutilized potential. Opportunities for innovative work to catalyze change within governments do exist, particularly under conditions of increased decentralization. Collaboration between NGOs and governments to realize more of the potential and exploit more of the opportunities implies working together in a mutually interdependent fashion.

Many types of relationships have developed between NGOs and governments in agriculture including:

- Support for marginalized regional administration, as in Mali (Roche 1991);
- Training of government and NGO staff and farmers in participatory methods (see case 8.5);

- Development of alliances during training courses, leading to increased job satisfaction on part of government staff.
- Research and research dissemination. One study (Farrington et al. 1993) found it least common for NGOs to generate technology which government disseminated, more common for NGOs to disseminate results of research conducted by NARSs, and most common of all for NGOs and NARSs to conduct research jointly. In this mode the NGOs generally operate in a more obviously, and often on-farm, adaptive mode than the NARSs. This is partly attributed to NGOs' frequent practice of adapting and scaling down technologies originally developed by NARSs for resource-rich farmers.
- Consortia of government, NGOs, and farmers' organizations for joint planning and coordination. In Ecuador, such collaboration has been planned to lead to regional agricultural technology development committees, in which government organizations, NGOs, and farmers' organizations would all have voting power.

Case 8.5. The Aga Khan Rural Support Programme (India), Gujarat

The NGO AKRSP(I) fully involves villagers in the process of planning and implementing watershed development and management. AKRSP(I) acts as a facilitator in this process, which has resulted in environmental and economic change led by local institutions. AKRSP(I) identified village training needs, and this training was provided by government in formal style (in classrooms). But farmers said they learned little in this environment, so AKRSP(I) developed an alternative participative and interactive training strategy. Government staff came to observe and participate. Farmers themselves became extension volunteers (EVs) and trainers, and were more effective and efficient in training other farmers.

This cadre of EVs now conduct their own participatory planning using PRA methods. In February 1992, at the time of an International PRA Roving Workshop in Kabripathar village, Bharuch District, Gujarat, a nonliterate woman, Raiben, acted as facilitator for other women to carry out a village census on cards, to show people, assets, and livestock. Other village volunteers facilitated the mapping of degraded forest, sampling with 20 m by 20 m quadrats, counting and measuring standing trees and rootstock, and making decisions about numbers needed of different species. Village volunteers have even told AKRSP(I) staff that they need not bother to turn up when a PRA is to be conducted. Some of the volunteers are also being requested to come as consultants to help other villages conduct PRAs. The approach and methods seem, then, in this instance, to be self-spreading (Shah et al. 1991; Shah 1999).

These new state-society relations have significant implications (see Curtis 1991). There are benefits from synergism, from greater efficiency of resource use, and from NGOs and farmer organizations becoming more accountable. There are also costs and dangers. The state's capabilities may be weakened in two ways: through NGOs substituting for government activities; and through a brain drain to NGOs, as NGOs are increasingly able to attract skilled people away from the public sector, even though this may enrich NGOs with professionals who understand government bureaucracies.

International Agricultural Research and the CGIAR

The CGIAR Institutions

The IARCs (International Agricultural Research Centres) of the CGIAR (Consultative Group for International Agricultural Research) have a professional influence out of all proportion to their size and budgets. Agricultural scientists worldwide see the IARCs as centers that embody and set standards of professional excellence. Through their training of national scientists, their international networking of research programs, their publications, and their prestige, the IARCs spread and sustain the dominant concepts, values, methods, and behavior of agricultural science. Still basking in the afterglow of the Green Revolution, they still predominantly accept and propagate the transfer of technology paradigm.

The CGIAR system has responded to the increasing priority attached to the environment, the management of natural resources, and sustainability in agriculture. The shortcomings of commodity-based research have been increasingly recognized, and much discussion has focused on an ecoregional approach to research in the CGIAR to complement or replace it. The new approach proposed seeks to achieve this by focusing on ecoregions, by better and more equal collaboration with NARSs, and by cooperation between IARCs. No single organizational model is foreseen, but there is a valuable set of organizational principles. The new approach will "operate on a regional basis; focus on an important agroecological zone with a serious degradation problem; combine natural resources management and production objectives; employ a multidisciplinary approach; include both natural and social sciences; involve national research institutions and other partners in a synergistic way; adopt flexible systems of governance and priority setting; and ensure global coherence and flexible mechanisms" (TAC 1993).

There is a powerful case, though, that a second Green Revolution can only be achieved through decentralization, farmer participation, and diversification, and through scientists coming closer to farmers. The CGIAR exists to fill global gaps. Yet it could do more about two major gaps that need to be filled for a second Green Revolution (Conway 1997).

The first gap is the development and dissemination of methods for analysis conducted by farmers themselves. The assumption has been that farming systems research has to be done by professionals. Yet recent experiences with participatory rural appraisal (PRA), including innovations by the International Centre for Living Aquatic Resources Management (ICLARM), indicate that farmers have a far greater ability than agricultural or other professionals have supposed to conduct their own appraisal, analysis, experimentation, monitoring, and evaluation.

The second gap is the need for approaches and methods for changing the behavior, attitudes, and beliefs of scientists. A striking finding of recent experience with participatory methods is how powerfully inhibiting is the normally dominant behavior of professionals with farmers — lecturing, criticizing, advising, interrupting, holding the stick, and wagging the finger. The astonishing time it has taken to realize the analytical capabilities of farmers can be attributed to this almost universal tendency of outsiders. The gap, then, is experiential training approaches and methods to enable scientists to change.

Since these two gaps remain largely unrecognized and neglected by the CGIAR, they are liable to persist as major impediments to a second Green Revolution. The danger is that those who are already pioneering the new paradigm within the system will remain marginal, and others will be discouraged from joining them or starting up on their own. If this occurs, the prestige and influence of the CG system will have an adverse conservative effect, inhibiting change and discouraging innovation. On the other hand, if the IARCs were to take a lead in developing and disseminating the new participatory approaches, their impact could be vast and could both support and gain from those in national systems and in those NGOs that are working in the same direction.

To support the development and dissemination of participatory approaches and methods within and outside the CG system, there is a need to form new alliances and to strengthen those that already exist.

Opportunities for Alliances with NARSs, NGOs, and Farmers' Groups

Groups of professionals within some IARCs have already been conducting successful participatory research in partnership with other organizations and groups. These include or have included:

- post-harvest potato technology research with Peruvian farmers, from the International Potato Center (CIP) (Rhoades and Booth 1982);
- bean research with Bolivian, Colombian, and Rwandan farmers and NGOs, from the International Center for Tropical Agriculture (CIAT) (Ashby et al. 1989);
- aquaculture systems research and development with Malawian and Filipino farmers, from ICLARM (Lightfoot and Noble 1992);
- women in rice systems program, from the International Rice Research Institute (IRRI) (Paris and Del Rosario 1993);
- upland conservation research and development in the Philippines and elsewhere, from IRRI (Fujisaka 1991; Garity 1999);
- agroforestry research in East Africa (Sanchez 1999);
- pigeon-pea research with women farmers in Andhra Pradesh (Pimbert 1991) from the International Centre for Research in the Semi-Arid Tropics (ICRISAT);
- soil and water conservation research with Indian NGOs and farmers, from ICRISAT (Kerr and Sanghi 1992);
- countrywide network for potato research in Philippines, UPWARD (User's Perspective with Agricultural Research and Development) at CIP (UPWARD 1990);
- continentwide network for farmer participatory research for alley farming and agroforestry, AFNETA (Alley Farming Network for Tropical Africa), supported by International Institute for Tropical Agriculture (IITA), International Livestock Centre for Africa (ILCA), and International Council for Research in Agroforestry (ICRAF) (AFNETA 1993).

These programs are, however, not the norm. Those individuals who have succeeded in developing and using participatory approaches have tended to be isolated and marginalized within their institutions. Given the few female scientists in the system, it is especially striking how many of the pioneers are women. At least until recently, they have been more recognized and respected in the outside world than by their colleagues.

Often it has been the NARSs, and even more so NGOs, that have been in the lead methodologically with participatory approaches, and with training. These have been pioneered in India by MYRADA, AKRSP, ActionAid, OUTREACH, SPEECH, Seva Bharati, and other NGOs, and by agricultural universities, such as the Narendra Deva University of Agriculture and Technology and the Tamil Nadu Agricultural University; in Kenya by CARE, World Neighbors, ActionAid and other NGOs, and by the Ministry of Agriculture; and in the Philippines by the

University of the Philippines, Los Banos, and the University of the Visayas. The question is whether the CGIAR system as a whole, and the IARCs individually, will embrace participatory approaches and methods, their development, dissemination, and use, as core professional activities, or whether these will remain on the fringe.

Local Institutions

Types of Local Institution

Recent years have seen an extraordinary expansion in collective management programs throughout the world, described variously by the terms community management, participatory management, joint management, decentralized management, indigenous management, user-participation, and co-management (Pretty and Ward 2001). The uniting factor is that "these have in common the prevalence of face-to-face interpersonal relationships, which are naturally more frequent and intense within groups and communities than within localities" (Uphoff 1992). Local institutions function in a wide range of ways.

- to organize labor resources to help produce more;
- to mobilize material resources to help produce more (credit, savings, marketing);
- to assist some groups to gain new access to productive resources;
- to secure sustainability in natural resource use;
- to provide social infrastructure at village level;
- to influence policy institutions that affect them;
- to improve access of rural population to information;
- to improve flow of information to government and NGOs;
- to improve social cohesion;
- to provide a framework for cooperative action;
- to help organize people to use their own knowledge and research to advocate their own rights; and
- to mediate access to resources for a select group of people (Pretty 1995a).

These advances in social capital creation have been centred on participatory and deliberative learning processes leading to local group formation in six sectors: 1) watershed/catchment management; 2) irrigation management; 3) micro-finance delivery; 4) forest management; 5) integrated pest management; and 6) farmers' research groups.

Local groups and other institutions have been relatively neglected in agricultural research, extension, and development. This is another symptom of agricultural development that focuses on technology rather than on the organizational and institutional setting. Yet all the positive experiences in sector A of the conceptual model (fig. 9.1) have built upon existing institutions or helped to develop new ones. Local institutions can have many positive effects. Besides those previously listed, these include enhancing local capabilities, attracting and developing local leadership, with increasing responsibilities through growth, and diversification into more activities. The potential of local groups still remains largely unrealized.

What, then, can be done both to encourage the greater adoption of group-based programs for environmental improvements and to identify the necessary support for groups to evolve to maturity? Clearly, international agencies, governments, banks, and NGOs must invest more in social and human capital creation and ensure the transition is made from dependence to interdependence, which in turn helps to build assets. The danger is not going far enough, and being satisfied with any partial progress. As Ostrom (1998) puts it: "creating dependent citizens rather than entrepreneurial citizens reduces the capacity of citizens to produce capital." The costs of development assistance will also inevitably increase; establishing new organizations is not without cost. It is clear that more will have to be invested on public social goods to get more improvements in natural capital.

Problems with Local Groups

These local groups do have shortcomings. First, initial or existing conditions may lead to or perpetuate inequity. Groups of women or of the poorer are easily overlooked. Some community-level institutions securely establish and legitimize unequal access to natural resources, as with tank management and water allocation in Tamil Nadu during times of water scarcity (Mosse 1992). Also, if only one institution is present in the community, with powers to refuse membership, then (as with farmers' clubs in Malawi) the poor and women are liable to be excluded (Kydd 1989).

Second, external interventions can create problems. They are liable to warp and weaken local institutions. There are dangers that the state will suffocate local initiative and responsibility, or capture and harness local initiatives and resources for other purposes. Local politicians may also seek to take over local successes or gain reflected glory from them.

Third, problems arise during the evolution of groups. Growth in size can threaten effectiveness: too large groups can allow social hierarchies to dominate, such as in Kenya (Huby 1990). Groups are sometimes more effective in their early years: as they grow in size, confidence, and prominence, their power and position can bring them into new conflicts; and the original leaders may not build up secondary leadership, creating an internal vacuum. A diversity of local institutions can also lead to factionalism and conflict unless attention is paid to articulation between groups and federation to higher level bodies.

Strategies to Overcome Problems

These problems have been largely overcome by the supporting organizations involved in the successful cases listed above. Caution is needed in drawing general lessons from experience. Interventions can threaten local institutions' operations, so there may also be dangers in the co-option of local institutions as a general strategy. Some precepts can, however, be suggested from comparative experience for reliable local institutions that act on their own and also exercise demand for the research and extension they require.

- Where there has been little spontaneous local organization, external agents can play a positive role in change, often by concentrating first on rural context rather than content. They may mobilize resources and act as a broker between interest groups, or they may create demand for local institutions by beginning with awareness and articulation of local needs and interests, as in cases in Ecuador and Bolivia, where issues of land tenure and marketing were addressed before planning research and extension activities (Bebbington 1991).
- Responsible leadership is crucial. It is encouraged where groups select their own members and make their own rules, as with MYRADA credit groups (Fernandez 1992). Good leaders need adequate rewards to guard against unofficial or corrupt practices.
- Training, where it is involved, is best to help people gain new problem-solving skills. This is more useful than technical training. Local people can then take on the roles of researcher and extensionist, and by so doing increase efficiency and effectiveness through horizontal diffusion by farmer-to-farmer training and extension.
- Perhaps the most important strategy is to find ways of helping local institutions to come together and federate, with small groups at the base (e.g., extended kin groups) represented by wider and stronger institutions at higher levels.

Educational and Learning Organizations

Formal Educational Institutions

The Biased Structures of Agricultural Universities and Facilities

- They are frequently organized along authoritarian rather than participatory management lines.
- Management positions are often held on basis of seniority rather than management skills.
- Creative and eccentric innovation is rarely tolerated.
- Institutional rewards, particularly senior authorship of papers, promotes individual and isolated research, making many institutions lonely places.
- Organizations become introspective and resistant to new ideas, processes, and changing environmental circumstances.
- Staff development, if it exists, is frequently in the form of refresher training, where content (new faces) is the primary input, rather than a balance between content and the development of new management or learning skills.
- Explicit or implicit status divisions become set in stone, for example, researcher versus extensionist, natural versus social scientist (Ison 1990).

Universities and their agricultural faculties are often the most conservative of agricultural organizations. They have been slow to adopt innovative ideas, methods, and staff development activities. They remain in the conceptual straitjacket of positivism and modernization, arising partly out of the functional and practical demarcation of research and teaching, and the focus on teaching rather than learning (Pearson and Ison 1990). Agricultural universities thus have a poor record in training professionals to be problem solvers. Most have developed structures that reflect the proliferation of disciplines that have emerged over the past thirty years. An innovative field or area of study is usually accommodated by adding on a new sector, without basic restructuring. Many farming systems research (FSR) courses, for example, have implied the creation of new courses or departments, thereby treating FSR as another discipline or commodity (Gibbon 1992). New ideas have hardly ever stimulated radical rethinking or restructuring.

The most fundamental need is to enable universities to evolve into communities of participatory learners. Academics must become involved in learning, learning *about* learning, facilitating the development of learners, and exploring new ways of understanding their own and others' realities. Participatory learning implies mutual learning — from farmers, from students' own learning, and from academics. There are some researchers in agricultural universities who do work closely with farmers in a participatory mode. But these participatory approaches in the field with farmers have had only slow and slight influence on the style of teaching and learning in universities with students. More radical change is required. The education system does not need patching and repairing; it needs transformation.

One example of how educational institutions can take on a new role for sustainable agriculture comes from Honduras. Since 1988, scientists at a small agricultural college in El Zamorano, Escuela Agrícola Parameri-cana, have been working to build the capacity of small farmers to control pests without pesticides (Bentley 1992). This is done by teaching a short course for farmers to fill in key gaps in their knowledge. Farmers' knowl-edge is already profound, but there are aspects of pest control they do not know about. They know about, for example, many aspects of the devastat-ing disease maize ear rot, but not about the details of fungal fruiting bodies and spore production. Farmers have many words to describe social wasps, but do not know that solitary parasitic wasps exist. They do know that pesticides are toxic, but equate smell with toxic strength and so have no means of perceiving chronic toxicity: "they generally apply pesticides with no protective gear, often early and smoking, clearing stopped up nozzles with their mouths allowing pesticide from the backpack sprayer to drip down their backs. Farmers think that because they don't get ill as they spray, they must be building up resistance to the agrochemicals" (Bentley 1992).

The successful new learning is based on the collaboration between farmers and scientists (case 8.6). Small-scale farmers help to set scien-tists' formal research agendas. Collaborative work results in the develop-ment of better technologies than either university staff or farmers could invent alone.

Informal Learning

Because of the widespread failure of the formal educational sector to provide the necessary learning environments for the development of new professionals, it has been other institutions that have led the way. These have chiefly been NGOs from both the North and the South. Enlightened individuals in government organizations, NARSs, and CG institutes, as well as farmers have played their part. The investment is not in knowledge, in the formal sense, but in attitudes, behavioral changes, and facilitation skills. Training is centered on learning by doing and bringing scientists, extensionists, and farmers together to negotiate and learn from each other on personal level. The impact on attitudes can be significant.

Case 8.6. Learning about Pest Control without Pesticides in Honduras
The key to the collaboration is the participatory mode of teaching and experimentation. Farmers are taught by scientists using local terminology; they observe fungi under microscopes; they collect insects from the field and watch parasitoids emerge; they observe wasps returning to nests with insect prey; they put caterpillars on maize plants and watch ants carry them off within minutes. Scientists from the college have documented a wide range of experiments that farmers have conducted after courses:

- one farmer intercropped amaranth among intercropped vegetables to encourage predators;
- one farmer noticed worms in his stored potatoes and so placed the box on an ant nest; the ants cleaned the pests out, and he then transplanted ant nests to his farm;
- one farmer described taking parasitic wasp cocoons found on his farm to a neighbor's farm to increase the spread of wasps.

Follow-up to the course is coordinated with local NGOs and the groups of farmer extensionists, who are visited regularly by college scientists. These visits also mean that information on farmers' needs is taken back to the Crop Protection Department at El Zamorano. Small-scale farmers are thus helping to set scientists' formal research agendas, as well as learning more sustainable farming practices (Bentley 1992).

There is growing experience in this informal sector in farmer-to-farmer extension, visitation, and peer-training. These take many forms. Most common are farmer exchange visits, in which farmers are brought to the site of a successful innovation or useful practice, where they can discuss and observe benefits and costs with adopting farmers. Professionals play the role of bringing interested groups together and facilitating the process of information exchange. During the visits, participants are stimulated by the discussions and observations, and many will be provoked into trying the technologies for themselves. For farmers, "seeing is believing," and the best educators of farmers are other farmers themselves (Jintrawet et al. 1985). Such farmer-to-farmer extension has resulted in the spread of Leucaena contour hedgerows in the Philippines (Fujisaka 1989); peanuts after and sesame before rice in northeast Thailand (Jintrawet et al. 1985); management innovations for irrigation systems in Nepal (Pradan and Yoder 1989); velvetbeans for green manuring in Honduras (Bunch 1990); and a range of watershed protection technologies in India and Kenya (Mascarenhas et al. 1991; Hinchcliffe et al. 1999).

As local people develop the capacity to learn from and to teach each other, so they develop further their own capacity to conduct their own research. There are many recent innovations in farmers' own analyses that point the way to innovative learning and self-spreading. In India, villagers who have been trained as extension volunteers by AKRSP(I) are now training the staff of other NGOs in participatory and interactive learning methods. Farmers also work on the radio as broadcasters in Niger and Peru (McCorkle et al. 1988) and monitor research and conduct surveys (Jiggins and de Zeeuw 1992).

These approaches all build the capacity of local people to conduct their own investigations and solve their own problems. All have shown that such informal learning is a low-cost method of enabling farmer groups to adapt, choose, and improve their farming systems. They also provide leadership experience for villagers and present role models that they can aspire to emulate.

Conclusion

The intention and will to adopt new values, approaches, and practices are prerequisites for change and cannot be assumed. But even when they exist, both institutions and individuals face difficulties. In institutions, standardization, simplification, and speed stand out as recurrent dangers, pursued in the interests of wider and more rapid application. As Sumberg (1991) has put it: "it would appear absolutely essential to avoid the temptation of a rapid institutionalisation of farmer-participatory research. It was this . . . that eventually limited the overall impact of farming systems research. . . . There is a strong irony in the tendency for approaches that have developed out of a need to deal with diversity, variability, complexity etc, to become institutionalised in such a way that whatever positive contribution they might have been able to make is effectively marginalised."

For individuals, especially those trapped in conventional organizations, there are problems. In outlining the new professionalism we do not wish to discourage those for whom, in their current institutional context, there may seem so little room to maneuver that it is out of reach. There are many pathways and many small steps that can be taken toward it. Nor should the new professionalism be seen as an alternative that completely replaces the old. It is, rather, a complementary and corrective model. The old and the new have mutual strengths. For the new, both drive and restraint can be exercised so that its spread can be sure, sustained, and self-improving. Each setting will have its own best sequence and strategy for change. Learning how to evolve and spread the new professionalism must itself be a slow and sensitive learning process.

NOTES

The writing of an earlier paper on which this article is based was made possible by financial support to the Sustainable Agriculture Programme of the International Institute for Environment and Development (IIED) from the Swedish International Development Authority (SIDA), the Swedish Agency for Research Cooperation with Developing Countries (SAREC), and the British Overseas Development Authority (ODA). Another version of the paper was presented to the 1992 Beyond Farmer First workshop, which was also supported by the Ford Foundation and the International Development Research Center (IDRC). It was also published as an Institute of Development Studies discussion paper (Pretty and Chambers, 1993). We are grateful to John Thompson, Ian Scoones, and David Gibbon for helpful comments on earlier drafts. The paper has also benefited from a wide range of comments and discussions by participants at the Beyond Farmer First workshop.

1. The principal critiques, analyses, and advances have come from the field of naturalistic enquiry (Lincoln and Guba 1985); from nonlinear science of chaos and fractals (Gleick 1987); from historical contingency and linear uncertainty (Gould 1989); from open systems contextual science (Russell and Ison 1991; Checkland 1981); from quantum physics (such as from the theories of Heisenberg and Schrödinger); from the philosophy of symbiosis (Kurokawa 1991); from postmodernism (Harvey 1989); from a new pedagogy (Freire 1968; Lynton and Pareek 1990); from historical sociology (Abrams 1982); from adaptive management in development (Holling 1978; Mearns 1991; Pretty and Scoones 1991; Uphoff 1992c); from action science and reflection-in-action (Schon 1983; Argyris et al. 1985; Schon 1987); and from organizational management theories and practice (Peters and Waterman 1982; Peters 1987; Handy 1989; Senge 1990).

2. A selection of terms for systems of participatory and social learning include: Action Planning, Agroecosystems Analysis (AEA), Beneficiary Assessment, Citizens' Juries, Community Audits, Community Profiles, Community Visions, Development Education Leadership Teams (DELTA), Diagnostico Rurale Participativo (DRP), Evaluacion Rural Participativa (ERP), Farmer Par-

ticipatory Research, Farming Systems Research, Future Search, Groupe de Recherche et d'Appui pour l'Auto-Promotion Paysanne (GRAAP), Méthode Active de Recherche et de Planification Participative (MARP), Open Space Technology, Parish Appraisals, Participatory Appraisal (PA), Participatory Analysis and Learning Methods (PALM), Participatory Action Research (PAR), Participatory Forest Resource Assessment (PFRA), Participatory Monitoring and Evaluation (PME), Participatory Poverty Assessment (PPA), Participatory Research Methodology (PRM), Participatory Rural Appraisal (PRA), Participatory Rural Appraisal and Planning (PRAP), Participatory Technology Development (PTD), Participatory Urban Appraisal (PUA), Planning for Real, Process Documentation Research, Rapid Appraisal (RA), Rapid Assessment of Agricultural Knowledge Systems (RAAKS), Rapid Assessment Procedures (RAP), Rapid Assessment Techniques (RAT), Rapid Catchment Analysis (RCA), Rapid Ethnographic Assessment (REA), Rapid Food Security Assessment (RFSA), Rapid Multiperspective Appraisal (RMA), Rapid Organisational Assessment (ROA), Rapid Rural Appraisal (RRA), Real Time Strategic Change (RTSC), Regenerated Freiréan Literacy through Empowering Community Techniques (REFLECT), Samuhik Brahman (Joint trek), Soft Systems Methodology (SSM), Theatre for Development, Training for Transformation, Village Action Plans, Village Appraisals, and Visualisation in Participatory Programmes (VIPP).

3. The NARSs were in Bangladesh, Ecuador, Guatemala, Indonesia, Nepal, Panama, Senegal, Zambia, and Zimbabwe.

REFERENCES

Abedin, Z., and H. Haque. 1989. Innovator Workshops in Bangladesh. In Chambers et al., eds, *Farmer First.* London: Intermediate Technology Publications Ltd.

Abrams, P. 1982. *Historical Sociology.* Shepton Mallet: Open Books.

Adnan, S., A. Barrett, S.M. Nurul Alam, and A. Brustinow. 1992. *People's Participation: NGOs and the Flood Action Plan.* Dhaka, Bangladesh: Research and Advisory Services.

AFNETA. 1993. *Workshop Report: Interim Research Committee Meeting in Research Planning and Methodological Development for Phase II AFNETA Research.* Ibadan: AFNETA/IITA.

Argyris, C., R. Putnam, and D. Smith. 1985. *Action Science.* San Francisco and London: Jossey-Bass Publishers.

Ashby, J., C. Quiros, and Y. Rivers. 1989. Experiences with Group Techniques in Colombia. In R. Chambers et al., eds., *Farmer First.* London: Intermediate Technology Publications Ltd.

Bagadion, B., and F. Korten. 1991. Developing Irrigators' Organisations: A Learning Process Approach. In M. Cernea, ed., *Putting People First* (2d ed.). Oxford: Oxford University Press.

Bebbington, A. 1991. Farmer Organisations in Ecuador: Contributions to

"Farmer First" Research and Development. *Sustainable Agriculture Programme Gatekeeper Series* SA26. London: IIED.

Benor, D., J. Harrison, and M. Baxter. 1984. *Agricultural Extension: The Training and Visit System.* Washington DC: The World Bank.

Bentley, J. 1992. Promoting Farmer Experiments in Non-Chemical Pest Control. Paper for joint IIED/IDS Beyond Farmer First: Rural People's Knowledge, Agricultural Research and Extension Practice Conference, 27–29 October, Institute of Development Studies, University of Sussex, UK. London: IIED.

Bunch, R. 1990. Low Input Soil Restoration in Honduras: The Cantarranas Farmer-to-Farmer Extension Programme. *Sustainable Agriculture Programme Gatekeeper Series SA23.* London: IIED.

Campbell, A. 1994. *Landcare: Communities Shaping the Land and the Future.* St Leonards, NSW: Allen and Unwin.

Chambers, R. 1992a. The Self-Deceiving State. *IDS Bulletin* 23 (4): 31–42.

———. 1992b. Rural Appraisal: Rapid, Relaxed and Participatory. *IDS Discussion Paper 311.* University of Sussex, UK: Institute of Development Studies.

———. 1992c. Methods for Analysis by Farmers: The Professional Challenge. Paper for 12th Annual Symposium of Association for FSR/E, Michigan State University, September 13–18.

———. 1992d. Spreading and Self-Improving: A Strategy for Scaling-Up. In Edwards and Hulme, eds., *Making a Difference,* 40–47.

———. 1993. *Challenging the Professions: Frontiers for Rural Development.* London: Intermediate Technology Publications Ltd.

———. 1997. *Whose Reality Counts? Putting the First Last.* London: Intermediate Technology Publications.

Chambers, R., A. Pacey, and L. A. Thrupp. 1989. *Farmer First: Farmer Innovation and Agricultural Research.* London: Intermediate Technology Publications Ltd.

Chand, S., and B. Gurung. 1991. Informal Research with Farmers: The Practice and Prospects in the Hills of Nepal. *Journal of Farming Systems Res.–Extension* 2 (2): 69–79.

Chapman, N. 1988. The Impact of T&V Extension in Somalia. In J. Howell, ed., *Training and Visit Extension in Practice.* London: Overseas Development Institute.

Checkland, P. 1981. *Systems Thinking, Systems Practice.* Chichester: John Wiley.

Constantino-David, K. 1992. The Caucus of Development NGO Networks: The Philippine Exercises in Scaling Up NGO Impact. In M. Edwards and D. Hulme, eds., *Making a Difference? NGOs and Development in a Changing World.* London: Earthscan Publications Ltd.

Conway, G. R. 1997. *The Doubly Green Revolution.* London: Penguin Books.

Critchley, W. 1991. *Looking after Our Land: New Approaches to Soil and Water Conservation in Dryland Africa.* London: Oxfam and IIED.

De los Reyes, R., and S. Jopillo. 1986. *An Evaluation of the Philippines Partici-

patory Communal Irrigation Program. Quezon City: Institute of Philippine Culture.

Devavaram, J. 1999. Paraikulum Watershed, Tamil Nadu. In Hinchcliffe et al. 1999.

Drinkwater, M. 1992. Knowledge, Consciousness and Prejudice: Developing a Methodology for Achieving a Farmer-Researcher Dialogue in Adaptive Agricultural Research in Zambia. Paper for joint IIED/IDS Beyond Farmer First: Rural People's Knowledge, Agricultural Research and Extension Practice Conference, 27–29 October, Institute of Development Studies, University of Sussex, UK. London: IIED.

Edwards, M., and Hulme, D. 1992. *Making a Difference? NGOs and Development in a Changing World.* London: Earthscan Publications Ltd.

Farrington, J., A. Bebbington, K. Wellard, and D. Lewis. 1993. *Reluctant Partners? NGOs and the State in Sustainable Agricultural Development.* London: Routledge.

Farrington, J., and S. Biggs. 1990. NGOs, Agricultural Technology and the Rural Poor. *Food Policy,* December, 479–91.

Fernandez, A. 1992. *The MYRADA Experience: Alternate Management Systems for Savings and Credit of the Rural Poor.* Bangalore: MYRADA.

Fowler, A. 1992. Prioritizing Institutional Development: A New Role for NGO Centres for Study and Development. *Sustainable Agriculture Programme Gatekeeper Series SA35.* London: IIED.

Freire, P. 1968. *Pedagogy of the Oppressed.* London: Penguin Books.

Fujisaka, S. 1989. Participation by Farmers, Researchers and Extension Workers in Soil Conservation. *Sustainable Agriculture Programme Gatekeeper Series SA16.* London: IIED.

———. 1991. A Set of Farmer-Based Diagnostic Methods for Setting Post "Green Revolution" Rice Research Priorities. *Agricultural Systems* 36: 191–206.

Ghimire, K., and M. Pimbert. 1997. *Social Change and Conservation.* London: Earthscan Publications.

Gibbon, D. 1992. The Future of Farming Systems Research in Developing Countries. In K. Raman and T. Balaguru, eds., *Farming Systems Research in India: Strategies for Implementation.* Rajendranagar, Hyderabad: NAARM.

Gibbs, G. 1981. *Teaching Students to Learn.* Milton Keynes: Open University Press.

Gill, G. 1993. OK, the Data's Lousy, but It's All We've Got (being a critique of conventional methods). *Sustainable Agriculture Programme Gatekeeper Series SA38.* London: IIED.

Gleick, J. 1987. *Chaos: Making a New Science.* London: Heinneman.

Gould, S. J. 1989. *Wonderful Life: The Burgess Shale and the Nature of History.* London: Penguin Books.

Guijt, I., and J. Pretty., eds. 1992. *Participatory Rural Appraisal for Farmer Participatory Research in Punjab, Pakistan.* Islamabad: Pakistan-Swiss Potato Development Project, PARC; London: IIED.

Handy, C. 1989. *The Age of Unreason.* London: Business Books Ltd.

Harvey, D. 1989. *The Condition of Postmodernity.* Oxford: Blackwell.

Heinrich, G., F. Worman, and C. Koketso. 1991. Integrating FPR with Conventional On-Farm Research Programmes: An Example from Botswana. *J. Farming Systems Res.—Extension* 2, no. 2: 1–15.

Hinchcliffe, F., J. Thompson, J. Pretty, I. Guijt, and P. Shah. 1999. *Fertile Ground: The Impacts of Participatory Watershed Development.* London: IT Publications.

Holling, C. 1978. *Adaptive Environmental Assessment and Management.* Chichester: John Wiley and Sons.

Hope, A., S. Timmel, and C. Hodzi. 1984. *Training for Transformation.* Harare: Mambo Press.

Ison, R. 1990. Teaching Threatens Sustainable Agriculture. *Sustainable Agriculture Programme Gatekeeper Series SA21.* London: IIED.

Jiggins, J., and H. de Zeeuw. 1992. Participatory Technology Development in Practice: Process and Methods. In C. Reijntjes, B. Haverkort, and A. Waters-Bayer, eds., *Farming for the Future.* Netherlands: Macmillan and Information Centre for Low External Input Agriculture (ILEIA).

Jintrawet, A., S. Smutkupt, C. Wongsamun, R. Katawetin, and V. Kerdsuk. 1985. *Extension Activities for Peanuts after Rice in Ban Sum Jan, N.E. Thailand: A Case Study in Farmer-to-Farmer Extension Methodology.* Khon Kaen: Khon Kaen University.

Kerr, J., and N. Sanghi. 1992. Indigenous Soil and Water Conservation in India's Semi Arid Tropics. *Sustainable Agriculture Programme Gatekeeper Series SA34.* London: IIED.

Kiara, J., M. Segerros, J. Pretty, and J. McCracken. 1990. *Rapid Catchment Analysis in Murang'a District, Kenya.* Kenya: Ministry of Agriculture.

Kuhn, T. 1962. *The Structure of Scientific Revolutions.* Chicago: Aldine.

Korten, D. 1990. *Getting to the Twenty-first Century: Voluntary Action and the Global Agenda.* West Hartford, CT: Kumarian Press.

Kurokawa, K. 1991. *Intercultural Architecture: The Philosophy of Symbiosis.* London: Academy Editions.

Kydd, J. 1989. Maize Research in Malawi: Lessons from Failure. *Journal of International Development* 1:112–44.

Lightfoot, C., and R. Noble. 1992. Sustainability and On-Farm Experiments: Ways to Exploit Participatory and Systems Concepts. Paper for 12th Annual Farming Systems Symposium. Michigan State University, 13–18 September.

Lincoln, Y., and E. Guba. 1985. *Naturalistic Inquiry.* Newbury Park: Sage Publications.

Lynton, R., and U. Pareek. 1990. *Training for Development* (2d ed.). West Hartford, CT: Kumarian Press.

Mascarenhas, J., P. Shah, S. Joseph, R. Jayakaran, J. Devavaram, V. Ramachandran, A. Fernandez, R. Chambers, and J. Pretty. 1991. Participatory Rural Appraisal. *Sustainable Agriculture Programme RRA Notes* 13. London: IIED.

Maurya, D. M. 1989. The Innovative Approach of Indian Farmers. In Chambers et al., eds., *Farmer First.* London: Intermediate Technology Publications Ltd.

McCorkle, C., R. Brandsletter, and D. McClure. 1988. *A Case Study on Farmer Innovation and Communication in Niger.* Washington, DC: Communication for Technology Transfer in Africa, Academy of Educational Development.

Mearns, R. 1991. *Environmental Implications of Structural Adjustment: Reflections on Scientific Method.* IDS Discussion Paper 284. University of Sussex, UK: Institute of Development Studies.

Merrill-Sands, D., S. Biggs, R. Bingen, P. Ewell, J. McAllister, and S. Poats. 1991. Institutional Considerations in Strengthening On-Farm Client-Oriented Research in National Agricultural Research Systems: Lessons from a Nine-Country Study. *Experimental Agriculture* 27:343–73.

Merrill-Sands, D., and M.-H. Collion. 1992. Making the Farmers' Voice Count: Issues and Opportunities for Promoting Farmer-Responsive Research. Paper for 12th Annual Farming Systems Symposium, Michigan State University, 13–18 September.

Mishra, P., and S. Madhu. 1988. Social Security through Social Fencing, Sukhomajri and Nada, North India. In C. Conroy and M. Litvinoff, eds., *The Greening of Aid: Sustainable Livelihoods in Practice,* 22–28. London: Earthscan Publications Ltd.

Mitlin, D., and D. Satterthwaite. 1992. Supporting Community Level Initiatives. In M. Edwards and D. Hulme, eds., *Making a Difference? NGOs and Development in a Changing World.* London: Earthscan Publications Ltd.

MOALDM. Passim. Annual and Quarterly Reports of Catchment Approach Planning. Nairobi: Soil and Water Conservation Branch, Ministry of Agriculture Livestock Development and Marketing.

Morales, H. 1992. NGO Networks in the Philippines. In M. Edwards and D. Hulme (eds.), *Making a Difference? NGOs and Development in a Changing World.* London: Earthscan Publications Ltd.

Moris, J. 1990. *Extension Alternatives in Africa.* London: Overseas Development Institute.

Mosse, D. 1992. Community Management and Rehabilitation of Tank Irrigation Systems in Tamil Nadu: A Research Agenda. Paper for GAPP Conference in Participatory Development, July 9–10, London.

Mullen, J. 1989. Training and Visit System in Somalia: Contradictions and Anomalies. *Journal of International Development* 1:145–67.

Norman, D., D. Baker, G. Heinrich, C. Jonas, S. Maskiara, and P. Worman. 1989. Farmer Groups for Technology Development: Experiences from Botswana. In R. Chambers, A. Pacey, and L. Thrupp, eds., *Farmer First.* London: Intermediate Technology Publications Ltd.

Ostrom, E. 1998. *Social Capital: A Fad or a Fundamental Concept?* Center for the Study of Institutions, Population, and Environmental Change, Bloomington: Indiana University.

Paris, T., and B. Del Rosario. 1993. Overview of the Women in Rice Farming

Systems Program. Paper presented at the IRRI Rice Research Seminar Series, January 7.

Pearson, C., and R. Ison. 1990. University Education for Multiple Goal Agriculture in Australia. *Agric. Systems.*

Peters, T., and R. Waterman. 1982. *In Search of Excellence.* New York: Harper Row.

Pimbert, M. 1991. *Participatory Research with Women Farmers* (video, 33 mins.). Hyderabad: ICRISAT.

Poffenberger, M. 1990. *Joint Management of Forest Lands: Experiences from South Asia.* New Delhi: The Ford Foundation.

Porter, D., B. Allen, and G. Thompson. 1991. *Development in Practice: Paved with Good Intentions.* London: Routledge.

Pradan, N., and Yoder, R. 1989. Improving Irrigation Management through Farmer to Farmer Training: Examples from Nepal. *International Irrigation Management Institute Working Paper no. 12.* Kathmandu.

Pretty, J. 1991. Farmers' Extension Practice and Technology Adaptation: Agricultural Revolution in 17–19th Century Britain. *Agriculture and Human Values* 8 (1–2): 132–48.

———. 1995a. *Regenerating Agriculture: Policies and Practice for Sustainability and Self-Reliance.* London: Earthscan Publications; Washington, DC: National Academy Press; Bangalore: ActionAid.

———. 1995b. Participatory Learning for Sustainable Agriculture. *World Development* 23, no. 8: 1247–63.

———. 1998. *The Living Land: Agriculture, Food Systems and Community Regeneration in Rural Europe.* London: Earthscan Publications.

Pretty, J., and R. Chambers. 1993. Towards a Learning Paradigm: New Professionalism and Institutions for Agriculture. Sussex, U.K.: Institute of Development Studies.

Pretty, J., and I. Scoones. 1991. Local Level Adaptive Planning: Looking to the Future. *Sustainable Agriculture Programme RRA Notes* 11:5–21. London: IIED.

———, eds. 1989. *Rapid Rural Appraisal for Economics: Exploring Indicators to Tree Management in Sudan.* London: IIED; Khartoum: Institute of Environmental Studies.

Pretty, J., and P. Shah. 1997. Making Soil and Water Conservation Sustainable: from Coercion and Control to Partnerships and Participation. *Land Degradation and Development* 8:39–58.

Pretty, J., and H. Ward. 2001. Social Capital and the Environment. *World Development.* Forthcoming.

Pretty, J., J. Thompson, and J. K. Kiara. 1995. Agricultural Regeneration in Kenya: The Catchment Approach to Soil and Water Conservation. *Ambio* XXIV, no. 1: 7–15.

Rahman, M., ed. 1984. *Grass-Roots Participation and Self-Reliance.* New Delhi: Oxford and IBH Publication Co.

Rhoades, R. 1989. Evolution of Agricultural Research and Development since

1950: Toward an Integrated Framework. *Sustainable Agriculture Programme Gatekeeper Series SA12.* London: IIED.

Rhoades, R., and R. Booth. 1982. Farmer Back to Farmer: A Model for Generating Acceptable Agricultural Technology. *Agricultural Administration (Research and Extension) Network Paper 11.* London: Overseas Development Institute.

Röling, N. 1992. Facilitating Sustainable Agriculture Changes Policy Models. Paper for joint IIED/IDS Beyond Farmer First: Rural People's Knowledge, Agricultural Research and Extension Practice Conference, 27–29 October, Institute of Development Studies, University of Sussex, UK. London: IIED.

Roche, C. 1991. ACORD's Experience in Local Planning in Mali and Burkina Faso. *Sustainable Agriculture Programme RRA Notes* 11:33–41. London: IIED.

Rogers, A. 1985. *Teaching Adults.* Open University Press, Milton Keynes.

Russell, D., and R. Ison. 1991. The Research-Development Relationship in Rangelands: An Opportunity for Contextual Science. Plenary paper for 4th International Rangelands Congress, Montpellier, France, April 22–26.

Russell, D., R. Ison, D. Gamble, and R. Williams. 1989. *A Critical Review of Rural Extension Theory and Practice.* Faculty of Agriculture and Rural Development, University of Sydney, Australia.

Schon, D. 1983. *The Reflective Practitioner: How Professionals Think in Action.* Aldershot, UK: Avebury.

Senge, P. 1990. *The Fifth Discipline: The Art and Practice of the Learning Organisation.* London: Century Business.

Shah, P. 1999. Participatory watershed management programmes in India: reversing our roles and revising our theories. In Hinchcliffe et al. 1999.

Shah, P., G. Bharadwaj, and R. Ambastha. 1991. Participatory Impact Monitoring of a Soil and Water Conservation Programme by Farmers, Extension Volunteers, and AKRSP. In J. Mascarenhas et al., eds., Participatory Rural Appraisal. *Sustainable Agriculture Programme RRA Notes* 13:127–31. London: IIED.

Sumberg, J. 1991. NGOs and Agriculture at the Margin: Research, Participation and Sustainability in West Africa. *Agricultural Administration (Research and Extension) Network Paper 27.* London: Overseas Development Institute.

TAC. 1993. *The Ecoregional Approach to Research in the CGIAR.* Report of the TAC/Center Directors Working Group, TAC Secretariat, FAO, Rome.

Uphoff, N. 1990. Paraprojects: A New Role of International Development Assistance. *World Development* 18:1401–11.

———. 1992. *Learning from Gal Oya: Possibilities for Participatory Development and Post-Newtonian Social Science.* Ithaca: Cornell University Press.

Wijayaratna, C. 1985. Involvement of Farmers in Water Management in Gal Oya, Sri Lanka. In *Participation Experiences in Irrigation Water Management.* Proc. of Expert Consultation on Irrigation Water Management, Yogyakarta and Bali, July 1984. FAO, Rome.

CHAPTER 9

Does Food Security Require Local Food Systems?

Molly D. Anderson and John T. Cook

An overriding goal of international agricultural development policy is the elimination of poverty-related food insecurity, hunger, and malnutrition. Sustainable food supply systems are vital to the success of any development strategy because subsistence needs must be met before other quality-of-life issues can be addressed. This article examines the relationships between the goals of food security and sustainable development. We argue that localized food systems can meet needs for food, maintain environmental quality, and promote better political representation in food-system choices. Local food systems do not imply termination of trade or exclusive reliance on local resources, but they encourage local environmentally responsible use of resources for food production and supply as the first choice. Strong local food-supply systems are a critical barrier against some of the economic, cultural, and environmental vulnerabilities that emerge in communities as a result of globalization of food supplies.

The connection between food security and local food systems in the United States is the main focus of this article. Although hunger and food insecurity are most commonly seen as problems in low-income or developing countries, recent studies documenting the prevalence of hunger and malnutrition in industrialized countries have made clear that high aggregate national income and food security do not necessarily go hand in hand. The United States wields considerable power in the global food business and possesses one of the largest per capita GNPs in the world (U.S. Bureau of the Census 1996). Yet according to the most recent estimates of food insecurity in the United States by the U.S. Department of Agriculture, 31.2 million people live in food-insecure households (Hamilton et al. 1997; Bickel et al. 1999). Likewise, hunger has re-emerged during the 1980s and 1990s in other wealthy industrialized nations, such as Australia, Canada, New Zealand, and the United Kingdom.

The growth in the number of food-insecure people manifests in the increasing usage of emergency food supply systems (Riches 1997).

The route to achieving food security in developing nations is seen most commonly as involving increased food production through application of modern agricultural techniques. In a study of the food production outlook through the year 2010, the United Nations estimates that increased yields will account for 66 percent of production growth in developing countries, and increased cropping intensity will account for an additional 13 percent (Alexandratos 1995, 170). The World Bank also supports the assertion that production increases can accommodate the effective demand of the increasing world population (Crosson and Anderson 1992).

With the problem defined as insufficient food production, the solution appears to be increased agricultural productivity; and the means of achieving that solution seem obvious. Plucknett and Winkelmann (1995, 182), well-respected professionals who have worked with the U.S. Agency for International Development, the World Bank, and the Consultative Group on International Agricultural Research, argue that "technology has been the most reliable force for pushing agriculture toward higher productivity throughout this century." They suggest an array of technological advances that will help farmers achieve continuing output increases: genetic engineering, using genetic material maintained at −10 degrees Celsius in quality-controlled gene banks; biological test kits for in-field identification of viruses and other diseases; and expert computer systems. Like many other agricultural development theorists, they stress the importance of continued investment in agricultural science and technology.

There is, however, growing evidence that food insecurity will not be eliminated solely by increasing production, although technological advances that maintain environmental quality are certainly *part* of the answer. Lappé and Collins (1982) emphasized that increasing production while ignoring *who* is in control of productive assets can create even greater impoverishment, food insecurity, and hunger. For example, African agricultural development programs have provided credit and training exclusively to men, despite women's dominant role in household food production. Although women in sub-Saharan Africa grow and sell between 80 and 90 percent of food for family and local consumption, they receive less than 1 percent of the total credit available to agriculture. This has contributed to increases in inequities between female and male agricultural producers and greater hardship for women; over the last twenty years the number of rural women living in absolute poverty has increased by 50 percent, while the percentage of rural men in absolute poverty increased only 30 percent over the same time period (UNPF 1997).

During the past half-century the environmental costs of industrialized agricultural production systems have been severe. Far from being a tangential point, environmental degradation is intimately connected with food security. Much of this degradation results from agricultural mismanagement or overexploitation of natural resources for food production. Environmental degradation that leads to declines in resource productivity reduces the prospects of future world food security, making this goal more difficult to attain. Mismanagement in agricultural production has caused moderate to severe soil degradation of about 17 percent of the world's vegetated land since 1945 (Oldeman et al. 1990). Salinization due to improper irrigation techniques is widespread, although its effects on productivity are difficult to estimate. Recent studies report that salinization has reduced productivity on 15 million hectares in developing countries, caused up to 30 percent lower yields of major crops in Egypt and Pakistan, and lowered crop yields on irrigated land in the United States by 25 to 30 percent (Postel 1993). Agriculture is the primary source of nonpoint pollution of streams, rivers, and coastal areas, leading to eutrophication and hypoxic zones that affect commercial fisheries. Fertilizer runoff into the Mississippi River contributes 56 percent of the excess nutrients that have created a large hypoxic zone in the Gulf of Mexico, according to the U.S. Geological Survey (Beardsley 1997).

The long-term environmental costs of food production must be considered in evaluating whether a society meets sensible criteria for sustainability, such as those proposed by Meadows et al. (1992):

- rates of use of renewable resources do not exceed their rates of regeneration;
- rates of use of nonrenewable resources do not exceed the rate at which sustainable renewable substitutes are developed;
- rates of pollution emission do not exceed the assimilative capacity of the environment.

Contemporary global industrialized agricultural systems violate all three of these conditions.

Reformulating "food security" as "community food security" attempts to include other influences on and consequences of food supply beyond national income and levels of agricultural production. Community food security is relevant in redefining the goals of agricultural development and food policy in both industrialized and developing nations. This essay considers some of the main problems with the concept of food security that can be effectively addressed by broadening it to "community food security," examines local food systems as ways to share information and power in food supply more equitably, and presents cases of successful "relocalization" of food supply. We believe this examination of local food systems in the United States will help to identify ways that other nations can better promote community food security.

Problems with the Narrower Concept of Food Security

Food security is defined as

> access by all people at all times to enough food for an active, healthy life and includes at a minimum: a) the ready availability of nutritionally adequate and safe foods; and b) the assured ability to acquire acceptable foods in socially acceptable ways (e.g., without resorting to emergency food supplies, scavenging, stealing, and other coping strategies). Food insecurity exists whenever [a or b] is limited or uncertain. Hunger . . . and malnutrition are potential, although not necessary, consequences of food insecurity. (Anderson 1990, 1575)

This definition, compiled by the Life Sciences Research Office of the Federation of American Societies for Experimental Biology, was synthesized from definitions that emerged in the economic development literature of the 1960s and 1970s (reviewed in von Braun et al. 1992). In that literature, food security is considered primarily at the individual, household, state, and national levels. It is assessed by discrepancies between net import needs and import capacity or other comparisons of aggregate food demand and supply (state or country level); intake surveys (individual and household levels); anthropometric data (individual level); or with various proxies such as change in socioeconomic indicators, demographic characteristics, hunger surveys, or demand on the emergency food-supply system (FAO 1996).

Attempts to remediate food insecurity or the related problems of hunger and malnutrition in the United States and internationally have rested on several assumptions with implicit ethical weights.

1. Food is not a basic right, comparable to freedom from physical molestation or its threat. People must produce their own food, or buy it with earnings from socially approved activities.
2. If individuals have enough money, they are food secure. Therefore, food security is promoted most directly by augmenting

individual and household income, or the ability to earn that income.

3. Ability to pay carries with it the right to consume as much food as a person wishes to buy (i.e., no moral obligation exists to limit one's own consumption to promote more equitable consumption of food and food-related resources among the world's people, current and future).

4. The source of food (who grows it and where) is irrelevant to food security. Ability to pay carries with it the right to buy food of whatever quality, type, and source is preferred by the customer (i.e., consumers have no moral obligation to support particular kinds of production regimes).

5. Natural resources needed for food production are inexhaustible or readily substituted. In procuring food, it is not necessary to consider the environmental externalities of producing and transporting it (i.e., no moral obligation exists to conserve or restore natural resources used in food production).

6. The price system operating within a free-market economy will lead to the optimum location and scale of food production activities in each country.

The underlying problem with these assumptions and the programs based on them is that they treat food supply as if it were isolated from the physical environment and sociocultural context in which it is produced and consumed, and in which food insecurity arises. Taking food out of the context in which it is produced and consumed obscures important existing problems and can even create new problems.

Food security studies at the individual, household, state, or country level cannot adequately explain factors at the community level that affect food access; and the predominant emphasis on the household level excludes the homeless and refugees who suffer from inadequate food supplies. Many people with incomes above the poverty level who live in poor communities or communities with high levels of social fragmentation have limited access to food, for example, due to absence of retail food markets, lack of transportation, high crime rates in the neighborhood, or ongoing military conflict. Community dynamics that affect food access include the level of investment in public resources (for example, transportation infrastructure), the quality of that investment (for example, buses versus freeways), and the quality of social relationships and interaction (for example, whether women can safely use public transportation).

Emphasis on income generation as the solution to food insecurity has contributed to heedless overconsumption of environmental resources, threatening the capacity of future generations to produce the food they need. For example, resource-intensive agricultural and aquacultural technologies have been promoted in developing countries as ways to supplement income by producing foods for export, often without regard for their sustainability. This is well-documented for both the Green Revolution and the new "Blue Revolution" of aquaculture (Stonich et al. 1997).

Farm-based communities and fragile networks of knowledge about locally adapted agricultural production are being lost or destroyed by action stemming from the assumptions that who produces food where is irrelevant, and that these decisions are optimally determined by the price system. Concentration of power *away from* smaller producers and consumers, and *to* large-scale farms and agribusiness corporations contributes to loss of farms, farmers, and social accountability in agriculture. Small- and mid-scale farmers in many parts of the world who do not benefit from economies of scale are going out of business due to international or extraregional competition and rising operating costs.

Although concentration of food production on large farms in certain geographic areas — such as California, Florida, or Mexico — may be a more efficient way to produce food from a narrow economic perspective, there are high costs involved that are not internalized in the price system. These include the loss of farms and farming communities in other regions of the United States, loss of knowledge about local farming conditions and effective ways to cope with them, and loss of control or means of influencing important decisions about agricultural production. The advantages of "economic efficiency" — lower food costs and greater year-round availability of seasonal crops to consumers — must be balanced against these negative effects.

However, there are few avenues available to the public for input into decisions about trade-offs between public interests and the interests of financially and politically powerful players in the agricultural sector. The processes of vertical integration in agribusiness and concentration of ownership of farms and retail food outlets insulate decision making about food production and distribution from social accountability, as power over the food system concentrates in a shrinking set of people (Gussow 1991; Tansey and Worsley 1995). Even for communities with abundant food, the nutritional and cultural meanings of their food can be easily distorted as overconsumption by those who can afford it becomes "normal" (Goodman and Redclift 1991; Iggers 1996).

In the United States, individuals and households without enough food are able to seek help from public and private food assistance networks. There are at least twelve different government-supported public programs that provide food or resources for purchasing food, established since hunger was first recognized as a public-policy issue during the Great Depression of the 1930s (Poppendieck 1997). These public assistance programs are supplemented by massive private networks of "emergency" food providers: food pantries, soup kitchens, shelters, and the food banks and Prepared and Perishable Food Rescue Programs that supply them.

However, the safety net of public and private food providers is not adequate to meet current needs. For example, a 1997 assessment of food stamp participation rates using the best available data showed that only 71 percent of those eligible to use food stamps actually used them (Stavrianos 1997). Private networks cannot accommodate the *previously existing* demand for their services, much less the fourfold increases in demand anticipated with 1996 changes in the U.S. welfare system (Cook and Brown 1997).

The inability to meet basic food needs contributes to a tightening spiral of poverty and malnutrition that affects tens of millions of Americans each year. Lack of access to nutritious food reinforces poverty through malnutrition. For example, malnourished adults often do not have the strength and stamina to work effectively or fend off illness. Children who do not get enough of the right kinds of food suffer from impaired cognitive development and reduced immunity to diseases (CHPNP 1993; Pollitt 1994). Food access for poor people has deteriorated with the increasing polarization of socioeconomic opportunity, in which the poor and affluent are increasingly concentrated and isolated from each other. If current trends continue, most of the world's impoverished people will live in urban areas in the next century, in neighborhoods characterized by extreme poverty with little opportunity for escape. Affluent people will cluster in enclaves where they have little or no contact with poor people (Massey 1996).

The public and private networks that have been put in place to deal with hunger and food insecurity have failed to solve these problems. Part of this failure is due to a phenomenon for which Ivan Illich coined the term *paradoxical counterproductivity.* Institutions, once they pass a certain threshold of size and intensity, often produce the opposite of their stated intentions. Schools make people stupid; medicine and medical intervention make people sick (Illich 1971, 1975). In the realm of food production, pesticides and the ways they are promoted by agro-industries create "superpests" (Wargo 1996). In the realm of food supply, food assistance programs appear to create greater food insecurity. Treating food insecurity as an emergency, rather than an endemic consequence of deep-rooted problems with a community and its reliance on the global food system, has distracted attention from ways that community resources can be augmented so that food supply is more predictable and subject to local control. A crisis-intervention orientation, relying on the availability of external aid, precludes planning for local self-reliance and hunger prevention and may actually erode community resources.

There are many reasons for paradoxical counterproductivity, some attributable to the general logic of institutional development and some specific to particular circumstances. First, as institutions get bigger, they tend to eliminate the possibility for other kinds of responses to the problem they were created to address (Schwartz 1997). This sometimes happens deliberately, as when the American Medical Association resists midwives or alternative practitioners encroaching on its territory, or when the National Cattlemen's Association tries to impugn vegetarianism. But it also happens inadvertently, as when roads designed to improve transportation become so congested that traffic is stalled for hours, yet walking or riding a bicycle is no longer safe because of traffic volume.

A second reason for paradoxical counterproductivity is that as an institution develops and grows, its size and economic power can lead people to view it as the solution to an expanding range of problems. For example, people who were previously tolerated by their families or neighborhoods as just somewhat eccentric are viewed as "mentally ill" and in need of professional care, as mental health professionals and institutions become ubiquitous (Schwartz 1997). Of course, institutionalization and professional treatment are sometimes thoroughly appropriate. The point is that effective alternatives for coping with social problems often become dysfunctional, as formal bureaucratized "solutions" become more powerful.

In addition to these general problems, food assistance programs can exacerbate hunger and food insecurity in several ways:

1. Food-assistance institutions give the illusion that the problem is being addressed adequately. The very fact that hunger and food insecurity become less visible while continuing to exist, or even to grow, deters public awareness, outrage, and action.

2. The tendency to evaluate public and private food assistance networks predominantly in terms of economic costs and benefits works against creating effective solutions to inequities in the food system. Not only do economic evaluations of food programs leave out nonmonetary costs and benefits (externalities), they also fail to include in the balance all the monetary benefits that go to middle- and upper-class Americans. In 1993, total federal government benefits, including (a) Aid to

Families with Dependent Children; (b) means-tested benefits such as food stamps and child nutrition programs; (c) non–means-tested assistance programs such as social security and farm price supports, and (d) tax expenditures, such as tax deductions and credits, amounted to $1.1631 trillion, of which 86 percent was received primarily by middle-class and wealthy recipients (CHPNP 1995). Yet means-tested benefits alone are most often the focus of economic evaluations of whether taxpayers can afford to aid the poor and hungry.

3. Food assistance networks cannot "fix" hunger and food insecurity because powerful reciprocities exist between food insecurity and agribusiness/food industries. The food-assistance programs were conceived initially as a way to deal with agricultural surpluses and were administered with a priority on benefits to agricultural producers, not hungry people (Poppendieck 1997). This legacy has shaped their evolution. The U.S. government buys commodities from growers to support farm prices, and it redistributes this "surplus" to private food banks and public food-assistance programs, in addition to using some for foreign aid. Although the commodity programs have been justified as benefiting low-income consumers (Browne et al. 1992), they have not always worked as planned. Higher food prices and restricted supplies due to government farm programs cost U.S. consumers between $5 and $10 billion in indirect or welfare costs between 1982 and 1988 (Faeth et al. 1992). Thus, the stability of producers' income is supported by shifting costs from producers to consumers (poor as well as wealthy).

Additional reciprocities exist for food processors and retailers who donate surplus and damaged goods that would otherwise diminish their profits and partially recover their losses through tax write-offs. Reciprocity has also been documented between direct provider agencies (e.g., soup kitchens or pantries) and clients: workers sometimes take home food, or a church might "use" the food-provision service as a vehicle to fulfill its religious or social role (Daponte 1996). None of these reciprocities are necessarily bad. Some benefit consumers at all income levels, and some benefit volunteers at provider agencies who are themselves quite poor. However, they create a network of interlinked interests that works against putting the formal emergency food-access system out of business.

4. Food-assistance networks or institutions cannot eliminate hunger and food insecurity, finally, because their primary motivation generally becomes to perpetuate themselves. Food assistance programs serve a critical function by getting food to hungry people, but they do not help build food security. They simply reinforce the safety net designed to catch people who are already suffering from food insecurity.

Community Food Security: An Alternative Approach

These major problems arising from a narrow definition of food security have led to efforts to reformulate the basic concept (Anderson and Cook 1999). One reformulation likely to affect international programs dealing with food security appeared in the Rome Declaration on World Food Security (1996). This declaration emphasizes the role of sustainable management of natural resources, the elimination of unsustainable patterns of consumption and production, the need to ensure equality between men and women, and the revitalization of rural areas.

Many of these themes are reiterated in the U.S. Community Food Security Act, included in the 1996 Farm Bill. Projects funded under this act must "be designed to meet the food needs of low income people, increase the self-reliance of communities in providing for their own food needs, and promote comprehensive, inclusive, and future-oriented solutions to local food, farm and nutrition problems" (CFS News 1996). The meager funding available thus far for Community Food Projects ($1 million during the first year of implementation and $2.5 million the second year) has gone to community-based organizations to expand their current projects. Examples of funded projects are new farmers' markets for low-income neighborhoods, community farms and gardens, and city or regional food councils. These are valuable efforts, but small steps toward widespread community food security.

A key component of these newer definitions of food security is attention to building local capacity to produce and distribute food and control food supplies. Creating a local food economy can be an effective way to revitalize communities (Feenstra 1997). Careful planning is needed to keep decision-making power within the community rather than losing it through dependence on external sources of food. Increased investment in localized food production can meet many of the diverse community needs more effectively than globalized food systems because it can give priority to community and environmental integrity before corporate profit-making (which tends to drive corporate investments in agricultural technology and food supply). Community food security planning also seeks to augment social capital (as defined by Putnam 1993) by helping community residents achieve some control over their own food supply while reinforcing social identity and cohesion.

The major advantage of localizing food systems, underlying all other advantages, is that this process reworks power and knowledge relationships in food supply systems that have become distorted by increasing distance (physical, social, and metaphorical) between producers and consumers. This distance has contributed to the social and environmental problems associated with global food supply. Corporate interests of large agribusinesses have been inserted between producers and consumers, mediating and extracting profits at each step of food supply, often excluding considerations of public welfare. By simplifying food supply in local food systems, knowledge about how to produce and distribute food can be restored to a community rather than being held exclusively by interests outside that community, who have no particular stake in improving the quality of life there. Opportunities are created at the local level to produce food with greater use of local inputs, and to control what will be grown and when. This allows increased self-reliance, as food producers become less dependent on imported food or external inputs needed for food production, which may be expensive or available erratically. Local food production also allows preservation of locally adapted, locally valued foodways because the producers and consumers either are the same people or are in close contact with each other.

The second important advantage of local food systems is that they can involve community-level economic investment, which keeps multiplier effects local. Economic investment is made in local food systems through entry of new farmers, expansion of existing farms, new food-processing businesses, and new or expanded local markets. The decline of community-level investment has been a major cause of declining farm-based communities, but new investment can reverse this trend.

The third advantage of local food systems is that they enable better environmental stewardship of producing landscapes. Local food production and growers are easily visible to community residents, in contrast to the unseen farms and workers of distant regions. Closer physical connection between production and consumption allows greater attention to the environmental externalities of food production. People living in the local food system's scope can see the effects of farming on their landscapes; and they can experience the advantages of protected green space, a healthier environment, and greater biodiversity that result from environmentally responsible food production. As community residents become aware of the effects of different farming practices on resources, they are more likely to acquire an understanding of natural resources as vulnerable and limited. Awareness of the vulnerability of natural resources can lead to increased motivation to protect those resources, and an increased sense of the power communities have to restore landscapes if they encourage appropriate farming methods.

A fourth advantage of local food systems is increased community cohesion, identity, and viability. This can occur in several ways, but usually involves major improvements in the aesthetic quality of communities. Farming and gardening can provide an anchor or focus for a community's sense of identity. Gardening and food production in urban areas has been a successful means of restoring community pride, reducing crime, and revitalizing unattractive vacant land that had become dumping sites or magnets for illegal activity. Community gardens have become learning environments where community members can share information about food, nutrition, and a host of other topics, including environmental concerns, issues of social and economic justice, safety, and other family concerns. Farming and gardening often lead to improvements in and careful maintenance of open space. They contribute to unique community or regional character, and they can become commercially beneficial as sources of affordable produce and through agritourism. Examples of successful agritourism include pick-your-own apple orchards in upstate New York and central Massachusetts, and the vineyards and wineries of California and New York.

Reaping the benefits of local food systems requires education about food production and consumption alternatives, creation of a robust local marketing infrastructure, and increased opportunities for local involvement at each stage of food supply. Community food security education can help overcome the sense of alienation from food supply that globalization fosters. Marketing venues in which local foods are labeled to distinguish them from foods from other sources and point-of-purchase information about production alternatives are available allow people to affect their community's environmental and social quality through food purchases (Anderson 1998).

Building Community Food Security through Local Food Systems

Building a food system that serves those who do not have adequate food access requires efforts on many fronts. The most fundamental reform in food systems reverses the first assumption of food-security models listed above by ensuring food security as a basic human right, one that is required for the enjoyment of all other rights (Shue 1980). Without food security, people may be unable to enjoy other rights such as freedom from violation of property, rights to public education, and rights to free speech. Although several international documents have been produced calling for rights to food security (e.g., FAO 1996; UN 1991), implementation and enforcement ultimately must be on the local level. Many cities have established food policy councils to promote improved food security. These have had mixed success, depending on factors such as the historical and political context, staff and budget support, and composition of the council

(Dahlberg 1994). Two of the strongest food policy councils at present are in Toronto and in Hartford, Connecticut.

Next, greater public participation in food-system and land-use choices that affect the public interest is essential to reverse the trend toward increasing concentration of decision-making power within agribusinesses. Public monitoring and encouragement of social accountability for agribusiness also can improve its impacts on social welfare. For example, several nongovernmental organizations, including the Women's Environment and Development Organization, have designed codes of conduct for multinational corporations (e.g., WEDO 1995) to bring their activities into congruence with democratic political structures.

Positive actions that build local food systems and information networks are needed, however, in addition to those aimed at limiting the less desirable aspects of global food supply. First, opportunities for public participation in land stewardship could increase the public sense of responsibility for natural resources and the potential for public stewardship of these resources. The town of Weston, Massachusetts, has successfully managed a town forest and farm for more than a decade, giving residents opportunities to work in food production and taste or use the fruits of their labor (Donahue 1999).

Second, partnerships and coalitions among different organizations working on food system reform can be effective. Such partnerships are necessary to raise credibility, provide a voice to those who are politically disempowered, and allow people working in different facets of the food system to learn from each other. Productive partnerships include those between growers or agricultural businesses and their local customers; between environmental and agricultural interests; and among antihunger organizations, state or local governments, and consumer organizations. City- or statewide food policy councils are one example of such coalitions. Other examples include sustainable agriculture working groups in most regions of the United States that have integrated food access concerns with production issues. Producers in the Hudson River watershed and the City of New York have worked together to establish successful incentives improving drinking-water quality by implementing better fertilizer management practices. The Massachusetts Audubon Society, one of the earliest environmental organizations in the United States, has partnered with Boston State Hospital to create a large urban garden that helps provide food and work for low-income people, while using open space more productively.

Third, community food security requires improved opportunities for those who wish to produce, process, or distribute food, to slow the trend toward increasing concentration of production and supply. Investment in this kind of change should be local to obtain the fullest benefits. It can include sponsorship of training programs or other support for growers shifting to more environmentally sound practices, job training, job-finding networks, and support for starting new food-business ventures. Community-supported agriculture is one example of a business venture that works to the mutual benefit of farmers, consumers, and the environment. Consumers buy shares in a farm and its output, thus reducing financial risks that may be associated with conversion to more environmentally sound practices.

Community food security implies more deliberate choices regarding food trade. Within a community food security perspective, it is not desirable to consume inexpensive food if to do so requires that agricultural workers or environments are harmed at distant locations. From this perspective, availability of inexpensive fruits and vegetables that are out of season locally, for example, is not desirable if it requires exploitation of farm workers or small producers and degradation of environments in tropical or subtropical locations.

The final aspect of creating community food security is strengthening informal networks that provide social support along with food. Building community food security implies building *community*, not just food security. This may be the hardest task, because there are so many forces in modern U.S. society working against community cohesiveness. But stronger communities, with the networks of care that they encompass and foster, are the most important security against hunger and lack of access to high-quality food.

Local Food Systems in a Global Food Economy

To illustrate the application of some of the principles of community food security, we will describe three types of projects that have made substantial progress toward goals of improved food access, economic opportunity, and environmental stewardship, using combined strategies of public education, partnerships, innovative marketing strategies, greater local economic investment in food supply, and community-building.

1. *Farmers' market development in low-income U.S. neighborhoods.* Several cities have attempted to improve markets for local fruit and vegetable growers and facilitate access to high-quality fresh produce for low-income people by establishing farmers' markets in inner-city neighborhoods. Except for certain ethnic minorities, low consumption of fresh fruits and vegetables correlates with low household income level. However, health advantages of higher consumption levels (five or

more servings per day) are well-documented (Frazao 1995), and if farmers' markets increase consumption of fresh fruits and vegetables, strong health benefits are anticipated. Farmers' markets give the public direct contact with growers, and they provide an alternative, in a setting conditioned by local values and culture, to uniform, mass-produced food (Lyson et al. 1995).

Farmers' market projects for low-income neighborhoods have been initiated by the Food Project in Boston, the Sustainable Farming Center in Austin, the Coalition for Community Food Security in Los Angeles, and the Farmers Market Trust in Philadelphia. Some of these projects target particular ethnic groups (e.g., Hispanic and African-American neighborhoods in Austin). The nonprofit organization Just Food in New York City has recently begun a project sponsored by the USDA's Northeast Region Sustainable Agricultural Research and Education Program to investigate the feasibility of increasing ethnic markets in New York as a strategy to help local farmers increase their sales. A parallel effort was initiated in 1996 by Massachusetts Extension to grow different varieties of produce important in Caribbean cuisine and to sell them in farmers' markets in and near Boston.

Although suburban farmers' markets have been very successful in a number of metropolitan areas, central-city farmers' markets face unique challenges. In Boston, market managers have encountered some difficulty engaging farmers who are willing to sell at the market, and the related problem of small volumes of shoppers willing or able to patronize the market regularly (personal communication, Oct. 20, 1997, Martha Boyd, The Food Project). The Farmers' Market Nutrition Program, pioneered in Massachusetts, allows customers to buy farmers' market produce with food stamps or WIC coupons. This is a successful way to overcome some of the difficulty of purchasing produce on a low income. Sponsors of farmers' markets in other cities have experimented with different types of food and nutrition education programs to encourage residents to use the markets.

2. *Fair-trade coffee: Equal Exchange.* The globalization of coffee production has followed a familiar path, with poor wages and working conditions for small producers and farm workers and considerable environmental degradation accompanying booming profits for major coffee exporters. Farm communities have suffered as well from the degradation of soil and water quality. Equal Exchange is an employee-owned for-profit corporation in Canton, Massachusetts, which imports coffee directly from fifteen small-producer cooperatives in Central America, South America, and Africa. Approximately 70 percent of their coffee is

certified organic. A large percentage is *shade-grown,* that is, produced in a biodiverse forest as opposed to a full-sun monoculture that destroys habitat for migratory birds and other animal and plant species.

Since Equal Exchange deals directly with producers and retailers and avoids several intermediate brokers, it can pay producers a higher price for coffee while selling to U.S. customers at prices comparable with other gourmet coffees. The increased price has enabled producers to improve their farms and communities. Equal Exchange has an aggressive promotional and educational campaign to educate consumers about the advantages of "fair trade." The "fair trade" principles espoused by Equal Exchange are based on four policies: (1) paying farmers a fair price; (2) providing pre-harvest credit; (3) transparency in the business relationship—open books and information exchange; and (4) trading with democratically run small-farmer cooperatives. In addition to the economic and trade benefits, fair trade strengthens community organizations that typically fulfill other social needs in the community such as health care and education. Through the fair-trade relationship, farmers gain access to markets and information they would never have had otherwise. Equal Exchange is part of a worldwide fair-trade movement that collectively imports and distributes 35 million pounds of coffee beans a year, or $200 million in retail sales, under various fair-trade labels and seals of approval in northern Europe, Japan, Australia, Canada, and the United States.

3. *Urban gardening in the United States and developing nations.* Food production in urban gardens is usually considered part of the informal economy because most is for local or household use. According to the USDA's 1987–88 Nationwide Food Consumption Survey, 16.4 percent of all U.S. households consumed fresh vegetables that were home produced, and 7.8 percent consumed home-produced fresh fruits (USDA/ARS 1994). The UN Development Programme acknowledges that accurate global figures on the numbers of urban farmers and amounts of food produced are not available, but it estimates that there may be several hundred million urban gardeners worldwide. In Dar es Salaam, one of every five adults in the city is a farmer, and over 60 percent of the peri-urban area of Bangkok is given over to vegetable production. Singapore has 10,000 licensed farmers and produces one-quarter of its locally consumed vegetables. New York City has more than 1,000 vacant lots available to community gardens, and Berlin has more than 80,000 community gardeners (UNPF 1996).

Urban gardens are important for aesthetic and social value as well as food production. A study of urban agriculture in and around Hartford estimated that backyard and community gardening produced between $175,000 and $300,000 annually in economic benefits, along with substantial social and psychological benefits (Nugent 1996).

Several organizations in the United States and other countries promote urban gardening. The American Community Gardening Association, the International Development Research Centre in Ottawa, City Farmer — Canada's Office of Urban Agriculture in Vancouver, and the Urban Agricultural Network in Washington, DC, stand out because of their size and scope. However, smaller organizations have been even more important in establishing gardens in low-income neighborhoods in individual cities. An evaluation of the Philadelphia Urban Gardening Project documented higher vegetable consumption (except for iceberg lettuce, celery, and fresh salad greens) and greater neighborhood social participation among gardeners than among nongardeners (Blair et al. 1991). Urban gardens combined with youth job-training, or rehabilitation of prison inmates or homeless people, have been especially promising programs because they deliver strong social benefits along with food (Hynes 1996).

Conclusion

Community food security and local food systems provide a framework for finding solutions to a variety of critical problems related to global food production and distribution. While local food systems cannot be expected to replace larger-scale agricultural production and trade as the world's primary source of food, they can supplement and complement larger-scale food systems in urgently needed ways.

Community food security builds on the narrower conceptual framework of household food security by recognizing a broader range of issues connected to ensuring "access by all people at all times to enough food for an active healthy life." A community food security approach:

promotes critical examination of the social, environmental, and ethical implications of how, where, and by whom food is produced, distributed, and consumed;

internalizes more of the costs and benefits that remain external to the price system;

encourages local production and distribution of food using environmentally sustainable methods;

builds local self-sufficiency through greater community cohesion, identity, and cooperation; and discourages exploitation of agricultural workers at all levels and encourages recognition of equity as an important aspect of food supply.

Local food systems can provide much-needed avenues for influencing food production in positive ways. Education about the ways local food supply decisions ripple out through the larger worldwide food web allows residents of local communities to become aware of how their food consumption impacts other people and environments distant from their own. Local food systems enable community residents to bring their aspirations and values to bear on the larger global food production system, rather than only their consumer preferences.

Community food security and local food systems should not be viewed as a threat to conventional food supply, but can more accurately be seen as a valuable complement to it. This approach to food security and supply has important potential for helping to bring global food production, and overall social and economic development, closer to sustainability.

REFERENCES

Alexandratos, Nikos, ed. 1995. *World Agriculture: Towards 2010. An FAO Study.* Chichester, UK: John Wiley and Sons; Rome: Food and Agriculture Organization of the United Nations.

Anderson, Molly D. 1998. *Consumer Education vs. Marketing: Which is the Best Lever for Food System Change?* Belchertown, Massachusetts: Northeast Sustainable Agriculture Working Group White Paper.

Anderson, Molly D. and John T. Cook. 1999. "Community Food Security: Practice in Need of Theory?" *Agriculture and Human Values* 16, no. 2: 141–50.

Anderson, Sue Ann, ed. 1990. *Core Indicators of Nutritional State for Difficult-to-Sample Populations.* Life Sciences Research Office, Federation of American Societies for Experimental Biology. Prepared for the American Institute of Nutrition with the Office of Disease Prevention and Health Promotion, Department of Health and Human Services, Washington, DC.

Beardsley, Timothy. 1997. Death in the Deep: "Dead Zone" in the Gulf of Mexico Challenges Regulators. *Scientific American* 277, no. 5: 17, 20.

Bickel, Gary, Steve Carlson, and Mark Nord. 1999. *Household Food Security in the United States, 1995–1998 (Advance Report).* Washington, DC: U.S. Department of Agriculture Food and Nutrition Service and Economic Research Service.

Blair, Dorothy, Carol C. Giesecke, and Sandra Sherman. 1991. A Dietary, Social and Economic Evaluation of the Philadelphia Urban Gardening Project. *Journal of Nutrition Education* 23:161–67.

Browne, William P., Jerry R. Skees, Louis E. Swanson, Paul B. Thompson, and Laurian J. Unnevehr. 1992. *Sacred Cows and Hot Potatoes: Agrarian Myths in Agricultural Policy.* Boulder: Westview Press.

Center on Hunger, Poverty and Nutrition Policy. 1993. *Statement on the Link between Nutrition and Cognitive Development in Children.* School of Nutrition Science and Policy, Tufts University, Medford, MA.

———. 1995. *America's Welfare System: Who Benefits and What It Costs.* School of Nutrition Science and Policy, Tufts University, Medford, MA.

Community Food Security News. 1996. We Did It! CFS Act Passes. *Community Food Security News* (winter/spring): 1, 6.

Cook, John T., and J. Larry Brown. 1997. *Analysis of the Capacity of the Second Harvest Network to Cover the Federal Food Stamp Shortfall from 1997 to 2002.* Center on Hunger, Poverty and Nutrition Policy, Tufts University School of Nutrition Science and Policy, Medford, MA.

Crosson, Pierre, and Jock R. Anderson. 1992. Resources and Global Food Prospects: Supply and Demand for Cereals to 2030. World Bank Technical Paper No. 184. Washington, DC: World Bank.

Dahlberg, Kenneth A. 1994. Food Policy Councils: The Experience of Five Cities and One County. Paper presented at the Joint Meeting of the Agriculture, Food and Human Values Society and the Society for the Study of Food and Society, Tucson, AZ.

Daponte, Beth Osborne. 1996. Private versus Public Relief: Utilization of Food Pantries versus Food Stamps among Poor Households in Allegheny County, Pennsylvania. DP#1091–96, Institute for Research on Poverty, University of Wisconsin-Madison.

Donahue, Brian. 1999. *Reclaiming the Commons: Community Farms and Forests in a New England Town.* New Haven: Yale University Press.

Faeth, Paul, Robert Repetto, Kim Kroll, Qi Dai, and Glenn Helmers. 1991. *Paying the Farm Bill: US Agricultural Policy and the Transition to Sustainable Agriculture.* World Resources Institute, Washington, DC.

FAO. 1996. *Rome Declaration on World Food Security. World Food Summit Plan of Action* (November). Rome: Food and Agriculture Organization.

Feenstra, Gail W. 1997. Local Food Systems and Sustainable Communities. *American Journal of Alternative Agriculture* 12, no. 1: 28–36.

Frazao, Elizabeth. 1995. *The American Diet: Health and Economic Consequences.* Agriculture Information Bulletin No. 711, Economic Research Service. Washington, DC: USDA.

Goodman, David, and Michael Redclift. 1991. *Refashioning Nature: Food, Ecology and Culture.* London and New York: Routledge.

Gussow, Joan Dye. 1991. *Chicken Little, Tomato Sauce and Agriculture: Who Will Produce Tomorrow's Food?* New York: Bootstrap Press.

Hamilton, William L., John T. Cook, William W. Thompson, Lawrence F. Buron, Edward A. Frongillo Jr., Christine M. Olson and Cheryl A. Wehler. 1997.

Household Food Security in the United States in 1995: Summary Report of the Food Security Measurement Project. USDA/FCS/OAE.

Hynes, H. Patricia. 1996. *A Patch of Eden: America's Inner-City Gardeners.* White River Junction, VT: Chelsea Green Publishing Company.

Iggers, Jeremy. 1996. *The Garden of Eating: Food, Sex, and the Hunger for Meaning.* New York: Basic Books, Inc.

Illich, Ivan. 1971. *Deschooling Society.* New York: Harper and Row.

———. 1975. *Medical Nemesis: The Expropriation of Health.* London: Calder and Boyars.

Lappé, Frances Moore, and Joseph Collins. 1992. *World Hunger: Ten Myths.* 4th ed. San Francisco: Institute for Food and Development Policy.

Lyson, T. A., G. W. Gillespie Jr., and D. Hilchey. 1995. Farmers' Markets and the Local Economy: Bridging the Formal and Informal Economy. *American Journal of Alternative Agriculture* 10, no. 3: 108–13.

Massey, Douglas S. 1996. The Age of Extremes: Concentrated Affluence and Poverty in the Twenty-first Century. *Demography* 33, no. 4: 395–412.

Meadows, Donella H., Dennis L. Meadows, and Jorgen Randers. 1992. *Beyond the Limits.* Post Mills, VT: Chelsea Green Publishing Company.

Nugent, Rachel A. 1996. The Sustainability of Urban Agriculture: A Case Study in Hartford, Connecticut. Produced as part of an AAAS/EPA Environmental Science and Engineering Fellowship. Department of Economics, Pacific Lutheran University, Tacoma, WA.

Oldeman, L. R., V. W. P. van Engelen, and J. H. M. Pulles. 1990. *World Map of the Status of Human-Induced Soil Degradation: An Explanatory Note.* 2d ed. Wageningen, the Netherlands: International Soil Reference and Information Centre.

Plucknett, Donald L., and Donald L. Winkelmann. 1995. Technology for Sustainable Agriculture. *Scientific American,* 182–86.

Pollitt, Ernesto. 1994. Poverty and Child Development: Relevance of Research in Developing Countries to the United States. *Child Development* 65, no. 2: 283–95.

Poppendieck, Janet. 1997. The USA: Hunger in the Land of Plenty. In Graham Riches (ed.), *First World Hunger: Food Security and Welfare Politics,* 134–64. Houndmills, Basingstoke, Hampshire, and London: MacMillan Press, Ltd.; New York: St. Martin's Press, Inc.

Postel, Sandra. 1993. Water and Agriculture. In Peter H. Gleick (ed.), *Water in Crisis: A Guide to the World's Fresh Water Resources,* 56–66. New York and Oxford: Oxford University Press.

Putnam, Robert. 1993. The Prosperous Community: Social Capital and Public Life. *American Prospect* 13:35–42.

Riches, Graham. 1997. Hunger, Welfare and Food Security: Emerging Strategies. In Graham Riches (ed.), *First World Hunger: Food Security and Welfare Politics,* 165–78. Houndmills, Basingstoke, Hampshire, and London: MacMillan Press, Ltd.; New York: St. Martin's Press, Inc.

Schwartz, David. 1997. *Who Cares? Redefining Community.* Boulder: Westview Press.

Shue, Henry. 1980. *Basic Rights: Subsistence, Affluence, and US Foreign Policy.* Princeton: Princeton University Press.

Stavrianos, Michael. 1997. *Food Stamp Participation Rates: January 1994.* Alexandria, Virginia: U.S. Department of Agriculture Food and Consumer Service.

Stonich, Susan C., John R. Bort, and Luis L. Ovares. 1997. Globalization of Shrimp Mariculture: The Impact on Social Justice and Environmental Quality in Central America. *Society and Natural Resources* 10:161–79.

Tansey, Geoff, and Tony Worsley. 1995. *The Food System: A Guide.* London: Earthscan Publications, Ltd.

UNICEF. 1991. The Convention on the Rights of the Child. In *The State of the World's Children,* 77–96. Oxford: Oxford University Press.

United Nations Population Fund. 1996. *Food for the Future: Women, Population and Food Security.* New York: United Nations.

USDA/ARS. 1994. Food Consumption and Dietary Levels of Households in the United States, 1987–88. Nationwide Food Consumption Survey 1987–88, NFCS Report No. 87-H-1.

Von Braun, Joachim, Howarth Bouis, Shubh Kumar, and Rajul Randya-Lorch. 1991. *Improving Food Security of the Poor: Concept, Policy, and Programs.* Washington, DC: International Food Policy Research Institute.

Wargo, John. 1996. *Our Children's Toxic Legacy: How Science and Law Fail to Protect Us from Pesticides.* New Haven: Yale University Press.

Women's Environment and Development Organization. 1995. Codes of Conduct for Transnational Corporations: Strategies toward Democratic Global Governance. WEDO Primer No. 1. New York.

CHAPTER 10

Community, Ecology, and Landscape Change in Zambrana-Chacuey

Dianne Rocheleau, Laurie Ross, Julio Morrobel, and Ricardo Hernandez

Gender Roles and Resource Management

During the past two decades foresters have turned increasingly to "farmers" as partners in the task of reforestation through social forestry and agroforestry programs. In some regions, such as sub-Saharan Africa and South Asia, the widespread recognition of women as farmers has led to the inclusion of women in farm forestry programs. However, in national and international circles in much of Latin America, including Central America and the Caribbean, a prevalent image of women as housewives and "not farmers" has masked the extensive involvement and the economic interests of women in agriculture, livestock management and forestry (Katz 1992; Townsend et al. 1994; Arriagada 1992; Momsen 1993; Urban and Rojas 1994; Silva 1991; Stonich 1993; Escobar 1995). To date, most social forestry and agroforestry programs in the region have emphasized fuelwood and have named women as the beneficiaries, while they have planned, implemented, and evaluated new technologies with men heads of household.

The extent and nature of women's actual participation in farming and forestry ranges from provision of family labor for men's cropping and forestry enterprises, to processing, marketing, and management of the products at household level, to full identification of women as farmers with direct responsibility for household food and/or cash crop production, including livestock and tree products (Collins 1991; Deere and Leon 1987; Deere 1990b; Silva 1991). Throughout the Dominican Republic both men and women are — to varying degrees — gardeners, farmers, livestock keepers and breeders, forest managers, forest gatherers, drawers of water, food processors, market vendors, and keepers of the natural and built environment. Any program that hopes to confront the

249

realities of rural ecologies and economies must recognize and work with both women and men in some combination of these pursuits.

For example, in the north, in the Cibao Valley and the Sierra the gender division of labor reflects the strong influence of Spanish traditions, with women identified more as housewives or as farmworkers (such as coffee harvesters) and not as farmers. While men may be the exclusive tillers of the land in much of this area, women do participate in both subsistence and commercial production as food processors and as keepers of small livestock (primarily hogs and chickens for both sale and home use). They may also act as farm managers and hire men's labor for some male-identified tasks (Flora and Santos 1986). In the Central Valley and the eastern edge of the Cibao Valley near Cotuí, gender identity is more strongly influenced by Afro-Caribbean norms and practices. The men and women share farm tasks under a more flexible ethos that leaves very broad scope for choice by individual women and their households, with many women identified proudly as farmers.

In every region of the country women and men differ with respect to labor, responsibilities, interests, and control in agricultural and forestry production and resource management. Their knowledge, experience, constraints, and opportunities are in many ways distinct, not by necessity but by custom and current practice. The work, knowledge, interests, and ideas of both women and men matter for resource management, and, conversely, natural resource policy and technologies matter to both women's and men's daily lives and their possible futures both separately and together.

What can resource management and rural development professionals do in the face of such complexity? It is unlikely that most resource management and agricultural professionals will become specialists in social analysis and group process, let alone gender analysis. However, there is no reason why they cannot work with social scientists and development/extension workers on participatory resource management approaches that explicitly deal with men's and women's distinct domains of work, interest, access, and control in resource management. It is also possible to learn to deal with difference — by gender, ethnic group, income level, or age — as part of the conceptual framework for project planning and daily practice. While very specialized skills and knowledge may require formal training and detailed investigation, the fieldwork of others can inform our work at the crossroads of gender, ecology, and community organization in rural landscapes. The lessons of this experience have equal value, whether our specialty is resource management, rural communities, or gender issues.

When working in complex circumstances that mix research and

development in a "laboratory" that is someone else's life and landscape, field experience may best be distilled as a story. The story may be more practical, more relevant, and often more appropriate than a replicable experiment or a set of fixed procedures. Often it makes sense of experience that is not replicable and may indeed be quite instructive (Rocheleau 1991). The case study approach, so widely used for teaching professional skills of all kinds, puts the story to work as a learning and teaching tool that integrates key concepts and skills within the complex context of real life situations. The story that follows illustrates several ways in which gender affects resource management and, conversely, how resource management technologies and policies affect men's and women's lives differently, and, in each case, profoundly.

The encounter between the Rural Federation in Zambrana-Chacuey and the Forestry Enterprise Project embodies both the promise and the pitfalls of social forestry programs throughout the world that attempt to combine reforestation with smallholder- or community-level production of tree products for home use and profit. By almost any standard measure the first decade of the collaborative effort of the Rural Federation of Zambrana-Chacuey and ENDA-Caribe[1] has been a resounding success. Over 85 percent of the more than 500 Federation-affiliated households in the region have planted timber trees on their farms. While some farmers have planted just a few experimental trees, many of them have converted tobacco plots to timber, while others have purchased new plots specifically to plant commercial timber for processing at the new cooperative sawmill.

Many farm families, however, have neither the land nor the cash to buy more land for monocropped timber trees and are unable to participate fully in commercial timber production. Additionally, some men farmers have converted women's multispecies patio gardens to timber trees, while other men have prevented their wives and children from planting trees with the project. Yet other women have received almost no information about the program. "Whose trees and in whose space?" has emerged as a key question in this initiative, along with the concern over the widespread promotion of single species timber lots in a landscape characterized by both ecological and economic diversity.

This case study attempts to sort out this complexity and to highlight ways that the Federation and ENDA's collaborative social forestry project can better serve the diverse interests of the entire rural population. We first present an overview of the national and regional context and the current ecological situation in the region. Next, we explore the gender- and class-divided interests in the social forestry project by tracing the introduction of *Acacia mangium* through the Federation to the diverse household economies and farm ecologies of its members. Four mini-studies of families in distinct but representative social, economic, and ecological situations demonstrate the ways that these factors converge to promote or inhibit participation in the timber project. We conclude with a set of recommendations that address technological, organizational, and tenurial transformations to diversify the timber production project both socially and ecologically.

Establishing the Framework for Agroforestry in Zambrana-Chacuey

The Dominican Republic has a long history of state involvement in the management and regulation of forests dating from the widespread clearing of valuable mahogany stands during the 1800s (Betances 1995; Rodriguez Liriano 1978). State policy has ranged from the strict prohibition of forest clearing for agriculture to direct appropriation of forest and farmlands by the state for parks and reserves, for its own commercial use, or for allocation to preferred clients of the ruling regime.[2]

For the majority of small farmers in the country, the forest was the context in which agricultural production and much of rural life was nested. During periods when the state favored expansion of plantation agriculture, forest cover in agrarian landscapes (now identified with "conservation") signified underutilized and unimproved land, while clearing of forest for agriculture (now labelled "deforestation") was legally recognized as an improvement. Smallholder farmers often lost their rights to land not under "productive use," which made forest lands particularly vulnerable to legal alienation by the state or local elites. Both smallholder and largeholder farmers felt compelled to clear forests or to plant commercial crops (coffee, cocoa, and fruit) in order to create and maintain land rights.

In 1967, state policy shifted toward resource management concerns to protect the watersheds of planned hydroelectric installations (Antonini, Ewel, and Tupper 1975). The legislature passed a law prohibiting the felling of any tree without the express permission of the newly formed, militarized forestry service (Direccion General Forestal, or DGF) (Veras 1984; Santos 1984; Geilfus 1994, 1996). In practice, the DGF often selectively enforced tree-cutting bans against poor smallholders, wood workers, and charcoal producers and awarded permits to commercial producers, local elites, and its own employees. Trees became untouchable resources as well as tenure liabilities for all but the most powerful rural farmers. However, intercropped coffee and cacao stands and multistory patio gardens created a "productive" context that sheltered a variety of forest trees without putting the land tenure of farmers at risk.

The decline of commodity prices for traditional tree crops—coffee and cocoa—over the last decade as well as the structural adjustment policies of the 1980s and 1990s brought a turn toward "nontraditional" agricultural exports (such as citrus, root crops, and pineapple)[3] (Raynolds 1994; McAffee 1987; Deere 1990a). Concurrent with these economic changes, ideologies of environment and sustainable development also gained prominence in national political circles (Lynch 1994). Both developments shaped the national context for reforestation during the last decade.

The residents of Zambrana-Chacuey have directly experienced the impact of Forestry Law 206, the falling market prices for their tree crops, and the complexities and contradictions between national trends in environmental protection and the push to expand nontraditional agricultural exports. This region has been targeted by DGF military anti-deforestation campaigns—such as the "Selva Negra" campaign, complete with helicopters—and by agribusiness corporations seeking to expand citrus and pineapple production. Smallholder farmers have turned to production of tobacco and/or cassava (*yucca*) cash crops on part of their holdings in order to survive the decline in coffee and cocoa prices. Now, Zambrana-Chacuey is the site of a forestry enterprise pilot project with widespread planting of timber trees as cash crops on smallholder farms. The project combines elements of peasant cooperatives and commercial outgrower models, coordinated jointly by a local farmers' federation and an international environment and development organization.

The Zambrana-Chacuey Region

Zambrana-Chacuey is a hilly region consisting of two districts at the edge of the fertile Cibao Valley and is home to roughly 12,000 people. It encompasses an area of 250 square kilometers with elevations ranging from 100 to 600 meters above sea level, and is located 10 kilometers from Cotuí, the capital of the Sanchez Ramirez province, and 100 kilometers to the north of Santo Domingo, the country's capital. While the zone once constituted a frontier for smallholder farmers in the 1960s, it has been transformed into a "sending area," with net outmigration due to land scarcity and rapid economic change.[4]

The once forest-covered region[5] exhibits both the scars of deforestation and the colorful brush strokes of cacao forests and homestead tree gardens. Currently the landscape supports a continuum of land use and cover types from rice and cattle on large expanses of flat land, to forests, coffee, and cacao on steep upland slopes and along stream banks.[6] Within and between these areas, farmers cultivate tobacco, citrus and other fruit trees, forested home gardens, and conucos (diverse plots of tubers — cassava, yam, sweet potato, and taro — and other vegetable crops). Most farmers raise small livestock, primarily hogs and chickens, and some people have specialized in charcoal production and other forest-based industries.

The majority of the residents of Zambrana-Chacuey are small-holder farmers engaged in a tenuous mix of subsistence and commercial agricultural production on one-half to two hectares of land per household. In many cases the plots already are considered "*micro*fundias" (as opposed to "*mini*fundias" — the usual term for smallholdings) and are no longer divisible into smaller units for the next generation. Absentee land speculators and ranchers as well as agribusiness corporations (Leche Rica Citrus and Dole Pineapple) continue to acquire more land in the region, in direct competition with smallholders.

Uneven land distribution and land tenure security have been key issues in the development of local organizations and the livelihood and land management strategies of rural smallholders. Most of the adults in the region report that they or their parents came there from other prime agricultural areas following eviction by commercial agribusiness or powerful largeholder farmers. Some families returned to Zambrana-Chacuey after having been illegally evicted decades before by powerful largeholders and clients of the Trujillo regime. Hundreds of households within the region acquired or formalized their land ownership rights between 1960 and 1990 through participation in land struggles with the state and local elites under the aegis of an active peasant federation. The Rural Federation of Zambrana-Chacuey is a focal point of regional identity and has largely defined the geographical and political boundaries for recent reforestation initiatives.

The Rural Federation of Zambrana-Chacuey

The Rural Federation of Zambrana-Chacuey has approximately 800 members (in 500 households) who belong to fifty-nine local farmers' groups, women's groups, youth associations, and most recently the Wood Producers' Association. Through networks of family, friends, and neighbors, at least 4,000 additional people are served by the Federation's programs. One of the founding leaders noted that "roughly 30% of the people in the region are in the Federation. They are mostly, but not all Catholic, and they are people who are conscious of struggle, helping neighbors and working collectively; [they are] small land holders, people fighting for land." The regional organization is linked to seventeen other peasant Federations in the *"Confederation Campesina de Mama Tingo,"* all spawned by a larger, national peasant movement (Lernoux 1982).

The foundations for the Federation can be traced back to the rural unrest that resulted from the large-scale evictions of peasant farmers from the Central Valley of the Dominican Republic by commercial agriculture, industry, and the state in the 1940s and 1950s (Rocheleau and Ross 1995; San Miguel 1992). A variety of community organizations — women's clubs, traditional church-based groups, youth associations, liberation theology-inspired religious groups, and marketing cooperatives — emerged in response to the evictions. In 1974, these disparate organizations converged to form the Rural Federation in order to protest the eviction of farm families during the expansion of the Rosario Dominicana gold mine in the region (Ross 1995).

The philosophies and goals of the original community organizations were incorporated into those of the Federation. In fact, the Federation continues to represent a coalition of three distinct currents within the broader rural movement.[7] Liberation theologians focus on human rights, social justice, and class struggles and see the Federation as a catalyst and agent of social change. The cooperative enterprises sector promotes the association of producers and consumers into groups to protect and promote their interests as small commercial farmers and traders in the local and national market. The traditional church-based membership views the Federation as representing local interests in securing infrastructure, services, and other "basic needs" — including land from the state — as well as acting as a buffer against outside encroachment. The leadership of the Federation has encompassed a broad spectrum of people with respect to class, ideologies, occupation, and locality. The commonly acknowledged founders and the current leadership include both women and men from all three wings of the Federation (Rocheleau and Ross 1995).

As a Federation at the regional level, the campesinos have organized land invasions and transportation strikes (Lernoux 1982). The Federation connects the campesinos to other regions of the country through its networks with other rural federations, empowering an often isolated segment of the population. The Federation also acts as a liaison between government agencies such the Secretariat of Agriculture and the small landholders in the provision of seeds and other agricultural inputs such as oxen and plowing equipment.

At the community level, groups organize *convites de trabajo* or work parties to perform tasks on members' farms. At times, men's and women's groups work together in complementary tasks (e.g., the men clear a member's land for a new conuco, while the women prepare food for the entire *convite* or a home garden for the same member). Some groups have established tree nurseries for fruit trees, coffee, and cacao, and some have organized cooperatives for buying and selling agricultural inputs. Many groups secure cropland plots for joint cultivation of food crops for home use, sale, and/or group fund-raising.

By 1993, the Federation owned land on which it had constructed a meeting place with cooking facilities, a primary school, and a cement block construction workshop. It operated a rural medical clinic staffed by a state-supported doctor and several nurses, as well as Federation volunteers. In a separate locale members constructed a workshop originally intended for women's and men's crafts that was later used to repair tools and more recently to construct furniture built from locally grown acacia. The fact that the Federation "marked" its territory is important in its own right. It demonstrated its members' commitment and belief that a future in the countryside was possible; it gave the Federation legitimacy in the face of outsiders; and it attracted ENDA-Caribe to the residents of Zambrana-Chacuey in 1982.

ENDA-Caribe and the Forestry Enterprise Project

ENDA (Environment and Development Alternatives) is an international NGO headquartered in Senegal. In the Dominican Republic, ENDA-Caribe, a regional branch, works with marginalized populations in both rural and urban areas, on agriculture, forestry, and health programs. From 1982 through 1995 ENDA pursued a farm forestry and sustainable agriculture program in collaboration with the Federation. ENDA staff and Federation farmers tested over sixty tree species (predominantly exotic trees) for growth potential in the zone. They identified *Acacia mangium,* the project's Australian "miracle tree,"[8] as a cash crop that yielded logs for milling within six to eight years of planting.

In the early stages of the project, the fame of this fast-growing tree spread through the Federation, as well as rumors that ENDA had negotiated with the forestry service (DGF) to grant the farmers official permission to harvest the acacia. Yet, doubts based on past experience with the DGF deterred the majority from planting. In 1990, ENDA and Federico de la Cruz,[9] a leader within the Federation with an affinity for forestry and a substantial plot of land, took the necessary step to prove to farmers that forestry was a viable and lucrative enterprise for the region.

Federico had been involved with the forestry project since its experimental phase, and had a number of acacia trees ready for harvest. A field day was planned at Federico's home to which the whole Federation, the media, other NGOs, and the head of forestry were invited in order to witness the legal felling of project trees. "Tree titles" were granted to some of the farmers present and a *ramada* (detached porch) was constructed with roundwood and poles from Federico's acacia plot. This event convinced the Federation members of the possibilities associated with forestry — largely because one of its own proved to them that forestry was indeed safe and viable (Rocheleau and Ross 1995; Geilfus 1996).

After this event, excitement about the trees, particularly the acacia, spread rapidly. As of 1992, there were 87 community nurseries and more than 300 household-based nurseries for timber and fruit trees. Overall, the project had planted 800,000 timber trees and 40,000 fruit trees, and it had 250,000 seedlings in nurseries (Valerio 1992). Roughly 85 percent of the Federation households had planted one or more *A. mangium* and other timber and fruit trees with the project.

Due to the accords between ENDA, the Federation, and the Forestry Department, many Federation members had been able to legally sell round wood or small stakes and poles at the farm gate. In order to organize transport, processing, and marketing of the timber, Federation members created a Wood Producers' Association. By October 1992 the Federation, the Wood Producers' Association, and ENDA-Caribe had started to construct a community-based sawmill and began to discuss the possible future of a forestry microenterprise.

The Ecological and Social Context in Zambrana-Chacuey

By 1993 hundreds of farmers were legally planting and harvesting *Acacia mangium* in Zambrana-Chacuey. The forestry fears of the past were giving way to promises of a locally controlled forestry enterprise (Geilfus 1996). Some Federation members, however, encountered obstacles to full participation in the production, processing, and sale of the acacia. The ECOGEN field research and subsequent analysis revealed which ecological situations were most conducive and which were most restrictive to acacia plantations. The research also determined which social groups — differentiated by gender and class — had been best able to take advantage of the benefits of forestry as well as which had been largely excluded or negatively affected. For purposes of this case study ecological differentiation in the zone is presented as a backdrop to the social context.[10] Land use types and species diversity — as indicated by numbers of trees, crops, and medicinal plant species — indicate ecological differences relevant to the adoption and impact of timber cash cropping. Gender and class differences relevant to timber cash cropping are grouped under three key elements of rural resource management in the region: land tenure; occupation, employment, and household division of labor; and the terms and structure of affiliation with the Federation.

Land Use, Land Cover, and Species Diversity

The variation in land use, land cover, and species diversity across farms and by individual farms matters to social forestry for three converging reasons. First, this clarifies the ecological opportunity costs of new species introductions and planting arrangements. Second, it illuminates the reasons that people may or may not choose to plant new trees on their farms and their placement of the new species. Third, by understanding who does and does not introduce these trees and why, we can evaluate alternative species possibilities, including local trees. Following is a brief description of the ecological situation in Zambrana-Chacuey. We also highlight these same issues throughout the description of the social context, to trace the ways that ecological and social differentiation create a matrix of possibility and constraint for acacia cash cropping.

The variation in patterns of land use and cover at the farm level creates very distinct ecological and landscape conditions for the incorporation of commercial timber. While all of the people surveyed had patios on their farms, 16 percent had nothing else; their entire holding was devoted to the house and a surrounding forest garden. At the other extreme, the larger holdings often included all seven land use types: patio, cropland, coffee/cacao stands, cañada (streambank forest), pasture, timber lots, and boundary plantings (table 10.1). A surprising 60 percent of all farms surveyed had blocks of timber and/or citrus trees, though the blocks were often small or newly planted.

TABLE 10.1. Presence of Land Types on Farms in Zambrana-Chacuey

Land-Use Type	Number of Farms	Percentage of Farms
Patio	45	100
Cropland	38	84
Border	33	73
Coffee/cacao	32	71
Cañada	29	64
Blocks of trees	27	60
Pasture	19	42
Fallow	12	26

The distribution of land use types is crucial for the introduction of acacia and for evaluation of its impact. Acacia is known locally as a "hot" tree, since it shades out or otherwise excludes other species. As a result farmers can only plant it on borders or in monocrop block plantings. Establishing a monocrop timber block with 50 to 200 trees would be quite different for people with holdings of 1/4 hectare in patio versus those with 5 hectares in a combination of patio garden, coffee, tobacco, cassava, pasture, and streambank forest. While the largeholders might substitute acacia for tobacco, the former might have to choose between a patio garden and an acacia timber lot.

Despite dramatic transformations in terms of land use and land cover over the years, the region has maintained a very high level of plant species diversity across all farms and by individual farms. The greatest number of tree, crop, and medicinal species per farm occurred in the patios — ironically, the smallest land use unit, the one closest to the home, and the one largely managed by women.[11] After the patio, the most species occurred in the remnant streambank forests (cañadas), then coffee and cacao stands, croplands, pastures, borders, and blocks.

Farmers in the region have previously incorporated monocropped plots of peanuts, tobacco, and cassava, as well as other cash crops intermixed within diverse food plots and forest gardens. Yet, the present economic demand for new cash crops, combined with the properties of the acacia, could threaten the present high levels of species richness in the region. Our analyses clearly demonstrated the degree of assimilation of acacia into all land use categories on the farms in Zambrana-Chacuey. The acacia constitutes one of the most frequently occurring species in patios, croplands, and border plantings though not always present in large numbers. It is increasingly being planted in pastures and to a lesser extent in cañadas and coffee and cacao stands. The growing incidence of acacia indicates a trend toward ecological simplification and homogenization of the landscape in Zambrana-Chacuey. In spite of ecological simplification and the uneven distribution of benefits from acacia cash cropping, there is still scope to transform and expand the current forestry project. The following section presents an examination of land, labor, and organizational factors that determine both the feasibility and the outcome of timber cash cropping in the region.

Gender and Class Dimensions That Influence the Receptivity to the Acacia

Differences in land tenure, livelihood strategies, and organizational affiliation present both opportunities and constraints for commercial timber farming by smallholders. These factors help to determine the general receptivity to commercial farm forestry, as well as conveying the constraints or hidden costs that many people face when trying to incorporate acacia. Each of these factors is, in turn, affected by class and gender. We begin with a discussion of land tenure, which directly affects land use and cover as well as species diversity on farmers' holdings.

Land is not equally distributed throughout the Federation's membership. There are no latifundistas — as understood in national terms — and the majority of farms owned by Federation members are best described as microfundias. On average, farmers "own" 1 to 1 1/2 hectares of land, which is usually divided among two or more plots. Forty-two percent of Federation members rent or borrow additional land for cash and subsistence cropping from neighboring largeholders who generally are not in the Federation. A sizable percentage of farmers in Zambrana-Chacuey are on state-owned or nontitled land; thus, they own not the land but the value of the *mejora,* or "improvements," such as cleared croplands as well as coffee, cacao, citrus, pastures, fencing, buildings, and, more recently, "legal" timber such as acacia.

Prior to the ENDA-DGF accords farmers often invoked a local saying, "To put trees on the land is to put the land in chains." The legal permission to harvest, process, and market the acacia has reversed the role of project trees in land tenure disputes, from tenure liabilities (as signs of abandonment) to tenure assets (as indicators of investment). This has encouraged many Federation members, especially largeholders,[12] as well as nonmembers to establish plantations of acacia and other recognized commercial timber trees[13] on their state and nontitled land to strengthen their land claims and tenure security as well as their income.

The 87 percent rate of timber planting among Federation members suggests that landholding size had little effect on the decision to plant acacia and other timber trees. Yet, the project was designed for people who could incorporate blocks of 50 to 200 project trees on their own landholdings. In this way, landholding size limited the scale at which many smallholder farmers could plant trees, thereby excluding many of these farmers from full participation in the Forestry Enterprise Project — including control of the benefits and the decisions about the direction of timber production.

If they had been involved more fully in project planning, many near-landless and smallholder farmers said they would have insisted on tree species more compatible with existing land use on very small plots — timber trees that could be intercropped, smaller trees for stickwood and poles, and more fruit trees. As a result of their exclusion from planning, these households with very small holdings are very vulnerable to loss of plant diversity, especially tree species if they plant acacia blocks. They are faced with trade-offs between their most diverse plots — patio, cañada, cropland, and tree crop stands — against timber blocks. In contrast, largeholders can trade off monocropped tobacco or cassava for timber and still retain patio gardens and diverse intercropped food plots.

Women, like near-landless families, face a land tenure barrier when attempting to control the benefits of forestry production. Many widows and some divorced or separated women own and manage their own farms (see case 4), while others with absentee or wage-laborer husbands are the de facto farm managers (a total of 20 percent according to a Federation survey in 1991). Yet, most of the women in the region (approximately 95 percent according to several surveys and 100 percent in our own sample) live in households legally headed by men and on land owned by husbands or male relatives.[14] As the following two examples demonstrate, the situation of women with resident husbands was strongly influenced by intrahousehold distribution of control over land and resources (see case 3).

Several women came forward in (or after) group meetings who wanted to plant acacia and other timber trees on household lands but could not do so for lack of clear tenure rights over even the patio, much less the cropland or other plots that they might have wished to convert to a timber lot. Most of them had already tried and encountered direct opposition from their husbands. One young woman who was a member of the Women's Association in her community planted several acacias on the patio, near the house. Her husband, who was not a Federation member, cut them down with his machete. She expressed a clear sense of injustice over her inability to control even the patio, which was commonly accepted as the woman's domain on the farm. In other cases the women had successfully established up to twenty trees on the patio or perhaps had even negotiated permission to plant part of the plot boundaries to timber. However, many women whose husbands were not Federation members or not actively involved in the tree project voiced an interest in planting blocks of timber. They were frustrated at not being able to control more than the patio and perhaps a piece of the property line.

Conversely, there were women whose husbands *had* planted acacia, perhaps without consulting them, at the expense of women's land or plants. In some cases women's vegetable gardens had been replaced by blocks of acacia. In other cases the multistory, diverse stands of fruit, timber, and cash crops on the patio are being overtaken by the very aggressive acacia. These women expressed skepticism about the timber production enterprise: "we have seen this before . . . peanuts, tobacco, now this acacia, they all take over our croplands and reduce the food which we can grow for ourselves." Several women noted that they would far prefer and might not resist a less "hot" tree that is more amenable to intercropping (Rocheleau and Ross 1995).

Overall, women's inability to control the acacia (whether they wish to cultivate it or to exclude it) has rendered their authority over all farm land — including the patio — increasingly vulnerable. Their inability to influence decisions about land use in regard to the acacia has implications for species diversity on the farm as well. The patio is the area on the farm with the highest rate of species richness. While women control this space, they do so without legal rights. This is highly significant for women's plants, for their participation in timber cash cropping, and for the future of forest and garden ecosystems in the region. Comparable to the case of people with very small farms, women have largely been left out of species and technology choices. They voiced an interest in timber trees amenable to intercropping as well as more fruit trees, and trees that produce smaller, more portable and readily harvested products to sell as needed for quick cash.

Livelihood Strategies: Household Differences

In response to unreliable markets, declining yields of cash and staple crops, and new employment opportunities, people in Zambrana-Chacuey have developed diverse livelihood strategies to produce subsistence goods and earn cash. While households vary substantially in the exact combination of income sources, production activities, and occupational specialization, agriculture plays a key role in almost all of the households, as do wage labor and/or trade. The nature of these strategies affects the interest and the capacity of households to engage in timber cash cropping or alternative forms of forest and agricultural production. It also influences the choice of species, planting arrangements, and land use practices.

The major cash crops in the zone are coffee, cocoa, tobacco, cassava, citrus fruits, and, increasingly, timber. The majority of families relied in part on the sale of cash crops for regular income as well as on small livestock sales (chickens and pigs) in times of cash shortages or emergencies. Yet, only two households relied solely on agriculture for their income. The overwhelming majority relied on a combination of regular income from wage labor, home-based production enterprises, and trade by one or more adults, as well as on the produce and the income from their fields. People earned cash through nonagricultural means by producing goods for sale in home industries, including food and crafts. Even prior to the forestry project, many households engaged in tree product enterprises as charcoal producers, woodworkers, and tree nursery entrepreneurs. One-third of the households in the Federation had at least one adult involved in trade (*compra-venta*). In most households some adults also engaged in wage labor — both on- and off-farm. The majority of households exhibited a high degree of economic diversification, yet there was a widespread sense of economic marginalization among farmers and rural residents (see case studies 3 and 4).

Household livelihood strategies, especially the extent of off-farm employment, trading, and forest products industries, have important and convergent implications for the expansion of smallholder timber cash cropping in the region. Timber constitutes a very promising nontraditional cash crop for smallholders in this region for two reasons. Timber is a more lucrative cash crop per unit land than any other currently available to smallholders, and it is low in both labor and capital input requirements. This cash crop is amenable to the allocation of more household labor to off-farm employment (wage labor or trading), or to management by one adult family member acting as the rural custodian of a split household.

This new commercial option offers an alternative to land sales and migration for smallholder households otherwise unable to maintain their holdings. As noted by several farmers, timber cash cropping would allow many farm households to move some members into towns or cities to obtain access to factory employment, secondary education, and health services as desired or required. This would permit the continued involvement of thousands of smallholders in crafting the patchwork of plant communities in the region, as opposed to concentrating land and land use decisions in the hands of largeholders and agribusiness interests. Yet, the degree of project specialization in acacia blocks may leave some households locked out of this economic activity, and it could result in the sale of some small holdings to local largeholders — keeping land in local hands but increasing local land concentration.

The cultural construction of gender among Federation members is flexible and does not preclude the active participation of women in agriculture and forestry and their identification as "farmers" (Rocheleau and Ross 1995). What differs between households is the way that tasks are divided, and the degree of women's versus men's authority and control in various activities. Survey results indicated that married women were more likely to be "in charge" of activities in home and patio spaces and to "help out" in other spaces (table 10.2).

In general, women are in charge of the activities that take place in the patio — including household activities such as cooking and cleaning, all or part of the processing of cash crops such as coffee, cocoa, and tobacco, and the management of small livestock (particularly goats, hogs, chickens, and rabbits). Women usually supervise the collection of fuelwood and water. Often they plant crops, such as pigeon peas, or have gardens in what are considered "men's" conucos. They "help" men prepare cropland for cultivation and also work during trips to bring food to the fields. Most women and girls also harvest agricultural products and tree crops, and some women market cash crops (coffee, cocoa, fruit). Some women own or manage their own coffee and cacao stands inherited from their parents. Women heads of household, those who take a special interest in farming, or those whose husbands work off-farm often take charge of all agricultural activities and identify themselves as "farmers."

Both women and men reported that women work with all types of trees — from fruit, coffee, and cacao to timber trees — and participate in all stages of production, including establishing nurseries, planting, maintaining, harvesting, processing, and marketing (table 10.3). Acacia (timber) stands out from these other tree crops in that women's labor is largely restricted to nursery and planting tasks, and they are virtually excluded from harvesting, processing, and marketing.

The project's ideology of men's and women's labor in agriculture and forestry differentiated acacia cultivation from other tree planting, which discouraged women's participation in this enterprise as managers or full partners. While the activities required to manage the tree are similar to any other tree crop or agricultural cash monocrop, the cultivation of the

TABLE 10.2.   Men's and Women's Management in Different Domains of Production

Domain of Production	Percentage of Women as Managers	Percentage of Men as Managers
Home	93.3	4.4
Medicinals	97.5	7.5
Vegetable gardens	92.6	22.2
Crops	51.1	79.1
Animals	78.5	35.7
Trees	39.6	93.1
Marketing	37.5	75

Note: The data are collapsed from more detailed reports of management tasks performed by women, men, children, paid labor, and combinations of all four groups. These figures represent all instances of women or men respectively reported as participants in management of these production domains.

acacia is being treated exclusively as "forestry." The identification of the Forest Enterprise Project as a male activity has also drawn heavily on international and national biases about forestry as a professionalized, male domain, rather than on regional and local perceptions of the division of labor in tree cropping (see case 2). This has both social and economic consequences in the lives of women and men farmers and in the distribution of tree species in the landscape.

Gendered livelihood strategies could undergo major changes if timber cash cropping in monocropped blocks takes root in Zambrana-Chacuey largely without women's participation. First, women would lose access to and control over whole classes of plants if they are reconfigured into monocrop enterprises — some of the plants would disappear from the household production repertoire and some would become cash crops under men's control in increasingly specialized production domains. In other cases women would have less production space in cropland or patio, would lose access to intercropping opportunities or partnership roles with their husbands in commercial croplands, and would retain less control over management of cash crop finances at the household level.

The ecological impact of women's exclusion from timber cash cropping activities might include partial or complete replacement of their diverse patio plots and/or cropland with monocrop timber blocks. The exclusion of women as partners in this enterprise could also thwart changes in the new timber enterprise, which women might otherwise render more diverse or adapt to intercropping.

TABLE 10.3.   Women's and Men's Forestry Activities (in percentages)

	Timber (n = 40)		Coffee (n = 40)		Cocoa (n = 38)		Fruit (n = 43)	
	Women	Men	Women	Men	Women	Men	Women	Men
Overall								
Work	45	85	68	88	58	87	65	81
Nursery	32	75	25	50	33	58	44	65
Planting	40	77	32	55	35	66	58	86
Maintenance	32	77	40	65	25	76	55	76
Harvest	7	35	75	47	87	74	58	65
Process	7	27	85	40	61	56	65	18
Market	5	35	42	67	33	69	30	58

Note: The responses indicate the percentage of households in which women and men participate in the activities listed for a given crop. This table collapses more detailed data on labor that distinguished between women only, men only, children only, paid labor, and various combinations of each. The numbers reported here include all the tasks in which men and women participated.

Organizational Affiliation

Besides varying in landholdings and livelihood strategies, the membership is also differentiated by the strength and structure of household connection to the Federation. Most Federation-affiliated households are linked by two memberships, yet the number of affiliations per household ranges from only one person's membership to as many as four memberships distributed among three or four people. The strength of a household's affiliation is reflected in the landscape as evidenced by the planting of timber tree blocks (as opposed to a few trees) at farm level. Sixty percent of the households sampled had planted acacia blocks by 1993, most of them connected to the Federation by two or more memberships.

The Federation is also a distinctly gendered organization as reflected in the patterns of affiliation of men and women. The gender differences in Federation membership occur both within and between households and between different associations. Household linkages to the Federation are structured by the gender of the members connected as well as their choice of organization.

As of 1993, women in Federation-affiliated households were mainly members of community Women's Associations (60 percent) and a small percentage were members of the local Farmers' Association (4 percent) and the Wood Producers' Association (4 percent). Nearly a third (32 percent) were not members of any association as individuals. While a similar number of men in affiliated households were nonmembers (38 percent), nearly half of the men (44 percent) were members of both the Farmers' Association and the Wood Producers' Association. A small percentage was affiliated with only one of these groups: Farmers, 11 percent, and Wood Producers, 7 percent (Ross 1995).

Men's and women's ability to control the acacia and gain access to the Forestry Enterprise Project differed substantially due to the selective affiliation of the project with the predominantly male Farmers' Association, and later the Wood Producers' Association. The patterns of household and project connection to the Federation determined in large part what knowledge entered the household, who controlled it, and who used it, as well as whose interests were represented in various activities. Over 20 percent of all Federation-affiliated households were linked solely by women, primarily through the Women's Associations, putting them at a distinct disadvantage for access to timber producer services channeled through the Farmers' Associations and the Wood Producers' Associations. The women's groups received commercially marginal projects such as small livestock production and household vegetable gardens instead of the timber production project.

The individual membership criteria for the Wood Producers' Association biased membership toward men with blocks of land amenable to monocropping and tended to deter both women and the near-landless. The individual membership fee also discouraged separate membership for both spouses in any given household. The minimum entry requirement of fifty trees planted in 0.05 hectare on their own land also restricted the ability of women and near-landless men to qualify for membership.

The lack of institutional linkages did not prevent women from planting the acacia — many women planted it as part of group efforts or as individuals. Rather, these barriers limited the *scale* at which the women could plant timber trees, which in turn affected their eligibility for WPA membership and the degree and quality of support that they received. Near-landless men, as well as those not interested in forestry, faced a different problem. The Wood Producers' Association was replacing the commercial and technical support role of the Farmers' Association in some communities, threatening ties to the Federation for those not producing timber (Ross 1995).

Federation membership is open to all smallholder farm residents of the region. The practical exclusion of women and the smallest landholders from the Wood Producers' Association contradicted the founding principles of the Federation, and the male orientation of the Forestry Enterprise Project conflicted with local practice in the gender division of tree cropping. These mismatches between local conceptions of subsistence and multispecies forestry and those introduced with the acacia created new divisions within households, communities, and the Federation as a whole.

Case Studies of the Present and Potential of Forestry in Zambrana-Chacuey

The expressions of gender and class differences within and between households and ecological differences within and between farms have created a matrix of constraints and opportunities for introduction of acacia by Federation members in the Zambrana-Chacuey region. The following four ministudies illustrate some of the ways that these social and ecological differences shape people's decisions when trying to incorporate acacia into their lands and livelihood systems.

The first demonstrates the positive potential of monocrop timber blocks exemplified by the replacement of tobacco with timber. The second case illustrates the gender stereotyping that accompanies acacia production and describes the acacia as a potential threat to the diverse assemblages of plants, family food supply in patios and croplands, and the cacao forests on farms. The third study portrays a family linked to the Federation only by the woman's membership. This study shows the constraints that smallholder families face with the acacia, compounded by the issue of gendered linkage to the Federation. Conversely, the fourth study discusses the potential for women in forestry when they have strong links to the Federation. Linkage to the Wood Producers' and Farmers' Associations would improve women's access to information and their decision-making power when it comes to the acacia. All four studies clearly demonstrate that there is room for species diversification as well as other modifications in the project to better suit the diversity both within the Federation as well as across the landscapes of the zone.

Case 1: Rafael and Maria: From Tobacco to Timber

Rafael Hernandez and Maria Lopez, a middle-aged couple, have transformed their land (4–5 ha) into a patchwork tree farm of monocropped acacia plots interspersed with blocks of intercropped food crops, the home garden and coffee stand near their home, and a few remaining plots of tobacco. Rafael and Maria's home is located at the edge of a clearing with the patio grading into a small intercropped coffee stand to one side, a small pasture along the other side of the house, and a large field of tobacco and tree seedlings stretching across the valley opposite from the house. The house and main fields are located in undulating topography along a well-traveled path less than one kilometer from the main road traversing the region from Cotui to the capital city, Santo Domingo.

For the last decade Rafael and his sons have planted most of the family lands and some rented lands to commercial tobacco crops, rotating with cassava for home use and sale. They also planted citrus in some fields and mixed food crops for household consumption (conucos) in one or two rented fields each year. Maria has focused her attention on the patio, medicinal plants, and "helping" with the coffee, cocoa, and tobacco production and processing. Her main domain is the house and surrounding patio.

Rafael was among the first in the Federation to experiment with the acacia and to commit substantial blocks of land to timber as a cash crop. He is also the first tree farmer in the region to build a cement block house with trees. He harvested his first plots, sold the logs with the assistance of ENDA and the permission of Foresta, and used the profits from the trees to purchase the necessary labor and materials to construct a substantial cement block house on a poured concrete foundation. Aside from the comforts and longevity of the structure, this type of house is a symbol of wealth and prestige. This has made Rafael and Maria's home into a kind of shrine to the success of acacia as a cash crop.

The timber tree has also transformed Rafael's place in the community. Never a very active Federation member in the past, he has become a leader in the Wood Producers' Association. Maria continues with her prior active role in the Sierrita women's association and her moderate level of participation in the medicinal plants and health project. Their son is an apprentice at the Federation's artisan project, having been drawn into ENDA and Federation activities by his father's intensive participation in the Forestry Enterprise Project.

Functional Niches for Trees and Tree Products
Rafael and Maria see timber cash cropping as their best strategy for the use of their land and labor. Rafael, in particular, has decided to replace most if not all of the tobacco plots on his property and to maintain some fields in cassava and tobacco rotations with trees, intercropping with acacia seedlings for the first two years of the six- to eight-year timber production cycle. He has successfully substituted timber for tobacco as his main cash crop and has demonstrated the technical and economic viability of acacia monocrop plantations as a permanent block or as a rotation with other cash and food crops.

Like tobacco (only more so), the acacia does not intercrop well, but produces more cash return per unit land than any other food and cash crop. The acacia is also said to protect against erosion and restore soil fertility,[15] while tobacco is notorious for soil depletion and provides little protection against erosion. The acacia also requires much less labor than tobacco and is more flexible in exact timing of operations. The acacia takes eight to ten years to mature for harvest (for milling as timber), at which time it yields more cash return than the same number of years in tobacco or any other crop currently raised in the region. The timber plantations, based on their recognition by the Forestry Department, have also strengthened the land tenure security and the value of the mejora (land improvements) on Rafael and Maria's lands.

Although no other functions compare in importance to the cash cropping and land tenure security benefits provided by the acacia, there is some scope for additional livelihood niches for trees on this farm. Rafael has also planted citrus trees as a second new cash crop, which can be intercropped, unlike the acacia. Maria and Rafael have little interest in "minor" forest or tree products since they still have enough land to keep animals that can serve the purpose of small-scale savings, investment, and insurance.

Spatial Planting Niches

Rafael and Maria have radically altered the landscape of their farm by substituting timber block plantations for tobacco plots, although they have not changed the overall template of rectangular blocks and ribbons. They have simply inserted a tree into a block formation previously dedicated to tobacco. They have also established fruit trees as an intercrop in pasture and in those food crop plots on their own property. Rafael sees no scope for such fruit tree planting on rented croplands. There is, however additional scope for fence-row planting of timber. There is little scope for separate planting of "conservation" trees on the contour for soil fertility improvement, although research suggests that the acacia itself, once harvested, may leave the soil in improved condition for one or two cycles of cassava or mixed food cropping. However, this function is clearly a by-product of timber production in the case of Rafael and Maria, not a major incentive for tree planting and not likely to be expressed as a contour intercrop in food crop plots. Finally, Rafael and Maria plan to purchase additional lands to plant blocks of acacia. While he sees the need and supports the idea, Rafael would not undertake group plantings or separate plantings on group sites, since he can afford to purchase more land or to replace crops with timber and plant food crops on rented land.

Overall the Forest Enterprise Project has had a major impact on the livelihood and landscape of this household. Given their experience it would be difficult to argue against substitution of acacia for tobacco on environmental, economic, or social grounds either in principle or in practice, outside of taking a purist preservationist stance. The acacia as cash crop has proven an attractive option for Rafael and Maria, who seek a more "sustainable," environmentally friendly cash monocrop and can afford to wait eight years to receive a return from those plots. It is a prime example of what Rick Schroeder (1993) has called the "commodity road to environmental stabilization." However, as in the case of tobacco and other monocropped cash crops, women in the region were quick to point out the danger that in smaller holdings acacia could displace diverse stands of food and mixed cash crops, and could make smallholders more vulnerable to fluctuations in the price of purchased food as well as the selling price of the commodity itself. The shift to timber as a kind of tall green tobacco thus carries both positive and negative connotations, depending on whose interests are at stake.

Case 2: Hernando and Marta—Cocoa, Dressmaking,
Monocrops, and Intercrops

At the age of sixty-eight, Hernando Perez is a largeholder cacao farmer who lives on a ridge overlooking a deep river valley in an outlying area of the region. The steep hillsides of the surrounding landscape are covered with multispecies cacao stands interspersed with occasional homesteads and conucos. The house is surrounded by a small clearing dotted with bright ornamental plants, medicinal herbs, and occasional fruit and timber trees. Sloping away from the back of the house, a very diverse patio garden dense with fruit, medicinal, and timber trees gives way to a mixed, densely shaded cacao stand. The main holdings of the family extend downslope to the river below, and across the road to a ravine on the opposite side of the ridge. The family supplements their cash income and food supply with various pieces of rented land on nearby slopes that they have planted to tobacco, cassava, garden vegetables, plantains, and mixed food crops.

Hernando, Marta, and their family depend heavily on the proceeds of cash cropping, with cocoa being the most important in a list that includes coffee, citrus, and tobacco. Two of their sons live on the same property with their families and help Hernando with cash crop production. Marta is a dressmaker whose creations are well recognized and sought after for special occasions and formal events. The business— which she runs from her home—provides her with an independent source of income. She also takes part (as a "helper") in some of the farm operations in coffee, citrus, and cocoa. She participates in several operations with most crops on the farm, including marketing of the products. Her role in timber production is more constrained, reflecting a highly gendered ideology of timber production, harvest, and marketing.

Hernando conveyed the strength of gender stereotyping about the new timber trees when he replied to questions about gender division of labor and control on the farm.[16] When asked if his wife was able to sell the citrus fruits, coffee, or cocoa from their farm he replied: "Of course. Marta could take some to market or she could negotiate a price and sell it to someone who comes with a truck or a car looking to buy. Either one of us can do that." The future sale of the recently planted acacia was a different matter. "Ah no. This is different. Growing timber is a very technical enterprise. *These trees must be measured in inches.*[17] This tree is a business for men!"

Marta is a well-known and specialized seamstress who designs and produces wedding dresses and silk party dresses. She was busy with customers at the time, presumably measuring them, in inches or something equally effective, to assure the good fit for which she is renowned. Ignoring Marta's obvious facility with measurement, Hernando's comments reflected the prevailing ideology that has accompanied the introduction of the acacia as a "men's business."

Functional Niches for Trees and Tree Products

The livelihood niche benefits for tree products on this farm include commercial timber, timber for home use, strengthening of land tenure rights, fruits and small wood products for sale, and boundary markers. There is very little additional room for nitrogen-fixing or soil-improving trees, aside from the amapola (*Erythrina poepoegiana*) and guama (*Guama* spp.) already ubiquitous in the cacao and coffee stands. The plots of mixed annual crops, pigeon peas, bananas, and plantains might benefit from contour planting of *Calliandra calothrysus* or *Acacia angustissima* to prevent soil erosion. However, Hernando would be unlikely to plant these in rented land unless there were a secure, proven market in small poles from the *Calliandra* and the owners would agree to the practice, which carries some possibilities of a subsequent tenure claim by the renters.

Spatial Niches for Planting Trees on Hernando and
Marta's Farm

The landscape niches for planting of acacia trees include a short length of the boundary along the main road, as well as blocks of land now occupied by multispecies, multistory cacao plantations. While new acacia blocks would displace the cacao stands entirely, these places also represent potential planting sites for timber, fruit, and other wood-product trees amenable to intercropping with cacao, coffee, plantain, banana, and citrus. Hernando is already interested in more corazón de paloma (*Colubrina arborescens*) and would probably be receptive to such trees as *Cordia alliodora*.

This example represents an important category of potential land use and landscape change in the region that has not been adequately addressed by the acacia block-planting option and that is not likely to be well served by such a technology if it is adopted. Although the major cocoa production areas are not as accessible or as visible as the tobacco zone, much of the land area in Zambrana-Chacuey is in cacao or coffee, and most of the households surveyed have some part of their lands planted to multistory, multispecies stands of cacao and coffee. In the major cocoa production regions the steep slope of the land is also ill-suited to monocropping and clear-cutting of timber, which is the current practice in acacia timber lots.

Case 3: Rosa and Ramon—Gendered Control over
Space and Gendered Affiliation in the Federation

For many farmers in Zambrana-Chacuey, the acacia and all other trees are still liabilities that expose them and their land to intervention by the DGF (Rocheleau and Ross 1995). Some view the acacia and the social forestry project with suspicion based on personal experience and bad luck with the DGF. For others, their nonaffiliation with the Federation translates into a lack of information about the social forestry–timber production project and a lack of faith in the types of safeguards the Federation and ENDA-Caribe can provide in dealing with the DGF. Rosa and Ramon's story illustrates the impact of a negative history with the DGF, combined with gendered affiliation with the Federation and gendered control over farm management. All three influenced this household's decision and ability to plant the acacia.

Ramon and Rosa Farias are a young couple with seven children. They live in a remote part of Rincon, on a small plot of less than 0.5 hectare that is fairly inaccessible under normal conditions and is even more isolated during the rainy season. Rosa is an active member and leader of her women's group, but Ramon is not a member of the Federation. He works full time off-farm, and Rosa manages their plot, which they only recently acquired with savings from his job along with income that Rosa provides through the production and sale of food and candy. By 1993 Rosa and Ramon had put nearly their entire holding into cassava. She had planted a household garden with a wide variety of vegetables, some fruit, and medicinals. They were jointly developing a coffee and cacao stand near the river and ravines that bound their land on two sides.

Earlier, upon learning about the forestry project, Rosa established a home nursery of 300 seedlings. Ramon, however, was against it. Their limited amount of land and his uncertainty about the market for timber and wood products influenced his decision. Most important, however, was Ramon's recent experience with the DGF (known locally as *Foresta*). As Rosa recounted:

> Last year Ramon was arrested by Foresta and held for days for cutting two palm trees at his uncle's house. He had purchased them to build our house. Someone reported him to Foresta and they took him away to jail. I was in Church and the neighbors came to tell me. I took the children to my mother's house, then went to Cotui. I had to pay the police to see him, and then I called his boss to say he couldn't be at work. The police asked for 1,500 pesos to release him, or for

him to work 30 hours in a reforestation site, or for the palm boards. Ramon had been taken before he cut the boards, so the neighbors helped to cut and carry them and we left them at the side of the road, where the Foresta man came to collect it.

Ramon was released after a couple of days and was lucky not to have lost his job. Yet Ramon's entrapment had a cost: his unwillingness to plant trees in the future.

After Ramon's release he didn't want anything to do with trees on our land. When my group got word of the tree project I made my small nursery. I wanted to plant them all on the borders and in blocks but Ramon said no. Finally the children and I pleaded to plant those three acacia near the edge of our plot.

Even if Ramon were more favorable to the idea of tree planting, this household still would face problems incorporating acacia onto their farm and complying with the minimum of fifty trees set by the Wood Producers' Association. Rosa recognizes that acacia is not the best tree species for their holding. She wishes that a "fresh" tree had been offered, one that could be intercropped with cassava. There is not much room to add blocks of acacia. Yet, they have a lot to gain from trees. We identified the functional niches that different tree species could play and possible physical landscape niches for them (Rocheleau, Ross, and Morrobel 1996).

Functional Niches for Trees
Cash crop trees such as coffee, cacao, and fruit species, as well as species that could service coffee and cacao stands by providing shade, would make the most important contributions to Rosa and Ramon's farm. Tree crops would provide food for the family and a seasonal source of cash. Another possible role for trees would be as a source of emergency cash in the form of small wood products such as poles. Smaller products could be easily and quickly harvested and sold for emergency and seasonal expenses. In this way, the tree would play a role much like that of small livestock in people's livelihood strategies. A concentration on smaller products would also address the difficulties that families living in remote areas face when trying to transport the large trunks of the acacia (Rocheleau, Ross, and Morrobel 1996).

Medicinal plants and trees fill another functional role on Rosa and Ramon's farm. Rosa's interest in traditional medicine and her involvement in the TRAMIL project could allow her to tap into this

Federation-ENDA initiative to market traditional remedies. Medicinal trees, shrubs, and plants could play a role in providing regular sources of income as well as remedies for family and friends. Nitrogen-fixing species could be incorporated for soil improvement as well an occasional source of cash from the sale of tree by-products. These functional roles for trees on small landholdings had not yet been addressed by the Forest Enterprise Project in 1993. While there are many possibilities for trees on Rosa and Ramon's farm, the option most actively promoted — timber — was probably Rosa and Ramon's least practical choice for incorporating trees onto their farm in the near future.

Spatial Niches for Trees
The challenge for Rosa and Ramon is to find the spatial niches for the acacia and other species on their small plot. The borders, both those that separate their holding from others as well as internal dividers, are certainly possible locations for timber trees. Trees that can be intercropped could be incorporated into coffee and cacao stands or in the patio or the garden. Given their limited holding, however, Rosa and Ramon would soon exhaust these planting spaces. This problem of land scarcity, which is hardly unique to Rosa and Ramon, suggests that aspects of the project must be broadened to accommodate families with very small farms. Access to group land or leased land for timber trees would alleviate the planting pressure on such farms.[18] Another programmatic change that would support Rosa's tree planting would be to funnel assistance and information about trees through women's groups and from the Federation to nonmember men in woman-affiliated households. This would help Rosa to alleviate Ramon's fears of the DGF. More overlap with other ENDA projects, in this case with the ethnobotany research or the medicinal gardens research, would also help the project to select trees with both cash and household value that smallholders could plant.

Case 4: Carmen—From Clandestine Charcoal Maker to Timber Producer

In a nearby community Carmen Ramirez's encounter with the enforcement of forest laws led her to a very different outcome than Ramon, based both on gender and on her close affiliation with the Federation. Not all encounters with the DGF permanently bias people's views of forestry, nor does a small plot of land preclude participation in the forestry project. A strong connection with the Federation as well as a history of deriving a livelihood from trees and tree products balanced Carmen's negative experience with the DGF. It enabled her to transform her 1/4 hectare plot into a patchwork of acacia blocks and dispersed fruit trees, which she hoped would soon be complemented by a block of acacia on her uncle's land (Rocheleau et al. 1995).

Carmen is a divorced woman with four school-aged children and has lived in Rio Blanco for twenty-two years. Carmen and her mother share a small plot of her uncle's land. Her home is adjacent to the highway and is a little over a kilometer from the Federation building where she works as the Federation cook and performs some administrative duties. Carmen and her mother are free to do as they wish with their small plot. They also have access to additional land further from the house, but her uncle has thus far given permission to cultivate only food crops on this land.

Carmen began to make charcoal after she and her husband divorced. As a single mother caring for children and an elderly mother in poor health, she was restricted in her ability to work off-farm. She sold vegetables, candy, and food from her home and began making and selling charcoal. She had learned the trade by helping her former husband to make charcoal. Although this activity was illegal without a permit she made this livelihood choice because it was her most lucrative economic option.

She recounts a frightening and dramatic encounter with Foresta in 1990 during the Selva Negra (Black Forest) Campaign against deforestation. Late one afternoon a Foresta crew sighted the smoke from her earthen charcoal kiln and landed its helicopter at her small plot near the house. Soldiers dressed in combat uniform and armed with automatic weapons pounded at the door and demanded to see her husband or to know his whereabouts. They assumed that she was lying to protect the man of the house when she confessed to making the charcoal. Finally when they were convinced that she was indeed the offending party, the soldiers said they would have to arrest her. "I told them to wait while I dressed the children, since they would have to come too." The soldiers hesitated, reluctant to take a woman *and her small children* into their custody. Rather than drag them to jail, the soldiers suggested that she find another livelihood. Meanwhile, they instructed her to avoid certain tree species and to selectively harvest other less valuable species for charcoal.

Carmen followed their advice about the trees and with friends and relatives sought an alternative occupation for the long term. Eventually Carmen secured regular employment as a cook and caretaker at the Federation Headquarters nearby. She heard through informal channels (to be exact, listening from the kitchen) about the plans for acacia tree sales, the sawmill, and the Wood Producers' Association. In this way, she learned more than many women about the early stages of the forestry project. She became an active tree planter and informal promoter among her women's group members, family, and friends.

She convinced her uncle to allow her to plant a block of acacia on the cropland that he allows her to use. She also planted most of her patio to fruit and timber trees. Currently, she has nearly 200 trees and seedlings on her 1/4-hectare plot. They are planted in rows as well as small blocks. With her knowledge, Carmen began to plant trees and encouraged the women in her group to start planting. Her experience with Foresta notwithstanding, Carmen trusts the Federation and ENDA to buffer the interactions between project participants and soldiers in the future.

Functional Niches for Trees

Unlike Rosa, Carmen has more independence in her decisions about how to use the land available to her, although she is dependent on permission to use the land of her uncle. She has focused on commercial plantation of acacia for timber as her best cash crop option for the future, and is less interested in coffee, cocoa, or "minor" tree products.

Timber production is a good choice for Carmen. Unlike Rosa, Carmen is the head of a household and has more freedom to plant the acacia. Additionally, the main highway runs right by her home, which facilitates transport of large logs. She is dedicated to the idea of a commercial timber enterprise and is very innovative in her approach to maximizing space on her farm for this timber tree. Yet, she too could benefit from additional timber species, especially species that could be intercropped with her fruit and cacao trees. She could also benefit from non–timber-producing species that produce poles and stakes instead. Fruit and medicinal tree crops would benefit Carmen for the same reasons as they would help Rosa — but Carmen is not as interested in these crops. Finally, tree species for soil improvement would be Carmen's lowest priority. Currently, she does not have a conuco and thus is not as concerned with the soil fertility of croplands. She relies on her job and eventually on money from timber, to buy the staple foods she needs.

Spatial Niches for Trees

Carmen faces serious land limitations, especially to incorporate a long-term monocrop. She has already lined the borders of her property with acacia and has established several small blocks of it on her land. If other tree species were offered by the project, she would be able to intercrop timber trees within her stands of fruit and cacao trees. Carmen, however, is committed to commercial forestry. The bottom line is that she needs access to additional land for timber blocks. If her uncle would enter an agreement with her that would give her permission to plant timber trees on his other land, Carmen would be able to expand her forestry production. Leased land, either for her as an individual or for her women's group, would also allow her to expand her timber production. In either case, the forestry project would have to spend some time listening to women's and smallholders' wishes, their constraints, and their concerns about species, leases, and group plots in order to better serve these two groups in timber cash cropping.

Carmen's story demonstrates that women can and do plant and derive livelihoods from trees in Zambrana-Chacuey. With permits from ENDA and with knowledge of the project she moved from an illegal forest-based activity into a government sanctioned one. Cultural norms do not restrict women from planting trees, but the clash in ideologies of gender and forestry between the Federation and ENDA restrict many women from participating. Carmen in many ways is in a unique position. Her job at the Federation proved very important in her knowledge about the project. As the head of a household she has relative control over her land and ability to make decisions about tree planting. Now that her mother has joined her and helps with child care, she is in a better position than many women to take independent decisions and to plant acacia. Like Rosa, Carmen could benefit from project assistance with either group land or leased land for acacia block plantations. Carmen favors a lease or sharecropping arrangement.

Carmen is an important source of knowledge for other women in her group who do not have the same type of connections to the Federation. Her example motivated other women in her group to plant, or at least to get their husbands or sons involved in the forestry project. This clearly demonstrates the need for women promoters in the Forest Enterprise Project and women representatives in the Wood Producers' Association. Her case also demonstrates that leased land for tree planting would increase women's control over an important income source, whether they be limited by lack of authority over household land or by the size of the plot or both.

Transforming the Forestry Enterprise Project:
Technological, Tenure, and Organizational Innovations

Two current trends within the project present ecological and social problems: (1) the simplification or replacement of plant associations in the regional landscape; and (2) the marginalization of women and near-landless households. Deliberate interventions by the Federation, ENDA, the DGF, and the people of the region could counteract these trends through technology, tenure, and organizational changes. The future opportunities for women wood producers, near-landless families, and more remote communities will hinge in part on the ability of the Wood Producers' Association (WP) and the Rural Federation (RF) to reconcile their respective mandates of production (WP), support of farmer/foresters (WP and RF), and advocacy for the poor (RF), and to cooperate to provide support for the diverse population of existing and potential wood-producers in Zambrana-Chacuey. Through our collaborative field research with the Federation, ENDA, and the Instituto Superior de Agricultura (ISA) we identified several specific courses of action grouped under technology, tenure and organizational structure.

Technology

The Federation, ENDA, and the Wood Producers' Association could better serve the interests of the near-landless and of women in general by diversifying the repertoire of species, spaces, products, and planting places for timber and other tree products. This strategy would address land constraints and displacement of food crops as well as transportation bottlenecks and farmer dependence on fixed arrangements for timber sale and transport. This would provide farmers with greater flexibility of planting choices as well as harvest and marketing options. There is a clear need for many different trees that can produce timber, small poles, specialty woods, and fruit and that can be safely intercropped with coffee, cacao, and food crops in gardens, croplands, homesteads, and riparian forests. Farmers have identified (and experimented with) several species of exotic and indigenous trees that could serve this purpose. For example, observations during field research yielded one clear possibility among the exotic trees amenable to intercropping. Several farmers had planted *Cordia alliodora* as part of early, informal project research efforts. By 1993, some of these trees had far surpassed the acacia in stature and growth rate, and prior experience in Costa Rica has already established the high value of *C. alliodora* timber and the feasibility of intercropping in multispecies stands of coffee.

Households and whole communities located far from motorable roads also need tree species that produce nontimber products (small poles, specialty wood, fruit) that can be transported by pack animals to markets or collection points. The participating organizations could better serve the full membership of the Federation by broadening the terms of technical assistance to include processing and marketing of a variety of tree products and to create and supervise portable sawmills in communities unable to transport logs to market.

Tenure

Tenure and credit innovations to support farm forestry can also transform the conditions of production for smallholders. While planting acacia for timber clearly increases land value, the dilemma of smallholders is that they must choose between food crops and a small block of timber. In addition to intercropping, one obvious solution is to lease land for tree farming, which 62 percent of those surveyed are willing to do under group auspices. That would require legal support to draft secure agreements as to land and tree ownership and management. Credit for land purchases by groups might also facilitate group planting of timber by the near-landless and by women who cannot secure more household land to plant trees. Two groups already have timber plots, and many groups have cultivated shared plots of food crops (such as cassava) or garden vegetables. Given the precedent and the level of demand, the development of group timber plots constitutes a viable option for women and the near-landless.

Organizational Innovations

Organizational changes could dramatically change the terms of women's and near-landless households' participation in forestry activities, particularly their share in the profits, the products, and the decision-making process. The Federation and the Wood Producers' Association could diversify the linkage of their activities to incorporate women's groups into forestry activities, as planners, participants, and critics. Women members and other groups without adequate land to plant trees require legal, social, and technical advice as well as financial support for forestry production.

One possible change is to introduce group membership in the Wood Producers' Association for women's groups or other community groups whose members are unable or unwilling to join separately. Family or household memberships could also help to bring in women whose husbands are already members. Either the Federation or the Wood Producers' Association could also appoint special technical and planning liaison people to meet with women's groups and other Federation groups about forestry activities and to solicit their opinions on pending decisions before the Association. This would allow for open discussion and debate, whether the members support or oppose the activity in question and whether they wish to adopt, reform, or resist a given techology or land use change. A complementary plan of action between ENDA, the Federation, and the Wood Producers' Association could specifically address the forestry concerns of women and near-landless households and, beyond that, could transform the ongoing forestry activities to serve all Federation members or at least to respond to all of their concerns.

Conclusion

The acacia has proven to be less than desirable in many ecological and social circumstances. Yet it would be a mistake to treat the success of smallholder timber production as a monolithic threat, to women, the poor, and the regional ecosystem; it is crucial to consider the alternatives, with and without the tree project. The same tree that may replace women's patio gardens, coffee and cacao stands, and remnant forests may also protect the land and people from other less desirable options. Timber is currently competing with tobacco, citrus, and pineapple for land in the region, and the latter two are controlled by large agribusiness corporations that displace smallholder farmers. Moreover, the timber cash crop option need not be limited to monocropped blocks of one species of timber tree under the exclusive control of men, as discussed earlier.

The evaluation of the experience to date and the exploration of possible future directions presents a challenge to address the complex gender and class-divided realities of the Zambrana-Chacuey region. In response to the problems and the opportunities identified by our field research effort we recommend changes in both policy and practice within this collaborative effort. Together with colleagues from the Federation, the Wood Producers, and ENDA, we discussed how to diversify both the species and planting arrangements, in the interests of biological diversity, watershed management, and social equity. We strongly encouraged all three institutions to promote and support group planting sites (by local Associations) for women in general and for those households with very small holdings. Finally, we suggested ways to directly link women and other excluded groups to the Forest Enterprise Project and the Wood Producers' Association. Each of these recommendations simultaneously addressed the need to include those groups previously excluded and to safeguard the rights of those who choose not to participate.

The successes, problems, and proposed solutions in this tale all incorporate a diversity of species, environments, and people. The distinct groups are both joined and divided on the basis of gender, class, locality, occupation, organizational affiliation, family composition, and personal histories. The outcome of this complex story matters not only for each of the concerned groups and for the region itself but has taken on a broader significance. The Forest Enterprise Project of Zambrana-Chacuey has become the model for a social and ecological experiment likely to be replicated at the national level and perhaps internationally. The experience of the people in this region with timber cash cropping also provides more general insights into the gendered social and ecological dynamics of land use and land cover change at global, national, and local levels. Finally, this story illustrates how we can use gender and class analysis of land tenure, livelihood, and landscape differences to identify both conflicts and complementarities, to map possible ecological and economic futures, and to transform policy and practice in particular places.

NOTES

This article was prepared with the assistance of Cristobalina Amparo, Cirilo Brito, Daniel Zavallos, participants from the Rural Federation of Zambrana-Chacuey, and ENDA-Caribe, Cotui, Dominican Republic. Portions of the article have appeared in Rocheleau et al. 1996 and Rocheleau and Ross 1995, and will appear in a Spanish language publication, *Revista Agroforesteria en Las Americas.*

1. ENDA-Caribe is a regional branch of ENDA (Environment and Development Alternatives), an international NGO headquartered in Senegal.

2. Clientelism penetrated every region of the country and every sector of rural production under the dictator Rafael Leonidas Trujillo, who ruled for thirty years until his assassination in 1961.

3. Cassava, yams, taro, and citrus are traditional subsistence food crops but nontraditional as export cash crops.

4. The capital, other urban areas, the semiarid southern flank of the Cordillera Central, and the drylands of the Cibao Valley as well as the forest edges of the Northeastern Coast have constituted destination areas for smallholder farmers over the last decade (Pedro Juan del Rosario, Personal Communication 1993).

5. The rolling hills were once covered almost entirely in humid and very humid subtropical lowland forests, according to the Holdridge Life Zone classification (Holdridge et al. 1971).

6. The streambank forests (cañadas) are a direct legacy of the Trujillo era, when the dictator decreed and strictly enforced a prohibition against tree cutting within thirty meters of any perennial stream.

7. For discussions of similar movements throughout Latin America see

Escobar and Alvarez 1992. For a history specific to the Dominican Republic see San Miguel 1992.

8. The acacia is — in local parlance — a "hot" tree, that does not intercrop well with annuals or other trees. It suppresses most understory growth within two to four years; for this reason, acacia must be planted on border lines and in monocropped block formations.

9. This and all subsequent names are pseudonyms to preserve anonymity.

10. For a more in-depth explanation of the ecological differentiation in Zambrana-Chacuey, please refer to Rocheleau, Ross, and Morrobel 1996.

11. For description and evidence of diversity in women's home gardens in other areas see Oldfield and Alcorn 1991; Doxon 1988; McCarry 1990; Pulsipher 1993; Kimber 1988; Rocheleau 1991.

12. Medium or even large landholders within the Federation would still be considered smallholders by regional and national standards.

13. Once the new role of acacia was established, federation members and ENDA staff sought and eventually obtained tree titles — for home use — for over twenty other tree species planted by various farmers under the auspices of the forestry project. This may yet open up the possibility for future negotiation about the availability (and economic and tenurial value) of whole forest stands and previously planted or protected trees (Rocheleau and Ross 1995).

14. The Federation conducted a self-census of one section of Zambrana-Chacuey in order to justify a request for electricity in the region. Twenty percent of the people named as heads of household on this list were women. Other formal surveys and the formal census of the zone, including ENDA's, state that women-headed households account for 3 to 6 percent of the population. The Federation's definition of head of household is based on who manages daily work and decisions.

15. While short-term trials suggest that the soil fertility for annual crops is restored after a planting cycle in acacia there is some question about the long-term viability of repeated acacia rotations. The rapid growth and high volume of biomass in the trees implies a major export of nutrients from the site and perhaps selective mining of some nutrients from the soil. ENDA Caribe and Instituto Superior de Agricultura (Julio Morrobel) have proposed further research on this topic.

16. Hernando had recently spent half a day in meetings and field visits with project staff and had enthusiastically committed himself and his farmers' association to a timber tree nursery and major planting initiative. His replies seem to reflect the gendered subtext of the project ideology as he read it.

17. Hernando referred here to the standard forestry measurement of tree diameter at breast height (DBH) used to assess the volume and in this case the value of standing timber.

18. Of those surveyed 62 percent of respondents expressed interest in planting trees on group land (local Farmer's Association or Women's Group land, or group-leased plots), provided that the leases were legally sound (Rocheleau and Ross 1995).

REFERENCES

Antonini, G., K. Ewel, and H. Tupper. 1975. *Population and Energy.* Gainesville: University Presses of Florida.

Arriagada, Irma. 1992. Mujeres Rurales de America Latina y el Caribe: Resultados de Programas y Proyectos. In Virginia Guzman, Patricia Portocarrero, and Virginia Vargas, eds., *Una Nueva Lectura: Genero en el Desarrollo.* Santo Domingo: Ediciones Populares Feministas, CIPAF, 1992.

Betances, Emelio. 1995. *State and Society in the Dominican Republic.* Boulder: Westview Press.

Brookfield, H., and C. Padoch. 1995. Appreciating Agrodiversity: A Look at the Dynamism and Diversity of Indigenous Farming Practices. *Environment* 36, no. 5: 6–11, 37–43.

Collins, Jane. 1991. Women and the Environment: Social Reproduction and Sustainable Development. In R. S. Gallin and A. Ferguson, eds., *The Women and Development Annual* 2:33–58. Boulder: WestviewPress.

Deere, Carmen. 1990a. *In the Shadow of the Sun: Caribbean Development Alternatives and U.S. Policy.* Boulder: Westview Press.

———. 1990b. *Households and Class Relations: Peasants and Landlords in Northern Peru.* Berkeley: University of California Press.

Deere, Carmen, and Magdalene De Leon, eds. 1987. *Rural Women and State Policy: Feminist Perspectives on Latin American Agricultural Development.* Boulder: Westview Press.

Doxon, Lynn E. 1988. Diversity, Distribution and Use of Ornamental and Edible Plants in Home Gardens of Honduras. Ph.D. diss., Department of Horticulture, Kansas State University, Manhattan, Kansas.

Escobar, Arturo. 1995. *Encountering Development: The Making and Unmaking of the Third World.* Princeton: Princeton University Press.

Escobar, Arturo, and Sonia Alvarez, eds. 1992. *The Making of Social Movements in Latin America: Identity, Strategy and Democracy.* Boulder: Westview Press.

Flora, Cornelia Butler, and Blas Santos. 1986. Women in Farming Systems in Latin America. In J. Nash, H. Safa et al., *Women and Change in Latin America,* 208–28. New York: Bergin and Garvey.

Geilfus, F. 1994. *Agricultural Innovation in the Dominican Republic: The Dynamics of Peasant Farm Systems in a Confined Environment.* Ph.D. dissertation, Université Catholique de Louvain, Louvain.

———. 1996. *From Tree Haters to Tree Farmers: A Twelve Year Experience in Social and Farm Forestry in the Dominican Republic.* Manuscript.

Holdridge, L. R., W. C. Grenke, W. H. Hatheway, T. Liong, and J. A. Tosi. 1971. *Environments in Tropical Life Zones: A Pilot Study.* Oxford: Pergamon Press, Ltd.

Katz, Elizabeth G. 1992. Intra-Household Resource Allocation in the Guatemalan Highlands: The Impact of Non-Traditional Agricultural Exports. Ph.D. diss., Department of Agricultural Economics, University of Wisconsin, Madison. Ann Arbor, MI: UMI Dissertation Services.

Kimber, C. T. 1988. *Martinique Revisited: The Changing Plant Geographies of a West Indian Island.* College Station: Texas A&M University Press.

Lernoux, P. 1982. *Cry of the People.* New York: Penguin Books.

Lynch, B. 1994. State Formation, Public Lands, and Human Rights: The Case of the Dominican Republic and Los Haitisses. Unpublished paper prepared for the XVIII International Congress of the Latin American Studies Association, Atlanta, Georgia, March 10–12.

McAffee, Katherine. 1987. *Storm Signals: Structural Adjustment and Development Alternatives in the Caribbean.* London: Zed Books.

McCarry, Nancy Stanford. 1990. Variation among Home Gardens in Guatemala: Reflections of Household Characteristics. Master's thesis, Department of Geography, University of Texas, Austin.

Momsen, Janet. 1993. Women, Work and the Life Course in the Rural Caribbean. In Cindi Katz and Janice Monk, eds., *Full Circles: Geographies of Women over the Life Course.* London: Routledge.

Oldfield, Margery, and Janis B. Alcorn. 1991. *Biodiversity: Culture, Conservation and Ecodevelopment.* Boulder: Westview Press.

Pulsipher, Lydia. 1993. He Won't Let She Stretch She Foot: Gender Relations in Traditional West Indian Houseyards. In *Full Circles: Geographies of Women Over the Life Course,* Cindi Katz and Janice Monk, eds., 122–37. New York: Routledge.

Raynolds, L. 1994. The Restructuring of Third World Agroexports: Changing Production Relations in the Dominican Republic. In P. McMichael, ed., *The Global Restructuring of Agro-food Systems.* Ithaca: Cornell University Press.

Rocheleau, Dianne. 1991. Gender, Ecology and the Science of Survival. *Agriculture and Human Values* 8:156–65.

Rocheleau, Dianne, and Laurie Ross. 1995. Trees as Tools, Trees as Text: Struggles over Resources in Zambrana-Chacuey, Dominican Republic. *Antipode* 27, no. 4: 407–28.

Rocheleau, D., L. Ross, and J. Morrobel. 1996. From Forest Gardens to Tree Farms: Women, Men and Timber in Zambrana-Chacuey, Dominican Republic. In D. Rocheleau, B. Thomas-Slayter, and E. Wangari, eds., *Feminist Political Ecology: Global Issues and Local Experiences.* London and New York: Routledge.

Rocheleau, Dianne, Barbara Thomas-Slayter, and David Edmunds. 1995. Gendered Resource Mapping: Focusing on Women's Spaces in the Landscape. *Cultural Survival Quarterly* 18 (4): 62–68.

Rodriguez Liriano, A. 1978. *La Historia Forestal de La Republica Dominicana.* Santiago, Dominican Republic: Instituto Superior de Agricultura (ISA).

Ross, Laurie. 1995. When a Grassroots Social Movement Enters a Development Partnership with an NGO: Overcoming the Barriers that Prevent Local Control over Modern Technology in Zambrana-Chacuey, Dominican Republic. Master's thesis, Clark University.

Santos, Blas, ed. 1984. *Foresta: Alternativa de Desarollo.* Santiago: Pontifica Universidad Catolica Madre y Maestra.

San Miguel, P. 1992. Los Campesinos del Cibao: Economia de Mercado y Trans-
formacion Agraria en la Republica Dominicana, 1880–1960. Manuscript.
Rio Pedras: University of Puerto Rico, and Santiago: Centro de Estudios
Urbanos y Regionales.

Schroeder, R. 1993. Shady Practice: Gender and the Political Ecology of Resource Stabilization in Gambian Garden Orchards. *Economic Geography*
69 (4): 349–65.

Silva, Paola. 1991. Mujer y Medio Ambiente en America Latina y el Caribe: Los
Desafios Hacia el Ano 2000. In Mujer y Medio Ambiente en America
Latina y el Caribe, eds., *Fundacion NATURA-CEPLAES,* 5–20. Quito:
Fundacion Natura-Ceplaes.

Stonich, Susan C. 1993. *"I Am Destroying the Land!": The Political Ecology of
Poverty and Environmental Destruction in Honduras.* Boulder: Westview
Press.

Townsend, Janet, Ursula Arrevilla Matias, Socorro Cancino Cordova, Silvana
Pacheco Bonfil, and Elia Perez Nasser. 1994. *Voces Femininas de las Selvas.*
Centro de Estudios del Desarrollo Rural, Mexico, and University of Dur-
ham, England.

Urban, Anne Marie, and Mary Rojas. 1994. Shifting Boundaries: Gender, Migration, and Community Resources in the Foothills of Choluteca, Honduras.
Clark University, Worcester, Massachusetts: International Development.

Valerio, M. 1992. Agroforesteria y conservación de suuelos. Unpublished
AGROSIL document. Santo Domingo: ENDA-Caribe.

Veras, J. 1984. Indice Cronologico de la Legisación sobre Asuntos Forestales en
la Republica Dominicana. In B. Santos, ed., *Foresta: Alternativa de
Desarollo.* Santiago: PUCMM.

Contributors

Gar Alperovitz is President of the National Center for Economic and Security Alternatives. He also is a Lionel R. Bauman Professor of Political Economy in the Department of Government and Politics, University of Maryland at College Park.

Molly D. Anderson is Associate Professor and Director of the Agriculture, Food and Environment Program at the School of Nutrition Science and Policy, Tufts University.

David Barkin is Professor of Economics at the Departamento de Produccion Economica at the Xochimilco Campus of the Universidad Autonoma Metropolitana in Mexico City.

Robert Chambers is a Fellow at the Institute for Development Studies, University of Sussex, Brighton, England.

John T. Cook is Deputy Director for Research at the Center on Hunger, Poverty, and Nutrition Policy at Tufts University.

Faye Duchin is Dean of Humanities and Social Sciences and Professor of Economics at Rensselaer Polytechnic Institute.

Neva R. Goodwin is Co-Director of the Tufts University Global Development and Environment Institute.

Jonathan M. Harris is Senior Research Associate at the Tufts University Global Development and Environment Institute.

Ricardo Hernandez is an independent consultant residing in Cotui, Dominican Republic.

Allan Hoben is Professor of Anthropology, Boston University African Studies Center.

Baylor Johnson is Professor of Philosophy at St. Lawrence University.

Julio Morrobel is Professor of Forestry and Natural Resources at the Instituto Superior Agrícola in La Herradura, Dominican Republic.

Robert L. Paarlberg is Professor of Political Science at Wellesley College and Associate at the Harvard Center for International Affairs.

Jules N. Pretty is Director of the Sustainable Agriculture Program, International Institute for Environment and Development, London, England.

Dianne Rocheleau is Associate Professor of Geography and Researcher at the George Perkins Marsh Institute, Clark University, Worcester, Massachusetts.

Laurie Ross is a community development consultant and doctoral student in Community Development and Planning at the University of Massachusetts-Boston.

Index

ActionAid, 212
Activists for Social Alternatives, 206
Aga Kahn Rural Support Programme, 206, 209, 212, 219
Agency for International Development, 157–60, 168
Agribusiness, 59, 80–82, 233
Agricultural development. *See* Agricultural development, emerging learning paradigm of; Food security; Resource management, rural development and
Agricultural development, emerging learning paradigm of. *See also* Food security; Resource management, rural development and
case studies, 199–201, 203–4, 209, 218–19
defined, 189–92
educational/learning organizations and, 216–19
governmental institutions and, 200–206, 208–10
institutional innovation, 195–200
institutional/organizational settings, 190–94
international research and, 209–13
local institutions and, 213–16
NGOs and, 206–10
participation, types of, 192–93
professionalism, 194–96
versus transfer-of-technology paradigm, 189–90
Agricultural Technical Improvement Project, 203

Alley Farming Network for Tropical Africa, 212
Alperovitz, Gar, 3–4
Anderson, Molly, 146–47
Aubreville, A., 159

Bangladesh Rural Advancement Committee, 207
Barkin, David, 6–7
Barnes, R. C., 154
Beckerman, Wilfrid, 2
Belman, Dale, 127
Biodiversity, 106–7, 131
Blaikie, P., 103–4, 153
Bookchin, Murray, 21
Brazilian Small Enterprise Assistance Service, 60–61
Brundtland Commission, 161
Buber, Martin, 20

Capitalism, 3–4, 14–15
CARE, 212
Case studies
agricultural technical improvement project, 203–4
desertification, 157–63
environmental reclamation, 163–65
forestry, 267–78
irrigation, 200
land degradation, 153–57
natural resource management, 201
pest control, 218
soil and water conservation, 199
watershed development and management, 209
Chambers, Robert, 145–46, 148

Cobb, John B., Jr., 21, 122
Collins, Joseph, 229
Collion, M.-H., 202
Commission for Environmental Co-
    operation, 128
Common property. *See* Property, com-
    mon
Common-property institution, de-
    fined, 34–35. *See also* Prop-
    erty, common
Common-property resource, defined,
    34–35. *See also* Property,
    common
Commons. *See also* Property, common
    distinguished from open-access re-
    gimes, 45n. 4
    global, 30–31, 37, 42–45
    as open-access resource, 33
Communism/socialism, 3–4, 14
Community-based institutions, de-
    fined, 19–21
Community Food Security Act
    (U.S.), 237
"Community inheritance," 26–28
Community investment, 25–28
Conservation Reserve Program, 182
Conservatism, 13–15
Consortium for International Develop-
    ment, 155, 157
Consultative Group on International
    Agricultural Research
    (CGIAR), 58–59, 70, 210–11
Cook, John, 146–47
Cruz, Federico de la, 256–57
Current Population Survey (U.S.),
    127

Daly, Herman E., 4, 21, 117, 122
Dasgupta, P., 2
Democracy, 16–18, 22–23, 28
Development, agricultural. *See* Agri-
    cultural development
Development, economic models of,
    3–4, 141–42
Development, hedgerow model of.

See Hedgerow model of devel-
    opment
Development, sustainable (theory
    of). *See* Sustainable develop-
    ment, theory of
Drucker, Peter, 22
Duchin, Faye, 4–5

Earth Summit (1992; Rio de Janeiro),
    162
ECOGEN, 257
Economic security, 22–25
Educational system, 72
Edwards, M., 207
El Serafy, Salah, 121
Employment, 22, 25, 86–87
Energy/power, 61–67
Entrepreneurs, 15–16, 69–72
Environment and Development
    Alternatives, 251–52, 256–57,
    279–81
Environmental degradation
    agribusiness and, 80–82
    case studies (Africa), 152–65
    economic analysis of, 94–97
    food security and, 230
    free trade and, 118–20
    market failures and, 123–25
    policy response to, 82–83
    population growth and, 96
    poverty and, 95–96
Environmental Enterprises Assistance
    Fund, 64–65
Environmental Kuznets Curve
    (EKC), 95, 125–26
Environmental policy. *See also* Envi-
    ronmental degradation; Trade,
    free versus sustainable
    case studies (Africa), 152–65
    policy narratives and, 151–52,
    165–69
Equal Exchange (organization),
    242–43
Equality/inequality, 16–19, 28–30, 33,
    126–28

Esty, Daniel C., 123, 131
European Economic Court of Justice, 119
European Union, 90, 132, 184
Extension agents, 57–59, 69–72
Externalities, 6, 119

Farmer First (conference), 189, 203
Farmer Groups, Resarch- and Extension-Oriented, 203–4
Farmers' Market Nutrition Program, 242
Fisheries, 43
Food security. *See also* Agricultural development, emerging learning paradigm of; Resource management, rural development and
community food security/local systems, 237–45
definition, traditional, 231
global economy and, 89–91, 101–2
problem, description of, 228–31
strategies for achieving, failed, 231–36
Food systems, local. *See* Food security
Forestry Enterprise Project, 251, 266–67, 278–82
Freeman, Richard, 127
Friedman, Milton, 15

GDP, defined, 8n. 1
Gender roles, 87–88, 229, 249–50, 261–67, 271–78
General Agreement on Tariffs and Trade (GATT), 90, 92, 122–23, 130–31
Global commons. *See* Commons
Global economy. *See also* Trade, free versus sustainable
consumption and production, separation of, 93–94
development, impact on, 89–98, 100, 107–8

economic analysis of, 94–97
failings of, 91–93
local food systems and, 241–44
rise of, 89–91
transnational corporations and, 89–93
Global Environmental Organization (proposed), 123, 131
GNP, defined, 8n. 1
Goodman, Paul and Percival, 23
Goodwin, Neva, 3, 5–6
Grameen Bank, 53, 64, 208
Green Revolution, 58, 70, 80–81, 84, 86, 176–77
Greenhouse gases, 44, 131
Grossman, Gene, 125
Growth, ideology of, 4

Hardin, Garrett, 30, 166
Haryana Forest Department, 201
Hayek, Friedrich, 13–14
Hedgerow model of development
defined, 52–57, 65–67
education, importance of, 72
entrepreneurs, extension agents, and, 69–72
examples, 57–65
failure of, 67–69
as SAEJAS, 50–52
Hines, Colin, 132
Hirschman, Albert, 103
Hoben, Allan, 143–44, 148
Howarth, Richard B., 2
Hulme, D., 207

Ibrahim, Fouad N., 160
ICLARM, 212
IICA (foundation; Costa Rica), 105
Income, unequal distribution of (statistics), 18–19
Inheritance, 26–27
Inter-American Bank, 65
Inter-American Foundation, 105
International Agricultural Research Centres, 210–11

International Center for Tropical Agriculture, 212
International Centre for Living Aquatic Resources Management, 211
International Centre for Research in Semi-Arid Tropics, 212
International Convention to Combat Desertification, 162
International Council for Research in Agroforestry, 212
International Institute for Tropical Agriculture, 212
International Livestock Centre for Africa, 212
International Monetary Fund, 91, 131, 179
International Potato Center, 212
International Rice Research Institute, 212
International Service for National Agricultural Research, 201

Jodha, N. S., 33
Johnson, Baylor, 4–5
Jordan, Bill, 23

Krueger, Alan, 125
Krugman, Paul, 120
Kuznets, Simon, 125. *See also* Environmental Kuznets Curve

Lamprey, Hugh, 160
Land tenure, 85–86, 176–78, 254, 259–62, 280
Lang, Tim, 132
Lappé, Frances Moore, 229
Lee, Eddy, 126
Lee, Thea, 127
Liberty, individual, 15–16, 21–25, 28

Madison, James, 29–30
Maler, K.G., 2
Marine Mammal Act (U.S.), 123
Maritain, Jacques, 23

Market mechanism, 6, 66, 78, 89–98, 124–25, 178–80
Marx, Karl, 29
Merrill-Sands, D., 202
Morobel, Julio, 146
Mortimore, Michael, 156
MYRADA, 206, 212, 215

Nakano, Dawn, 21
National Agricultural Research and Extension Systems, 200, 206, 208, 211–13
National Soil Conservation Programme (Kenya), 199
Nongovernmental organizations (NGOs). *See also* under names of particular organizations
  antipeasant bias and, 86
  emerging learning and, 206–13, 217
  hedgerow model and, 53–55, 73
  policy narratives and, 168
  political role of, 102–5
  rural poverty and, 83
  SAPs and, 97–98
Norgaard, Richard, 148
North American Agreement on Labor Cooperation (NAALC), 128–29
North American Free Trade Agreement (NAFTA)
  differential impact of, 105
  emergence of global economy and, 90
  energy resources and, 121
  environment and, 92, 95, 128–31, 179
  export-led economic growth and, 124
  free versus sustainable trade and, 126–28
  potential expansion of, 130
Northeast Region Sustainable Agricultural Research and Education Program, 242

Open-access resources, 33, 37–38
Ostrom, E., 34, 214
Our Common Future, 1, 8, 40–41
OUTREACH, 206, 212
Overseas Development Institute, 174
Ownership, worker, 19–21

Paarlberg, Robert, 144–45
Pareto optimality, 134n. 19
Plucknett, Donald L., 229
Policy narratives, defined, 151–52.
    See also Environmental policy
Population growth, 96, 175
Poverty
    degradation of agricultural resources and, 174
    development and, 77–79
    discriminatory public policies and, 84–89
    environmental degradation and, 80–82, 95–96
    feminization of, 87–88
    global economy and, 89–98
    rural, dynamics of, 83–84
    rural sustainable development and.
        See Sustainable development, theory of
Prebish, Raul, 89
Pretty, Jules, 145–46, 148
Profit motive, 4
Progressivism, 14
Property, common. *See also* Commons
    common-property resources and, 37
    conditions favoring, 38–39
    versus corporate property, 37–38
    defined, 34–37
    democratic social capital and, 42
    equality and, 41–42
    exclusion, difficulty of, 39
    institutions of, 4–5
    as means of protecting resources, 33–34

as more egalitarian than private property, 33
    versus open-access resources, 37
    resources, access to, 39
    resources, efficient use of, 39
    resources, protection of, 40–41
    systems, breakdown of, 175–76
Property, institutions of, 4–5, 25–27, 37–38. *See also* Land tenure; Property, common
Public goods, defined, 35

Quiggin, J., 33

Repetto, Robert, 121
Resource management, rural development and. *See also* Agricultural development, emerging learning paradigm of; Food security
    agroforestry
        context, ecological and social, 257–67
        context, legal and institutional, 252–57
    case studies, 267–78
    future directions
        land tenure, 280
        organization, 280–81
        technology, 279–80
        trends, 278–79
    gender roles and, 249–50, 261–67
    hedgerow model of, 57–59
    policy narratives and, 166–69
    problem, defined, 249–52
Resources, degradation of agricultural
    farming methods and, 176–78
    market failures and, 178–80
    political explanations for, 180–81
    political responses to, 181–84
    population density/growth and, 174–76
    poverty and, 80–82, 174
    power imbalances and, 174, 177–86

Rhoades, Robert, 190–91
Rocheleau, Dianne, 146
Rockefeller Brothers Fund, 61–62, 70
Rome Declaration on World Food Security, 237
Ross, Laurie, 146
Rostow, W. W., 3
Runge, C. Ford, 123, 131
Rural Federation, 251–52, 254–58, 260–69, 275, 279–81

SAEJAS. *See* Sustainable development, theory of
Sanctions, 36
Sandler, T., 44
Selden, Thomas, 125
Seva Bharati, 206, 212
Simons, Henry C., 22
Socialism/Communism, 3–4, 14
"Socially and environmentally just and sustainable development" (SAEJAS). *See* Agricultural development; Environmental policy; Sustainable development, theory of
Solar energy, 62, 64–67
Song, Daqing, 125
SPEECH, 206, 212
Stamp, Dudley, 159
State Department of Industry and Commerce (Brazil), 60–61
Stebbing, E. P., 158–59
Stiglitz, Joseph, 141–42
Stone, Christopher, 44
Structural adjustment programs (SAPs), 91, 97–98
Summers, Larry, 95
Sustainable development. *See* Sustainable development, theory of
Sustainable development, theory of. *See also* Agricultural development; Environmental policy
defined, 1–8

as framework for practice, 141–48
political theory/philosophy and
community investment, 25–27
democracy and equality, 16–19
egalitarian culture, 28–30
institutions, community-based, 19–21
institutional basis of liberty, 21–23
liberalism and conservatism, 13–16
planning and accountability, 23–25
time, uses of, 27–28
rural
biodiversity and, 106–7
failed regions, 105–6
food self-sufficiency, 101–2
general considerations, 98–101
local autonomous development and, 107–9
social and political underpinnings of, 102–5
"socially and environmentally just and sustainable development" (SAEJAS), 5–6, 50–52
versus unsustainable, 51
Swift, Jeremy, 158, 162
Synergos Institute, 71

Throughput, defined, 4
Tiffen, Mary, 156
Time, uses of, 27–28
Trade, free versus sustainable. *See also* Global economy
free trade, impact of, 7, 117–20
NAFTA, 128–30
social and distributional issues, 126–28
sustainable trade, 120–23, 130–32
trade, growth, and the environment, 123–26
"Tragedy of the Commons" (Hardin), 30, 166
Training and Visit system, 202

UNESCO, 160
United Nations, 1
United Nations Conference on
    Desertification, 161
United Nations Development Pro-
    gram (UNDP), 5, 50, 73, 243
United Nations Environmental Pro-
    gram, 160
Uphoff, N., 203–4
Urbanization, 88, 107–8
USAID, 65
User's Perspective with Agricultural
    Research and Development,
    212

Wealth, unequal distribution of (statis-
    tics), 26–27
"Whose Common Future?" 33
Williams, William Appleman, 30
Winkelmann, Donald L., 229
Wolff, Edward, 26
Women's Environment and Develop-
    ment Organization, 240
World Bank

economic growth, projections of,
    124
environmental and natural resource
    accounting and, 121
food security and, 229
free versus sustainable trade and,
    131
as funding source, 55, 59, 65
global economy and, 91, 95
measures of sustainable develop-
    ment, 1
nongovernmental organizations
    and, 97–98
policy narratives and, 168
spending cuts, demands for, 179
sustainable agriculture and, 157
World Commission on Environment
    and Development, 1, 8, 50
World Neighbors, 212
World Trade Organization, 92, 122–
    23, 131. *See also* General
    Agreement on Tariffs and
    Trade
World Women's Bank, 53